The Organized Family Historian

How to File, Manage, and Protect Your Genealogical Research and Heirlooms

Ann Carter Fleming
CG, CGL

Amy Johnson Crow, CG
Series Editor

Rutledge Hill Press®
Nashville, Tennessee

A Division of Thomas Nelson, Inc.
www.ThomasNelson.com

Published by Rutledge Hill Press, a Division of Thomas Nelson, Inc., P.O. Box 141000, Nashville, Tennessee 37214.

Some material in this publication is reproduced by permission of The Church of Jesus Christ of Latter-day Saints. In granting permission for this use of copyrighted material, the Church does not imply endorsement or authorization of this publication. Materials from Hollinger and Allen County Public Library are also reproduced by permission.

The following items mentioned in this book are registered trademarks or service marks: AAA, Adobe Acrobat Reader, Amazon.com, Ancestral File, Ancestry, Board for Certification of Genealogists (BCG), Certified Genealogical Lecturer, Certified Genealogical Records Specialist, Certified Genealogist, CG, CGL, CGRS, Church of Jesus Christ of Latter-day Saints, *Consumer Reports*, Cyndi's List, CyndisList.com, Family History Center, Family History Library, FamilySearch, FamilySearch.org, FirstSearch, Federation of Genealogical Societies, GEDCOM, Google, HeritageQuest.com, Hollinger Corporation, Microsoft Outlook, Microsoft XP, MS Excel, MS Windows, MS Word, National Genealogical Society, National Society Daughters of the American Revolution, Nintendo, OCLC, *PC Magazine*, PDF, Periodical Source Index, PERSI, MS Pocket Excel, MS Pocket Word, Research Outlines (FamilySearch), Roots Web, RootsWeb.com, Social Security Death Index, Sons of the American Revolution, *UpFront with NGS,* USGenWeb, USGS, Windows Explorer, WorldCat, Zip-drive.

Library of Congress Cataloging-in-Publication Data

Fleming, Ann, 1947–
    The organized family historian : how to file, manage, and protect your genealogical research and heirlooms / Ann Carter Fleming.
        p. cm.—(National Genealogical Society guides)
    Includes index.
    ISBN 1-4016-0129-4 (pbk.)
    1. Genealogy-Methodology. 2. Paperwork (Office practice)—Management. 3. Filing systems. I. Title. II. Series.
CS14.F54 2004
929'.1'072—dc22   2003022732

Printed in the United States of America

04 05 06 07 08 — 5 4 3 2

To Marie

Contents

Acknowledgments

ONE PERSON CANNOT COMPLETE A PROJECT SUCH AS THIS. IT TAKES a team of players, each with a different area of expertise ranging from expert genealogist to new family historian. My team consisted of the following colleagues, friends, and family: Joan Beach; Mary Berthold; Kay Freilich, CG, CGL; Ruth Ann Hager, CGRS, CGL; Cyndi Howells; Ilene Murray; Pam Porter, CGRS, CGL; and Ted Steele. This team provided advice, enthusiasm, critical thinking, and fresh ideas, all with a red pen in hand. I am extremely thankful for their help and friendship.

A project of this scope is time consuming and could not have been completed without the encouragement, patience, and support of my husband, Jim Fleming. He was always there to provide a better word or phrase when needed or to just listen. He never complained when he asked what I was making for dinner and my response was reservations. Thank you for your love and patience.

INTRODUCTION

Who Should Read This Book?

WHAT IS IN YOUR HERITAGE TRUNK? DO YOU HAVE FAMILY PHOTOS, heirlooms, journals, letters, quilts, and other family memorabilia? It is time to open this trunk and organize the prized possessions left to you by your forebears.

As a family historian, you probably started by keeping all your documents and notes in a three-ring binder. Before you knew it, that notebook grew into an overflowing four-drawer cabinet. What can you do? Organizing your heritage trunk or accumulated heirlooms, notes, photos, and family anecdotes is the first goal. Everything should have a place, you should know where it is, and it should be easily accessible when needed. Papers should be in a file folder, project folder, or notebook, not piled on the table or floor. Organize your photographs, as well as the books, with like items together.

Organizing your research is the second goal. Whether you use a desktop computer, laptop, or pencil and paper to record your research notes, the forms and worksheets provided in this book will help you identify, organize, and sort your research materials. These helpful tools enable you to analyze the names, locations, and time periods that are important to your family before you embark on your research journey.

All of the forms mentioned in this book are available on the enclosed CD. You can print and use the blank forms as needed. Many of the forms should be filled out before you go to a research facility. As you utilize the forms, the missing information will become obvious, pointing you in the right research direction and allowing you to make more efficient use of your research time. Armed with the appropriate forms, your next stop will be a courthouse or genealogical library.

This journey through your family history should be fun. As you unlock the puzzles of the past, each new piece of the puzzle falls into place. You establish the framework and then start filling in the holes. Where did those people come from? Why didn't they leave a trail? Those questions and many others come to mind as your journey progresses.

Once this information is gathered, entered, and documented, it is time to share your family history with others—the final goal, and perhaps the most intimidating. Although software programs can write family histories, those histories sound like a computer wrote them. Writing your family history yourself brings the greatest reward. Your family history needs your personal feelings and touches. By sharing that history, you help your descendants understand the sacrifices and hardships your ancestors encountered as they left footprints in time.

Organizing your family history is a big project. Taking on the responsibility of the family historian is one of those unpaid, time-consuming, and sometimes thankless jobs. However, if you develop a plan today and work on it a little at a time, it isn't so cumbersome. Besides, who better to do it than you?

Part 1
Organize Your Heritage Trunk

CHAPTER 1

Where Do I Start?

A FAMILY HISTORY PROJECT USUALLY STARTS WHEN A LOVED ONE PROVIDES a special photograph, letter, or statement that piques your interest. Perhaps a child inquires about an old photo and you cannot provide the names of the people in the portrait. Before long, you listen to, and perhaps record, oral histories from living relatives, read old letters and diaries, peruse census records, download related records, visit important family sites, photograph monuments, and read tombstones. Suddenly you have stacks of paper, recordings, printouts, photographs, and notes with more information than you ever imagined.

It is time to organize and divide your family history project into three parts (see Figure 1.1). First, organize your heritage trunk, which includes such items as books, CDs, files, heirlooms, maps, notes, photos, and research aids. Second, organize your

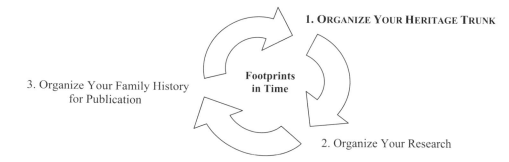

Figure 1.1 Phase one, organize your heritage trunk

research by dividing it into manageable pieces—worksheets can help with this task. Third, organize your family history for publication so that you can share your heritage with others. As you research, you move constantly from one part to another, each being necessary for the success of the other.

Plan Ahead

First things first! Develop a plan for your genealogy. Do you want to focus on only one or two surnames? Are you jumping in the deep water by working on both Mom's and Dad's families at the same time? Do you want to work on all families, generation by generation?

Some genealogists start their research by focusing on their eight great-grandparents; doing so provides an overview of the immediate ancestors. By the time you research all eight great-grandparents, you will have found a favorite family line or two. You may find yourself more interested in branches that you personally knew or perhaps the family of your living parent. You may also find that one family is more difficult to research, while another is much easier and more interesting.

My paternal grandmother and her family are my most interesting group of ancestors, since they arrived in St. Louis in 1780, thus making me a ninth generation St. Louisan. However, one of my cousins and I published a family history on my maternal grandmother's family. I am also interested in my husband's paternal family. Keep an open mind and remain flexible about which family you work on first or most often.

The genealogy bug has bitten you, or you would not be reading this book. Perhaps a cousin, friend, parent, neighbor, sibling, or even your spouse has the same interest. It is great to have a working partner. It is not necessary to work on the same family, but it is helpful to have someone to share your joy and disappointment at the library. If you need to travel to a research facility, a traveling companion makes the trip more enjoyable. Although you may not have such a partner today, one may well appear as you pursue this intriguing hobby.

Documents and Discussions

As a family historian, you probably want to know yourself and your family better. You can begin with a simple conversation with a parent, grandparent, or sibling. From such beginnings, you lay the basic forms of organization. Genealogists must organize and record bits and pieces of information in a logical order. Doing so makes the research easier and the finished product more comprehensible. The process may seem daunting, but it need not be so.

So Let's Talk

It's helpful to interview all relatives—the young, as well as seasoned veterans. You will find that when you interview various people about the same event, each person remembers something different. People have a different perspective on family members based on the age at which they interacted with them. An older sibling may recall grandparents that younger siblings never met. People who were children at the time of an event remember aunts, uncles, and grandparents only as old people. Cousins often have differing memories about grandparents. By interviewing all cousins, a clear

Interview Techniques

To conduct a successful interview, you should combine all the basic interview skills used by the media with your knowledge of the family and genealogy. It is acceptable to steer your interview in the direction you have planned. After you ask the question, let the interviewee answer the question. It is not a time to share everything you know; it is a time to learn new information. A well-respected veteran television anchorman once said, "A well-positioned, 'Oh?' speaks volumes." This is a case when less is more! Ask the same questions the journalist asks:

- Who?
- What?
- Why? (or why not?)
- When?
- Where?
- How? (or how long?)

picture of the grandparents develops. This comprehensive interviewing also broadens your knowledge and helps you sort out conflicting statements.

One day I asked my husband what seemed to be a simple question: When did you move to St. Louis? Several weeks later, we determined a close date. We interviewed the five siblings, made a timeline, and reviewed the facts with each person. The family left Illinois after the death of their stepfather; they moved to Florida to live near an aunt for a while, then traveled to Cleveland, and quickly went on to St. Louis. My sister-in-law remembers arriving in Cleveland in the winter—she was a teenager with a tan, and the girls at school were jealous. Every little detail is important when interviewing relatives. The stories included a funeral, school events, holidays, and a wedding. We started with a documented event and progressed through logical and known events. By compiling a timeline of all the shared facts, we were able to come up with the month and year. Close enough!

By interviewing my in-laws separately, conflicting information was uncovered. This event happened many years ago and everyone's memory was a little hazy on some facts. By compiling all the data, we were able to filter through the facts and determine the correct order. Such documented information, including birthdays, deaths, marriages, and graduations, serves as the foundation of your timeline.

Since we are in the age of technology, record the interviews on audiotape or videotape. Fifty years from now, along with the memories, you will have your grandparents, parents, or siblings on tape. Don't forget to record your own voice, as well.

Before the Interview

Before you interview anyone, you should request permission from all parties who will participate in the conversation. Even with permission, bear in mind that some people do not feel as comfortable talking to a recorder or camera. To make everyone more comfortable, try conducting some preliminary conversations. Inquire about family photos; looking at photos may prompt conversation, suggest new questions, and stir memories.

A little bit of preparation ensures a more enjoyable interview for you and your family members. Create a list of questions. It is your responsibility, as the interviewer, to keep the conversation on track. While one answer may lead to a new set of questions, don't forget your original plan, and get back to it as quickly as possible. Avoid questions that require only yes or no answers; you want details about events or people. The following list provides a guide for preparing an interview:

- Establish your goals for this interview.
- Prioritize your questions.
- Select a convenient time for you and the interviewee.
- Select a site without interruptions from phones, television, and doorbells.
- Limit the interview to one hour at a time.
- Request permission to record the interview.

The Interview

The interview should be a pleasant experience for all parties. If possible, conduct this conversation in person, eye to eye, so you can see reactions and facial expressions. If not, phone conversations are better than nothing. Request any interview in advance, and always tell the interviewee the subject of the conversation, thus providing him time to think about the subject.

Some family members may be apprehensive about talking with you. They may think you are trying to uncover some deep dark family secret. You are! However, what they thought was so terrible years ago is nothing today. Maybe Uncle Clarence was in jail for two months in 1925 for making moonshine. We can live with that! Some of the older family members will take their secrets to the grave. No matter how much you talk, they will not share those secrets with you. Just move on; there isn't anything you can do, and you don't want to upset the interviewee. Talk about another subject while developing a rapport with this person. If the interviewee gains confidence in you, maybe someday she will share those deep dark family secrets. But don't count on it!

When interviewing a parent's or grandparent's sibling, you want to ask general questions that apply to your direct-line ancestor, as well as the sibling. For example, if interviewing your grandmother's sister, you might ask the following:

- Were you and your sister born in the same town?
- How long did the family live at that location?
- What did your father do for a living?
- Did your mother work outside the home?
- Where did you and your sister go to school?
- What church did the family attend?
- Do you recall an event when you visited with your grandparents?

If you ask the question about visiting with her grandparents, she could say, "Yes, they lived next door for twenty years." She could say, "I only met them once when I was about ten and my family was on a trip to Montana." Your next question could be, "Montana?" Another response might be, "No, I never met them; they died when Mother was a baby." No matter what the answer, you may have new information.

Pose the questions to provide as much information about your grandmother as her sister—your interviewee. Analyze the answers as she talks. Is she telling you what you want to hear? Determine what information applies to your grandmother, as well as the interviewee. If one sister was born in New York City, was the other one? They probably went to the same school and church. Information about the parents and grandparents applies to both sisters. During this conversation, you hope to glean new information about your grandmother, as well as her sister. Here are some guidelines to follow during the interview.

- Ask short simple questions.
- Ask a question that will bring back memories of an era.
- Ask a follow-up question based on the previous answer.
- Restate a question by saying, "Now let me be sure I understand this correctly . . ."
- Try to avoid questions with yes or no answers.
- Try not to ask questions that will embarrass you or the interviewee.
- Make short keyword notes so that you are not distracted from the conversation.
- Do not read the questions directly from your tablet.

If several people are involved in the conversation, you can extend the interview time. Aunt Minnie may become frustrated if she does not remember some information. If that occurs, try to focus on a new area. If one person monopolizes the conversation, redirect new questions to the other person. Sometimes one-on-one interviews are better.

Talk to your relatives as often as possible. You may have dozens of conversations with Grandma, each in your tape collection. Each conversation will reveal new information. Many years ago, my Grandmother Carter had a slight stroke while visiting me. Over the next few weeks, we were together day and night and often talked about our family. I knew the basic facts about her parents, but as much as she tried, she could not remember new information about her family. Then three weeks after the stroke, while she sat in the waiting room of the doctor's office, Grandmother Carter said, "Ann, my mother and I traveled by train to Lebanon, Missouri, when I was a child. Uncle Otto picked us up in his buggy, taking us to his home in Plato." That was all she remembered. Conversation over!

I was so excited when she started the statement! I hurriedly tried to get to my emergency notepad, anticipating there would be a stream of information. I was disappointed with the limited information at first, but she gave me a place, name, and time period. With that information in hand, I found her mother's family, including Uncle Otto McLaughlin, in Texas County, Missouri. Without those few tidbits of information, I might still be looking for that family.

While conducting the interview, you should limit your part of the conversation. Ask the questions and respond appreciatively so the interviewee knows how important this conversation is to you. Make sure she knows you are paying attention. Do not gaze over her shoulder at the lunch preparations or talk to others during the interview. Just keep your relatives talking and listen carefully.

After the Interview

After the official interview, further information may be gleaned during casual conversation over dinner, at a picnic, or while sitting on the porch swing. Since everyone knows you are the family historian, it is natural for you to record information from conversations. Don't be afraid to ask questions during this casual conversation. Keep a pencil and notepad in your pocket or purse for those "emergency notes."

Carefully retrieve, label, and store the tapes after each interview. Clearly label the audiotapes with the date and location of the interview, and the names of the interviewee and anyone else heard on the tape. One fellow genealogist recorded the church memorial service for his mother. At that very difficult time, the family forgot to remove the tape from the tape recorder, and unfortunately the next Sunday's church service was recorded over the memorial service.

Before you store the tape, it's a good idea to transcribe the data so you have a written document of the conversation. The transcription also serves as an insurance package in case the tape is lost or damaged. You may want to copy the conversation tapes to a CD or DVD, providing a copy of both the transcription and electronic version to the interviewees. These recordings become part of your heritage trunk.

Document Decorum

Documents, including birth, marriage, and death certificates; deeds; wills; and letters are valuable resources that provide names, dates, and places. As you will do with photos, gather originals or copies from your extended family. When a family member shares a document with you, offer to photocopy the document at your expense and then return it promptly to the owner.

Now that you are the family historian, some relatives will graciously give you their family documents or photos. And be thankful the documents did not go out in the trash. All too often, family members discard documents during a cleaning frenzy. Keep a record of the original owner of each document and photo and the date you received it. As you progress with your family history to the point of writing a book or newsletter—or creating a Web site—it is polite to acknowledge the original owner of each item you use.

As you accumulate the photos, documents, and tape recordings, keep them in a container, basket, file folder, or preferably an acid-free box. Further information on this process is available in Chapter 4. Never take your original documents and photos on a trip, except for duplication. If you need to take a photo to a family reunion or to show a relative, always make a copy. If you think you need to keep a photo or document in your research notebook, always make a copy. Originals should stay at home since they are not replaceable.

An **ancestor chart** is a list or chart of ancestors from whom you descend.

Ancestor Chart

Ancestor charts are the road map for your family history. Researching your family history is a long journey, and everyone needs a good map. A four-generation ancestor chart is a diagram of your immediate ancestors. This chart, as shown in Figure 1.2, starts with you, then your parents and grandparents, and finally your great-grandparents. Most people can fill in three generations easily, but the fourth one is usually far more difficult. You may have known one, perhaps two, of your great-grandparents. Starting with yourself, fill in as much information as possible.

Ancestor charts come in various configurations. Many charts display four generations, while others

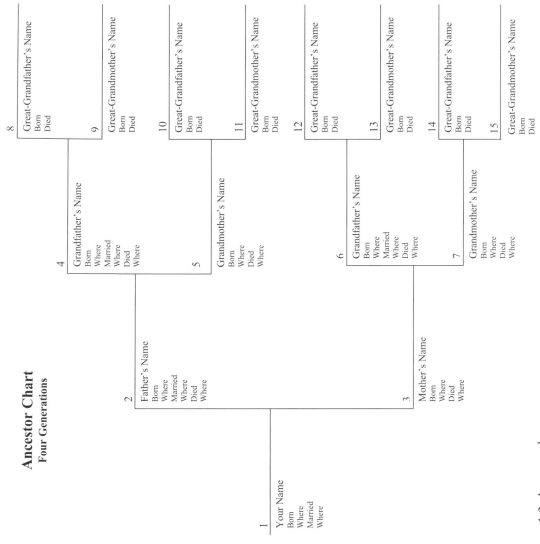

Figure 1.2 Ancestor chart

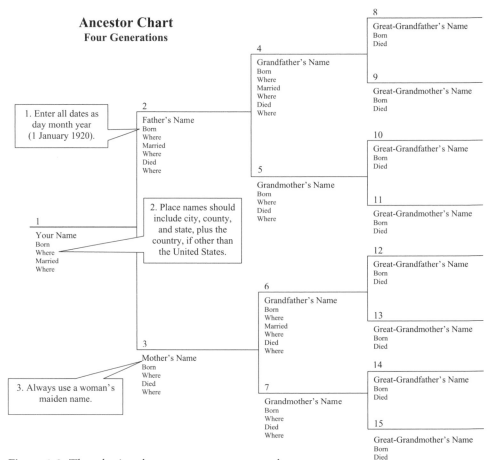

Ancestor Chart
Four Generations

1. Enter all dates as day month year (1 January 1920).

2. Place names should include city, county, and state, plus the country, if other than the United States.

3. Always use a woman's maiden name.

1. Your Name
Born
Where
Married
Where

2. Father's Name
Born
Where
Married
Where
Died
Where

3. Mother's Name
Born
Where
Died
Where

4. Grandfather's Name
Born
Where
Married
Where
Died
Where

5. Grandmother's Name
Born
Where
Died
Where

6. Grandfather's Name
Born
Where
Married
Where
Died
Where

7. Grandmother's Name
Born
Where
Died
Where

8. Great-Grandfather's Name
Born
Died

9. Great-Grandmother's Name
Born
Died

10. Great-Grandfather's Name
Born
Died

11. Great-Grandmother's Name
Born
Died

12. Great-Grandfather's Name
Born
Died

13. Great-Grandmother's Name
Born
Died

14. Great-Grandfather's Name
Born
Died

15. Great-Grandmother's Name
Born
Died

Figure 1.3 Three basic rules to use on an ancestor chart

show five or six generations. Some large fold-up or wall charts show fifteen or more generations at once. Genealogical software programs allow you to decide whether you want to print a four-, five-, or six-generation chart.

Start by filling in what you already know. List each person by his full name—not the name you know him by today. Be mindful that Grandma James was not born "Grandma James." She was born Julia Creely and was known by that name until she married John James. The first chart should start with you. Enter your name on the first line, adding your birth date and place, and your marriage information, if applicable (see Figure 1.3). Then add your father's name and information on the line marked "2." Do the same for your mother on the line marked "3." Enter the names of your

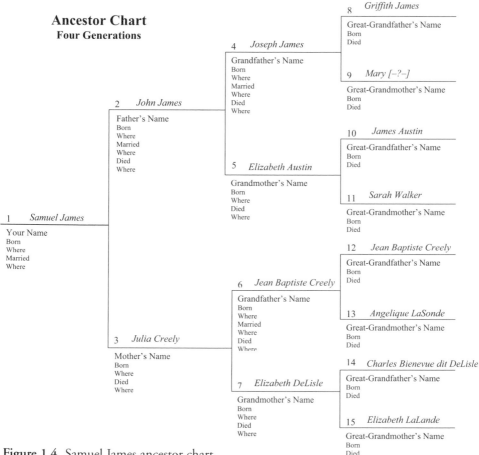

Ancestor Chart
Four Generations

1 — Samuel James
Your Name
Born
Where
Married
Where

2 — John James
Father's Name
Born
Where
Married
Where
Died
Where

3 — Julia Creely
Mother's Name
Born
Where
Died
Where

4 — Joseph James
Grandfather's Name
Born
Where
Married
Where
Died
Where

5 — Elizabeth Austin
Grandmother's Name
Born
Where
Died
Where

6 — Jean Baptiste Creely
Grandfather's Name
Born
Where
Married
Where
Died
Where

7 — Elizabeth DeLisle
Grandmother's Name
Born
Where
Died
Where

8 — Griffith James
Great-Grandfather's Name
Born
Died

9 — Mary [–?–]
Great-Grandmother's Name
Born
Died

10 — James Austin
Great-Grandfather's Name
Born
Died

11 — Sarah Walker
Great-Grandmother's Name
Born
Died

12 — Jean Baptiste Creely
Great-Grandfather's Name
Born
Died

13 — Angelique LaSonde
Great-Grandmother's Name
Born
Died

14 — Charles Bienevue dit DeLisle
Great-Grandfather's Name
Born
Died

15 — Elizabeth LaLande
Great-Grandmother's Name
Born
Died

Figure 1.4 Samuel James ancestor chart

grandparents and great-grandparents. Information about the men goes on the even-numbered lines and females on the odd-numbered lines. After entering all known data, you have your eight great-grandparents on one piece of paper. There may be gaps in the information, but you will fill in those pieces of the puzzle over time. This four-generation chart starts you down the road to uncovering your family's footprints.

Some family historians like to record surnames in all capital letters to differentiate given names from surnames. You can select this feature in the genealogical software programs (or turn it off). When writing charts by hand, feel free to choose the style with which you are most comfortable.

When you have more information than one chart will hold, start another chart. As in Figure 1.4, Griffith James, listed on line 8, should appear on line 1 of another chart.

Genealogical Guidelines

1. Enter all dates in the genealogical format—day, month, and year (1 January 1850). The year should contain four digits since you could be talking about 1950, 1850, or 1750.

2. Provide a complete description for each location: city, county, state, and country when outside the United States.

3. List all women by their maiden names. If you do not know a woman's maiden name, just leave the space blank until you locate the correct name.

Then his lineage is entered as far as it is known. Continue making additional charts when you complete one family line on the first chart.

Take copies of your charts when attending family holiday parties or reunions, visiting out-of-town relatives, or participating in other family events. The charts are great conversation starters for gathering family data. Having multiple copies allows two or more people to review them at a time. Otherwise, Uncle Fred may keep the charts the entire day.

You can either generate ancestor charts using a genealogical software program or write them by hand (I do both). As a family historian, you should keep a supply of blank ancestor charts to take on research trips and to share with others. You never know when new information will appear.

However the charts are created, you should be sure to share them with other family members and ask whether they have additional information. Seeing the information laid out on the charts often inspires new memories and may even lead you to new records. Cousins may be able to supply missing information. Perhaps you think Grandma died in California, but she really died in Virginia and was returned to California for burial.

As you track all of the new information you find, keep that original handwritten chart as your starting point. Years from now it will be interesting to compare your original chart to the current data. The comparison will give you a sense of accomplishment and will be fun to look at. Just by organizing your files and research, you will be amazed at the new information you can add to this chart.

Since the eight great-grandparents probably migrated from different parts of the United States or perhaps other countries, you can divide your research into different groups. For instance, one group could be the New England families, one the Illinois families, and another the German lines. If your ancestors immigrated to New York and the family still lives there, your research will be regional. On the other hand, if your ancestors migrated across the country, perhaps with each generation living in a different area of this country, your research will be nationwide.

You may consider researching only your father's surname. But that research is very limiting and you will miss the largest part of your ancestors. So if that plan crosses your mind, please reconsider. By looking at just one branch of the tree, you cannot see the entire family and you will miss some very interesting ancestors. After all, when you watch television, do you watch only one part of the screen? Of course not! Family history research works the same way: Be aware of the big picture so you don't limit the view.

> Retain a copy of your first ancestor chart to show what information you knew as you started your research.

On an ancestor chart, you are on the first line as number 1. Your father is on the line above you as number 2. Your paternal grandfather is on the line above your father, as number 4 and his father is number 8. As you can see in Figure 1.5, this is the only line in your chart that has continuous male descendants. Those four individuals are the only people you would trace if you were to trace only your surname. Look at all the ancestors you would be leaving out! If you are female, that line has stopped with you. However, you may have a brother who will continue the surname. All other lines in your family tree end with a female who marries and takes a new surname.

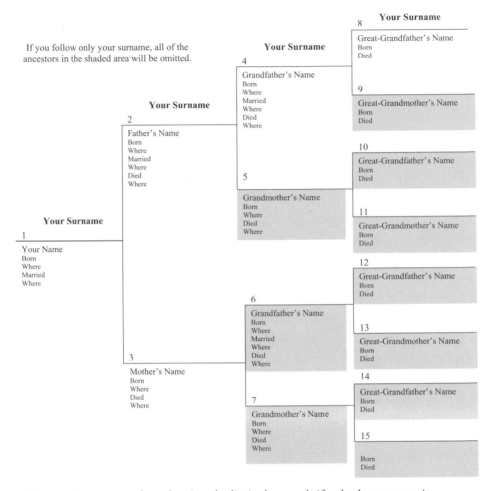

Figure 1.5 Ancestor chart showing the limited research if only the surname is followed

Family Group Sheet

If ancestor charts are the road map of your family history, family group sheets are the mileage markers. The family group sheet records information about each couple and their children on one sheet of paper. Make a family group sheet for every family unit, adding each child in chronological order. Then when a child marries, a new family group sheet will include the bride's and groom's names, with room for their children. If a person marries more than once, prepare a family group sheet for each marriage and record the children for each respective marriage on their parents' family group sheets. Figure 1.6 shows the first page of a blank family group sheet. Figure 1.7 shows

Family Group Sheet

	Name or Date	Place
Husband		
Born		
Married		
Died		
Buried		
Father		Mother
Other Spouse		Marriage Date & Place
Wife		
Born		
Died		
Buried		
Father		Mother
Other Spouse		Marriage Date & Place

	Sex	Name or Date	Place	
Children				
1st				
Born				
Died		Place	Cemetery	
Spouse		Marriage Date & Place		
2nd				
Born				
Died		Place	Cemetery	
Spouse		Marriage Date & Place		
3rd				
Born				
Died		Place	Cemetery	
Spouse		Marriage Date & Place		
4th				
Born				
Died		Place	Cemetery	
Spouse		Marriage Date & Place		
5th				
Born				
Died		Place	Cemetery	
Spouse		Marriage Date & Place		

Documentation

1.	
2.	
3.	
4.	
5.	
6.	
7.	
8.	
9.	
10.	
Prepared by & Date	

Figure 1.6 Family group sheet

Family Group Sheet

Page 2		Additional Children		
	Sex	**Name or Date**	**Place**	
6th				
Born				
Died		Place	Cemetery	
Spouse		Marriage Date & Place		
7th				
Born				
Died		Place	Cemetery	
Spouse		Marriage Date & Place		
8th				
Born				
Died		Place	Cemetery	
Spouse		Marriage Date & Place		
9th				
Born				
Died		Place	Cemetery	
Spouse		Marriage Date & Place		
10th				
Born				
Died		Place	Cemetery	
Spouse		Marriage Date & Place		
11th				
Born				
Died		Place	Cemetery	
Spouse		Marriage Date & Place		
12th				
Born				
Died		Place	Cemetery	
Spouse		Marriage Date & Place		

Documentation

11.	
12.	
13.	
14.	
15.	
16.	
17.	
18.	
19.	
20.	
21.	
22.	
23.	
24.	
25.	
Prepared by & Date	

Figure 1.7 Family group sheet, page 2

a second page that is available if needed. If there are more than twelve children born to any one set of parents, use page two again.

As you fill in the family group sheet, don't forget to document your sources. It isn't enough to have a name or date; family historians should record how and where they learned of that information. If you use a genealogical software program, you can enter the source citation once and then use it an unlimited number of times without any further data entry. Figure 1.8 shows a family group sheet partially filled in with abbreviated documentation for the Samuel James family.

If you use pencil and paper, it may be necessary to establish a shortcut version for your citations. Make a numbered list of your citations. This list should contain all the standard information needed for a citation: author, title, publication data, page numbers, and so on. Enter the citation number on the family group sheet adjacent to the fact you are documenting. This number serves as a cross-reference to your citation list, as shown in Figure 1.8.

As you do with the ancestor charts, take a supply of blank group sheets to family events. Ask each married couple to provide information about their family unit, recording dates and places of birth and marriage, along with other information. If other family members write the information, be sure you can read their handwriting

> A **family group sheet** is a form that contains information such as names, dates, and places of birth, marriages, and deaths for a single family—husband, wife, and their children.

before leaving the event. These sheets serve as your documentation for those facts.

It is a good idea to keep the family group sheets in a notebook or folder. Arrange the group sheets alphabetically by surnames, using tabs to divide the papers. You can divide them by your maternal and paternal lines or just group everything in alphabetical order. You can purchase a set of tabs with one tab for each letter of the alphabet. However, after a while one notebook will not hold that many pieces of paper. You can divide the sheets and notebooks into one for your paternal family and one for your maternal family. That decision is yours; use the method that works best for you.

Family Group Sheet

	Name or Date	Place
Husband	*Samuel James*	
Born	*16 September 1817*	*St. Ferdinand, St. Louis County, Missouri ①*
Married	*17 February 1838*	*St. Ferdinand, St. Louis County, Missouri ②*
Died	*15 July 1898*	*St. Ferdinand, St. Louis County, Missouri ③④*
Buried	*17 July 1898*	*St. Ferdinand Cemetery, St. Louis County, Missouri ③④*
Father	*John Griffith James ⑧*	Mother *Julia Creely ⑧*
Other Spouse	*None*	Marriage Date & Place
Wife	*Virginia Robertson*	
Born	*21 August 1820*	*St. Louis County, Missouri ①*
Died	*23 April 1903*	*Florissant, St. Louis County, Missouri ③*
Buried	*24 April 1903*	*St. Ferdinand Cemetery, Florissant, St. Louis County, Missouri ③*
Father	*William Robertson ⑥*	Mother *Sarah Baber ⑥*
Other Spouse	*None*	Marriage Date & Place

Children

	Sex	Name or Date	Place	
1st	M	*William Griffith James*		
Born		*1843*	*St. Ferdinand, St. Louis County, Missouri ①*	
Died		*1900*	Place *St. Louis County, Missouri*	Cemetery
Spouse		*Virginia Patton*	Marriage Date & Place *5 May 1864, St. Louis County, Missouri ②*	
2nd	F	*Virginia James*		
Born		*16 August 1850*	*St. Ferdinand, St. Louis County, Missouri ①*	
Died		*19 December 1939*	Place *St. Louis County, Mo ③*	Cemetery *Calvary Cemetery, St. Louis ③*
Spouse		*John Donahue Tobin*	Marriage Date & Place *11 November 1874, St. Louis County, Missouri ②*	
3rd	M	*Alphonse James*		
Born		*25 October 1856*	*St. Ferdinand, St. Louis County, Missouri ①*	
Died		*After 1901 ⑦*	Place	Cemetery
Spouse		*Eunice Bell Cable*	Marriage Date & Place *29 May 1886, Laclede County, Missouri ⑤*	
4th	F	*Jessie James*		
Born		*28 May 1862*	*St. Ferdinand, St. Louis County, Missouri ①*	
Died		*1919*	Place *St. Louis County, Mo. ⑩*	Cemetery *St. Martin's Cem., St. Louis ⑩*
Spouse		*John Bellville*	Marriage Date & Place *18 April 1883, St. Louis County, Missouri ⑨*	
5th				
Born				
Died			Place	Cemetery
Spouse			Marriage Date & Place	

Documentation

1.	*St. Ferdinand Catholic Church Baptismal Records, SLCL film 166*
2.	*St. Louis County Marriages, Recorder of Deeds, Bk 2: 85; Bk 11: 431; Bk 16: 442*
3.	*St. Louis Archdiocese Cemetery Index, St. Ferdinand Cem.; Calvary Cem.; St. Martin's Cem.*
4.	*Samuel James obit, St. Louis Post-Dispatch, 16 July 1898*
5.	*Laclede County, Missouri Marriage Record 2: 59*
6.	*William Robertson probate file, St. Louis Probate Office, no. 1118*
7.	*Samuel James probate file, St. Louis County Probate Office, no. 4986*
8.	*John James probate file, St. Louis Probate Office, no. 1087*
9.	*St. Louis County Marriages, 1: 197*
10.	*StLGS Old Cemeteries 1: 65*
Prepared by & Date	*Ann Carter Fleming, July 1995*

Figure 1.8 Samuel James family group sheet

As you uncover new original source data, be sure to add it to your files, charts, and genealogical software program, always documenting the sources at the same time you add the data to your files. If Jacob and Florence Dorf submit information for the family group sheet, the documentation should state their names as the providers and the date they provided the information. If their daughter, Rose Dorf Smith, provides the data, list her name and the date in the documentation. Add additional documentation to the computer program when you uncover birth certificates and marriage licenses. Then print a revised family group sheet.

Research Log

Now that you are beginning to accumulate paper, it is time to think about the overall organization before you become overwhelmed. The time to establish good research and organizational practices is at the beginning of this project. If you have not already started, begin keeping track of resources. By keeping a research calendar or research log, as shown in Figure 1.9, you will save time by not looking up the same information twice. Most professional researchers record the title, author, and publication data of a book or a URL before they even open it. At that point, the researcher does not know whether the book will yield new information or not. The research log should include every publication or Web site reviewed— even if nothing is found there.

You can maintain this log on paper or on the computer. Use a word-processing program, database, or spreadsheet, whichever method works best for you. Whether you use the computer or pencil and paper, do not hesitate to use multiple lines for one source. Take as much space as necessary; include enough information so that you will understand the purpose and results of each search tomorrow and next year. Recording a full reference the first time you use a source helps you find the resource easily if you need to examine that source again.

The log should include the date of research; the repository; the title, author, and publication data; and

> A **research log** is a document that records sources a researcher has reviewed and the results of those searches.

RESEARCH LOG

ANCESTOR'S NAME _____

LOCATION _____
(COUNTY, STATE, OR COUNTRY OF SEARCH)

Date of Search	Repository Name or URL	Purpose of the Search	Book or Film (Title, Author, City, Publisher, Year, Film Number, or URL)	Results

Figure 1.9 Research log

the results of the search. You can use a continuous log or one divided by surname, which is much easier to use and handle. Dividing the log by your ancestor's surname and then by location keeps the documents smaller and more concise. Provide enough information in the results field to identify the search, whether it was positive or negative. You may think you will remember every book or microfilm that you review, but you won't. Unless you record your research immediately, you will find yourself looking up the same information twice—an exasperating waste of time and energy!

Of course, sometimes it is necessary to look at the same book again after you find new information. For example, you believe that Julia Lynch and Jeff Anderson married about 1870, but you find no record. Then you find out the bride had been married previously to a man named James Rudd, so you look first for the Rudd-Anderson marriage and then the Lynch-Rudd marriage. There they are. Perhaps you find additional ancestors in the same county. Another visit to the same marriage index may be in order. By recording the purpose of each search, you know why you were looking at the book each time. In this example, the purpose of the first search was to locate the Lynch-Anderson marriage. The second search was for the marriage of Rudd-Anderson and then the marriage of Lynch-Rudd. Subsequent searches in that same county were made for Julia's siblings. In your research log, list the words "marriage," "county name," and "surnames." Otherwise, how will you know what you were looking for? Figure 1.10 provides an example of a research log.

Correspondence Log

Even in the electronic age, it is sometimes necessary to mail a letter via U.S. mail, particularly to government facilities, which often take a long time to reply to genealogical inquiries. It is a good idea to set up an "Open Correspondence" manila folder. By maintaining this folder, you will remember which inquiries are outstanding and how much time has passed since you mailed the letters. That helps you eliminate duplicate inquiries.

A correspondence log helps family historians remember whom they have contacted, that person's address, the purpose of the correspondence, and the mailing date. A paper or computer form will help this process. File the written correspondence with other family papers once you receive a response. Some researchers keep a correspondence log for electronic correspondence; others just store the e-mails in electronic family folders. You should create a printout of any electronic correspondence with

RESEARCH LOG

ANCESTOR'S NAME _____ *Anderson*

LOCATION _____ *Saline County, Illinois*
(COUNTY, STATE, OR COUNTRY OF SEARCH)

Date of Search	Repository Name or URL	Purpose of the Search	Book or Film (Title, Author, City, Publisher, Year, Film Number, or URL)	Results
10/1995	FHL	Anderson marriages	Saline Co. marriages FHL film no. 965056	Julia Anderson md James Rudd 9 Dec 1863 Further research required on this Julia.
10/1995	FHL	Anderson marriages	Saline Co. marriages FHL film no. 965056	No record for Julia Anderson & Jeff Lynch.
10/1995	FHL	Anderson marriages	Saline Co. marriages FHL film no. 965056 Bk A: 149	Margaret Anderson md William Lemmon 26 Nov 1863. (Julia's sister)
3/1996	GSSI Library	Check counties adjoining Saline Co. for Julia Anderson marriage	Judy Foreman Lee & Carolyn Cromeenes Foss, Pope Co Marriage Book 1813–1877 Vol 1, (np: pp. 1990), citing B: 513.	Julia Rudd md Francis J. Lynch 17 Sep 1865. Groom's name Thomas not Francis.
3/1996	GSSI Library	Julia Anderson Rudd Lynch marriage?	Williamson Co. marriages	Julia Rudd md Aaron Arnold 8 Oct 1887. Julia still married to Lynch! Copy in file.
3/1996	GSSI Library	Anderson marriages	Bernard Moore, Saline County, Illinois marriages, 1847–1880 (Thomson, Ill.: Heritage House, 1976), citing Bk A: 208.	Louisa Anderson md John Yancy 20 May 1866. (Julia's sister)
3/1996	GSSI Library	Anderson marriages	Bernard Moore, Saline County, Illinois marriages, 1847–1880 (Thomson, Ill.: Heritage House, 1976), citing Bk A: 134.	Indiana Anderson md John Culbertson 7 June 1862. (Julia's sister)
5/1996	Pope Co. Courthouse	Lynch-Rudd marriage	Pope County Courthouse marriage book	The index states Francis J. Lynch, but the marriage book names the groom Thomas J. Lynch. Julia is listed as Juliett Rudd.
10/1996	FHL	Lynch divorce?	Mary Brimm & Rebecca Schmook, Early Saline County, Illinois court records, divorce abstracts (Harrisburg, Ill.: Saline Co. Gen. Soc., nd), citing Bk T: 269, no. 57	Thomas Lynch-Julia (Anderson) Lynch divorce 18 October 1890.
10/1996	FHL	Anderson or Lynch marriages in adjoining counties	Williamson County marriages	Julia Lynch md Aaron Arnold 17 Oct 1890, see copy. Married one day before divorce dated!

Figure 1.10 Anderson research log

pertinent information, just in case the file is lost. Design your correspondence log (see Figure 1.11) in a word-processing program, spreadsheet, or database.

> A **correspondence log** is a list of letters and inquiries pertaining to genealogy; it contains the name, address, phone, fax, e-mail, family surname, date of correspondence, and a summary of the response.

When you send a letter requesting information, it is courteous to include a self-addressed stamped envelope (SASE). If you are asking the recipient to respond, the least you can do is pay for the postage. As a bonus, you will find the reply rate is better. Some reply letters fit in a No. 10 envelope, but if you are lucky, others need a larger envelope. You can send your address label and stamps unattached so that the responder has an option on the envelope to use. You still pay the postage and provide your accurate address. The sender supplies the envelope.

> **SASE** is the acronym for self-addressed stamped envelope. When corresponding by U.S. postal mail, it is courteous to pay for the return postage—and doing so increases your response rate.

When you receive a reply, record the date and results of the inquiry in the correspondence log. Remove the letter from the open correspondence folder, attach it to the reply, record the findings, take any necessary action, and file the packet in the appropriate file folder, according to your filing system. It may be necessary to review this correspondence in the future. Data that may not seem important today may become valuable pertinent information tomorrow or next year.

CORRESPONDENCE LOG

Surname of Interest	Name of Correspondent	Address	Request	Date of Request	Reply Results	Date of Reply	Action Item

Figure 1.11 Correspondence log

Genealogists can start organizing and recording their family histories by using a few simple forms, which are works in progress, changing each time they add new information. Take time to talk to your relatives, gleaning as much information as possible and properly recording the new data. Decide on a system to organize and store all your family documents to ensure easy retrieval when needed. By now, you may be asking yourself, "What do I do with all this stuff?"

CHAPTER 2

What Do I Do with All This Stuff?

PAPERLESS SOCIETY—SAYS WHO? PAPER, PHOTOS, DOCUMENTS, AND general "stuff" inundate family historians. Now if only we had some idea what to do with all that "stuff" we have found! "Stuff" is an official genealogical word covering a wide range of items in your heritage trunk, including books, documents, file folders, heirlooms, notes, photos, and whatever else you have collected.

When our ancestors traveled across the ocean on a ship or across the country by wagon, they stored all their worldly possessions in their heritage trunks. They were forced to be organized. Some of those same items may be in your heritage trunk today. Though you have more space today than your ancestors did, you still need to organize, identify, and containerize everything.

Where is your family memorabilia—in books, folders, boxes, drawers, or elsewhere? The first objective is to put like items together. Organize, sort, copy, purge, and file all the papers first, then review each document to glean and record new information. You may think this process is backward, but you probably started the stacks of paper with the best intentions of recording the new data and then filing the papers. If that method did not work, why not try this new plan?

Help Wanted: Filing

Organize Data

Does your family history currently reside in pile after pile of papers sitting on the floor, desk, dining room table, closet, or shelf? Do you know what you have and where it is? Finding the data is fun; filing it is frustrating. You can start to organize all of that "stuff" with just a few simple decisions. How do you usually think about your genealogy—by location, subject, or surname? File the way you think. What is right for one person may be wrong for another and vice versa.

> Do you want to file your photos with your documents and other papers? Probably not! Photos and regular paper do not mix well; keep a separate file or box for your photos. See Chapter 4 for tips on how best to organize photos.

Do you think about your family history by surnames? If so, file by surname. If you have a large overflowing file on one surname, subdivide within the surname by couples. There are just a few papers regarding the Creely family and hundreds on the James family. All Creely papers fit easily in one file folder. However, an extensive amount of research on the James family has produced a large volume of paperwork. Subdividing the James family papers by couples makes the folders easier to handle and allows for a more efficient retrieval system.

Another option for large surname files is to subdivide them by location. The James family started in Maryland, moved to Kentucky, migrated into Illinois, and settled in St. Louis, all before 1804. Folders for each location subdivide the surname. If the family lived in one location longer than another, you can divide a location file chronologically. The James family lived in St. Louis from 1804 until 1989. We can divide the St. Louis file by the two centuries or by increments of twenty-five or fifty years.

Since genealogists research by location, you may prefer to file by location. In some cases, one folder per state is sufficient; however, one folder per county is usually more manageable. If we file by location, everything on the James family and its collateral lines from Monroe County, Illinois, are filed together. Subdivide these files chronologically or by couples, as needed. On the file folder label, write the location name first and then any additional identifying information that will help you locate the correct folder.

The third option is to file all similar documents together: one folder for marriage records, another for birth certificates, and yet another for wills. It is advisable to assign an identification number to each document, assigning the next available number for that record type to each document. Marriages may start with M0000. The first marriage record will be M0001. The next marriage document, no matter who it is for or where it is from, will be M0002. In the front of each file folder, maintain an index with all numbers and documents listed for easy retrieval of the certificates. Computer programs are available to assist with this filing option. The program provides the number for the document when you enter the date and information. You not only have a paper copy, but also a computer list of your documents.

Filing Options

There are three basic filing options, but feel free to use a combination. You will find people who insist that one method, the one they use, is the best, and it probably is for their situation. Use the method that works best for you.

1. **Surname:** File records based on surname and then subdivide by couples or family units. You can also subdivide by location, listing the surname and city or state on the label.

2. **Location:** File your records based on location only. Documents from Virginia do not mix with documents from New York. Subdivide folders by state and then county or even further by city.

3. **Document Type:** File based on record type. Assign a sequential number to each document and list that number and document description on the folder index. File all of the marriage records together, death certificates together, and so on.

Whichever system you select, a blank sheet of paper attached inside the front of each folder makes a great place to jot down notes to yourself. If John James married Julia Creely in St. Louis, where do I file the marriage record? If filing by document, it goes in the marriage record folder. If filing by location, it goes in the St. Louis folder. If filing by surname, subdivided by couple, it goes in the James-Creely folder. If filing by surname, place the marriage record in the James folder with a cross-reference or notation in the Creely folder, "James-Creely marriage record in James folder." Decide where you will file marriage records. Should you file the marriage record in the folder for the groom or the bride? I use the groom's folder since that is the family surname researched thereafter. Place the marriage record in the couple's folder if that is your system.

Sort

Now that you have decided on a data-organizing system, it's time to start sorting those big stacks of papers. Find a convenient location in the house to sort all your genealogical papers—preferably a spot where the papers will be undisturbed for a day or so. An unused bed, a dining room table, the basement floor, or any other large area will suffice.

Take a small handful of papers at a time and divide them by the filing system you selected: surname, location, or document. Keep sorting your papers until those big stacks disappear. You now have like items together in numerous little stacks that are far more manageable. This is a giant step on the road to organization.

Copy

So far, we have sorted the papers, making little stacks out of the big piles. Now look at each stack separately and photocopy a few papers in each one. Most likely, the stacks have an assortment of paper sizes—8½ x 11-inch papers, index cards, old envelopes full of notes, a few photos, and possibly photocopies of documents or census records on 11 x 17-inch paper. See the problem here?

A good filing system contains information on 8½ x 11-inch paper, with the one exception listed below. This means no notes on the backs of envelopes, no index cards, and no scraps of paper. Odd-sized paper or envelopes make a disorderly file. Small pieces of paper are misplaced in file folders, easily getting attached to something else and eventually disappearing. Those envelopes with important notes jotted on the back cause the folder to be needlessly bulky. Establish good filing procedures by making everything the same size.

So gather the odd-sized papers and photocopy the notes onto the common paper size, 8½ x 11 inches. Copy the back of each scrap of paper that contains important facts or dates. Once you make the copies, discard the scraps of paper. But do double-check originals against copies before discarding anything. Make sure nothing is in the wrong stack and that you have a readable and complete copy.

The one exception I make is for photocopies on large paper. Census record photocopies are often on 11 x 17-inch paper so that the small print is legible. After all, what good is the copy if we cannot read it? Either fold the large paper in half, to 8½ x 11 inches, or keep a folder for oversized papers. If using an oversized folder, cross-reference this document on the note sheet inside the front of the folder.

Photocopy newspaper articles since the originals yellow and crumble over time. If you know the newspaper's name and place of publication, and the newspaper clipping does not contain that information, write it on the photocopy. The photocopy eliminates the need to handle the original document. Preserve the original newspaper article in an archival folder that helps retard disintegration. Newspaper articles leak acid, so they should not be stored next to valuable papers or photos. Chapter 4 provides further archival and storage information.

Photocopy Hint

When making a copy of any document or book, set the copier to 95 percent. That difference allows for white space on the edge where you can record your source citation without covering any part of the document or text.

If the stack contains photos, remove and file them with your other photos. Handle photos as little as possible, just like newspaper articles. Copies are good substitutes with which to work.

Purge

All too often, we needlessly save duplicate copies of the same information or documents. When sorting my files, I found ten-year-old computer printouts. Surely I have discovered new information over those ten years! Moreover, the data is in my genealogical software program and in the "in progress" written family history. Do I really need those old printouts? No! Be sure to list every fact elsewhere, then purge duplicate copies.

When purging, remove all paper clips from the folders. Paper clips are great, but not inside a folder. They become a nuisance, attaching to the wrong papers and cluttering the folder.

When you purge old notes, be cautious. You certainly do not want to throw out data that has not been entered elsewhere. You don't want to throw out the only copy of Grandpa's signature even if it was on the back of an envelope. You don't want to

Paper clips seem like a good way to keep papers together, but they really become a headache when the clip is caught on the wrong paper or the folder itself. They can also rust, which spells disaster for archival papers.

purge an important paper that was stuck between two unneeded papers. Once something is gone, it cannot be retrieved. A friend told me recently about a day twenty years ago when her husband's family was cleaning out a house after his aunt died. Someone went through the pictures and threw out every unidentified photo. Since my friend was new to the family and the "in-law," she did not say anything. Today my friend and her husband would love to have those photos. Whether you are working on documents, notes, or photos, be careful as you clean your files.

Filing Tools

File Folder Management

With the sorting, copying, and purging complete, you are ready to make file folders and labels. Determine the number of folders needed for each stack of papers. There are various types of file folders. The one-third-cut folders, compared to the one-fifth-cut ones, allow for a larger tab with more space for the folder name and description. Plus, most file folder labels are sized and designed for the one-third cut. One-half-cut folders are also available.

Should you use letter- or legal-sized folders? What type of filing cabinet do you have? If you have a basic two- or four-drawer filing cabinet, the assorted-cut folders are easy to read since the tabs are fully visible across the drawer. If you have a lateral filing cabinet (it may look like a piece of regular furniture that matches your desk), you may want to purchase one-position folders (folders with tabs all on the left, all on the right, or all in the center). The filing drawers in a lateral cabinet are the depth of a file folder and perhaps three feet long. You have to decide how you want to use the drawer. The folders can be placed in two rows facing the front of the drawer or in a continuous row facing one side of the drawer. If you use the continuous-row option, you will need to stand alongside the drawer to read the folder tabs. If you use an assorted cut, the tabs in the back of the drawer are much harder to read than if they were all in the center or front of the drawer. Before you purchase file folders and cabinets, *test drive* your storage area to find the system that works best for you.

Folders are available in basic manila or an assortment of colors. You should be able to find a different color for each of your eight great-grandparents' files. However, since one or two of those branches will need more folders than the others, you may end up with unusable colors and not enough folders in the most-used color. I suggest you use either a limited number of colors or all manila folders.

Accordion folders hold several manila folders, stand upright in the drawer, and take up less space than hanging files. You might want to consider some of these to hold related manila folders.

Though neat and orderly, hanging file folders tend to hold fewer files per drawer due to the thickness of the hanging rod at the top of each folder. On the other hand, hanging file folders do not fall over or slide down in the drawer. Most filing cabinets can accommodate standard folders, as well as hanging folders; just add or remove the hanging folders' framework. You must decide what type of filing system works best for you.

Notebooks

Some family historians use loose-leaf notebooks instead of file folders to store their data and documents. Just as with file folders, this system enables you to select the surname, location, or document filing system. Place a label on the spine and on the front of the notebook to make it easy to identify. If you have an available bookcase or shelf, arrange the notebooks for easy access.

With the notebook storage option, you can use clear plastic sleeves or hole-punched sheet protectors made for ring binders. Neither original documents nor their duplicates should be three-hole punched. Not only might you need to copy that document in the future, but the holes may destroy information on that document. Besides, three-hole-punched documents look awful!

Before you purchase any notebooks, consider the scope of the project. Do you need a one-inch binder or a three-inch binder? Do you anticipate 100 or 400 sheets of paper per notebook? A one-inch notebook holds approximately 250 sheets of paper; a three-inch binder holds about 750 pages. Which size notebook will work best for your project? Figure 2.1 shows the capacity of various sizes of ring binders.

	20-pound paper	**24-pound paper**
¼-inch binder	65	56
½-inch binder	130	112
¾-inch binder	195	168
1-inch binder	260	224
2-inch binder	520	448
3-inch binder	780	672

Figure 2.1 Ring binder capacity

Labels

File folder labels also come in an assortment of styles. Some are plain white, some solid colors, and others white with a colored line. Labels can be computer-generated, produced on a typewriter, or handwritten. Before printing or writing on the labels, test the size and color that work best for your file folders and storage area. Make sure each label is easy to read.

You may want some color coordination on the labels with the convenience of purchasing only one box of labels. In your word-processing program, make a folder named "Forms." Within that folder, make a *file folder* file. Use a large, bold font for each surname. You can highlight the name with pink, blue, or yellow. You could use pink highlighting for the wife's family, blue highlighting for the husband's family, and yellow for miscellaneous or general folders. You can assign each of the eight great-grandparents a separate color, if you like. A color printer or a set of highlighters is required for this option.

Using colored dots is a helpful way to identify file folders; blue and green dots could designate the paternal folders and red and orange dots signify the maternal lines. Dots are available in an assortment of colors and sizes at the office supply store.

Arrange the papers within each folder chronologically, alphabetically, or numerically. Continue the designated filing order, whether it is next week or next year. Being consistent is vital to maintaining your organization.

Since all genealogists love "the search," you may eagerly take on research projects for your neighbors or in-laws. Make a file folder for each of those projects, as well.

However, consider keeping those folders in a separate drawer or area so they are not interwoven with your family files.

Other Folders

As your research develops, you will see articles in magazines or newspapers about a place or event that you want to follow up on in the future. Make a topic or location folder to hold these articles. If you intend to do Native American research down the road, you may want to collect as much information on that topic as possible. If you plan to research in Virginia, save all those articles in a Virginia folder. Then when you are ready to do that research, the articles will be at your fingertips, not scattered hither and yon.

Project Folders

Current projects need to be at your fingertips. Keep those papers in a transparent colored or clear plastic project folder sealed on two sides. These folders travel well and are easily identifiable based on the assorted colors. It is easy to remember the red folder has one family, the blue folder has another, and the clear folder has travel information. Office supply stores sell these project folders in groups of five or ten in an assortment of colors or all clear. Because they are transparent, you can easily see and read the first page in the folder. If you are actively collecting documents on a particular family, use the project folder as a holding file until you are ready to file everything in the proper surname folder. Keep the project folders in a briefcase, a desktop file holder, a picnic basket, or any other container available for filing.

If your library does not allow three-ring binders in its research area, use the project folder as your research notebook. Assemble just the needed information to take into the library that day. You may even have your notebook in a locker or the car. The project folder keeps your papers from flailing across the table or floor.

The first piece of paper in your project folder can serve as a reminder or introduction of what is in that folder—for instance, "Research Trip" or "County Courthouse." This reminds you of the contents and at the same time keeps anything inside out of sight of others. If you use one of these folders for your medical or financial records, you do not want any of the pages visible to others.

These folders can also be helpful while working on a family reunion, holiday party, or special research project. When the event is over, move the folder contents to a regular folder, properly label the manila folder, and place it in a storage drawer. Then use the transparent folder for your next project.

Work Space

In a perfect world, every genealogist would have an office with a large desk, file cabinets, the most up-to-date computer equipment (including a scanner), bookshelves full of reference materials, and lots of room. However, we do not live in a perfect world. Perhaps you share a small desk with others, equipment is aging quickly, and reference material and storage space are limited. You have to make the best of your situation and use the space available. A computer, printer, and scanner require a certain amount of space. Some printers are also copiers, scanners, and fax machines that save desk space. Some computer desks use vertical space. If you have just one file folder drawer to use, keep your current project folders in that drawer, rotating folders in and out as the projects change.

If possible, keep like items together. Place the address book or Rolodex near the phone. Put the extra ink cartridges and at least a ream of paper near the printer and fax. Store the computer disks and data CDs near the computer. Ideally, everything should be kept in the area in which it will be used.

In your immediate work area, you probably have a phone. In that area, keep a spiral tablet, similar to the old-fashioned stenographer's pad, for notes. That way, the tablet is available when you need to write down a phone number, confirmation number, caller's name, random idea, or any other type of note. It is not necessary to search for the back of an envelope or small scrap of paper. In the tablet, record the date on each page. If necessary, transfer the data to the appropriate address book or file folder, or enter the information in your computer. Phone numbers should be permanently stored in a card file or address list. Do not remove pages from this tablet. Over time, this tablet becomes your memory and chronological history.

Another tool or option for recording your daily notes is a calendar with ample writing space for each day. The calendar serves as a diary of your activities, appointments, calls, and research. Keep track of your mileage and other tax-deductible expenses if you volunteer for your local genealogical or historical society.

Containerize Everything

Every good work area needs pens and pencils. Place them in a cup, basket, or any other suitable upright container. You may want to keep a pair of scissors and a magnifying glass in that same basket so they are easily available when you need them. You should store supplies, including paper clips, rubber bands, staplers, staple removers, and staples, in a drawer or desktop container.

Genealogists use many office supplies, including sticky notes, No. 10 envelopes, large manila envelopes, and address labels. If you share information by postal mail with your relatives, obtain the free Priority mail envelopes from the post office. Stronger than a standard 10 x 13-inch envelope, the Priority envelopes help the package arrive safely. Other mailing services also have special packaging.

If your work area is your lap and the surrounding floor while sitting in a comfortable chair, keep your supplies in a basket, box, or perhaps a portable container on wheels. A large basket, such as a picnic basket, provides a lid and moves easily from one spot to another. Some baskets come with a tray inside for those small items and ample space below for file folders. Plastic file boxes may have similar options. Discount stores and office supply stores offer moveable storage bins on wheels. This type of container certainly holds more than a box or basket. While shopping for a container, take a file folder with you to *test drive* the basket or container.

Storage Boxes

Once you set up an organized filing system, you can store reference materials in a file folder as you gather them. It is important to keep active files close to your workspace. Most family historians work on a few families at a time, with others waiting in the wings. Place the inactive files in a storage box, out of the way but easily accessible. The storage boxes may be in your closet or any other place that works for you.

Storage containers come in various sizes and styles. White cardboard boxes, often called bankers' boxes, have lids that lift off; others have pull-out drawers, as shown in Figure 2.2. If the boxes are placed on a shelf and are easily accessible, the lift-off lids may be the easiest

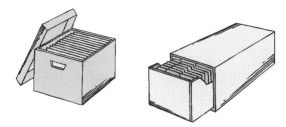

Figure 2.2 Storage boxes

to handle. If the boxes are stacked one on top of the other, the pull-out style is the most convenient. Both boxes are available at office supply stores.

Correct labeling is vital for storage boxes. It may be necessary to use the files again, so make a comprehensive contents list on the label. If possible, file alphabetically. If you have enough material for more than one box, you may want to sort by family: one box for Dad's folders and one for Mom's family folders.

In addition to the cardboard storage boxes, you can use file cabinets, moveable carts, or decorative boxes and baskets. Decide which storage container to use based on how much you have—and anticipate having—to store, the space available, and your budget. Before buying any storage item, decide where to put it in the house. Is there enough room for the drawers to pull out for easy access? Will this item look nice in your home? Will this storage item and area allow for growth? Develop a plan before making any investment.

Address, Phone, and Fax

An address book provides the lifeline for a family historian. Keep at your desk an address card file, computerized list, or actual book. In your family history address book, record every family history contact you make. This could be a distant cousin in another city, a volunteer at a genealogical or historical society, or a librarian or clerk at the local repository.

Record their names, addresses, phones, faxes, e-mail addresses, and any special information you know. Include the family surname that you share with this contact. Genealogists often forget the names of people in the current generation, but they do not forget the ancestor's name. Cards for your address book or box can be computer printed or handwritten. When you correspond with potential cousins by postal mail, phone, or e-mails, be sure to add their contact information to the correspondence log outlined in Chapter 1.

Package Labels

You can produce shipping labels on your computer for outgoing envelopes and packages. Your word-processing program has shipping label templates—or you can make your own. Purchase a package of address labels at the office supply store. Use the 3⅓ x 4-inch size, six labels per sheet, with room for both the ship-to address and the return address. Or purchase smaller labels, one for the return address, and one

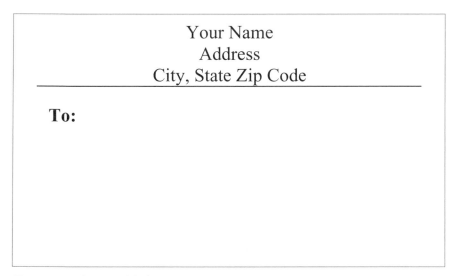

Figure 2.3 Shipping label

for the ship-to address. If you do not have a computer, write the ship-to and return addresses, as shown in Figure 2.3.

Business Cards

Business cards have a way of collecting in a drawer or in a stack on the desk. Either way, they are not in any order and are cumbersome to use. Purchase a business card holder or card sleeves for a three-ring notebook. Place the cards in the holder in an order that works for you. For instance, if you don't think you will remember his name, file Joe Smith, the plumber, under *P* for plumber rather than *S* for Smith. Likewise, I keep my genealogy contacts under the ancestor's surname rather than the contact's name. Will I remember that Mrs. Whoisit is a contact for the James family? Probably not. However, I will look under James when I want to contact her.

Have you ever considered a personal business card? Many people have professional business cards, but few have personal cards, as shown in Figure 2.4. Share the cards with fellow researchers or cousins whom you want to contact again. It is convenient to hand someone your personal business card with your name, address, phone number, e-mail address, and fax clearly printed. The recipient will appreciate the card and avoid transposing numbers.

Determine the necessary information to include on the card; select the colors, type, and font preferred; and then add any graphic or logo desired. You may want to print

Figure 2.4 Business card

a selected alphabetical list of your family surnames on the back of the card. These names can be changed or updated as needed. A business card is a great way to share information at a local genealogical meeting or even a national conference.

You can order business cards at an office supply store or design and print your own at home. Blank forms, usually ten cards per sheet, are available for your computer printer. You can print only a few cards at a time, in case something changes, or dozens, depending on your potential use.

You have sorted, copied, purged, and filed your family history documents, and your papers are now under control. However, organizing your files is not an overnight process. Before you rush off to the office supply store, consider your workspace and available tools. Use storage boxes if you need additional space. Now it is time to consider the books, CDs, and maps that family historians purchase to expand their knowledge on a particular topic. The next chapter reviews techniques to organize these items.

CHAPTER 3

Books, CDs, Maps, and Tapes

GENEALOGISTS OFTEN PURCHASE REFERENCE MATERIALS TO EXPAND THEIR knowledge on various regions of the country, specific states, land records, military events, or how-to topics. Reference materials are also great items to add to your birthday or holiday gift list. However, books, tapes, CD-ROMs, maps, journals, and other items can easily overwhelm you before long. This chapter discusses what reference materials are important, shows how to organize your materials and keep track of your holdings, and reviews ways to store and file these items.

Before you can store books and other items, you must analyze your collection and decide which resources you use most often. A dictionary, thesaurus, and your research notebook should be within arm's reach of your computer. You know which reference items you use most frequently; keep those near your desk. Place other reference books away from your immediate desk area—perhaps on a bookcase near your desk or in a convenient location in another part of the house.

Home Library: Paper and Electronic

Reference materials are necessary for family historians. Anglers buy new rods, reels, and lures and seamstresses buy yards of fabric, all because they may need it some day. Likewise, genealogists buy books, maps, and CDs. We like some books so much that we buy them twice, because we forgot about the first purchase. What can we do to organize these items?

Home Library

Family historians are usually avid readers. Most of us have a core collection of genealogical books and CD-ROMs. As researchers, we expand our home libraries with specialty books that include area-, topic-, and surname-specific books.

Depending on your area of research, your basic collection of books may vary slightly from that of other genealogists—you won't have a New England collection if

Home Library Core Collection

Your home library should include an excellent dictionary and thesaurus plus some or all of the items listed below. The collection should include locality- and state-specific resources and maps. Histories of particular counties, states, or countries are also helpful.

- *Evidence! Citation and Analysis for the Family Historian*, by Elizabeth Shown Mills (Baltimore: Genealogical Publishing Company, 1997). The ultimate book on documentation. The author, Elizabeth Shown Mills, explains why you should document, outlines the differences in sources, and provides examples of citations. As you write your family history, this book should be as close by as the dictionary.

- *Family History Library Catalog* CD-ROM, prepared by the Church of Jesus Christ of Latter-day Saints (Salt Lake City: Intellectual Reserve, Inc., 2002).

- *Handybook for Genealogists*, 10th edition, by George Everton (Draper, Utah: Everton Publishers, 2002). Provides the name of each county in every state. The address of the county seat, the date of formation, and maps provide an overview no matter where your research takes you.

- *The Source: A Guidebook of American Genealogy*, revised edition, edited by Loretto Dennis Szucs and Sandra Hargreaves Luebking (Salt Lake City: Ancestry Inc., 1997). Contains valuable information on a wide array of genealogical resources. If you need help understanding court records or the census, this book has the answers. It is the ultimate source reference book for genealogists.

your family arrived in New Orleans and always lived in the Midwest. However, everybody could benefit from the books and CD listed in the "Home Library Core Collection" sidebar on page 46. These classic references should probably be on every genealogist's bookshelf. Put them on your holiday and birthday wish list. These books may also be available at your local library; you may even find circulating copies that you can take home.

You probably have a great dictionary at home; however, if you can move it easily, it is not the full version of the *Oxford English Dictionary*. Since most of us cannot afford and don't have the space for the complete *OED*, why not use this extensive dictionary online for those hard-to-find words? Your local library may offer electronic access to the online subscription version of *OED*, both at the library and from your home. If it does, your tax dollars are working for you. If it doesn't, inquire about the possibility.

Another part of your collection may consist of area-specific books, those that discuss the history of your hometown, county, and state. Hometown could be the place you currently live or the hometown of your ancestors, whatever fits your research focus area. The resource materials might include a cemetery CD-ROM index, church history, deed abstract, marriage index, or state history. Another popular item is a how-to research book on your county or state. Topic-specific books cover a favorite subject, such as the Civil War. Perhaps you have visited numerous Civil War battlefields, purchasing books at each stop. The collection probably includes biographies of Civil War generals, both Union and Confederate.

Surname-specific books are family histories compiled by others. As your family history develops, dozens of surnames will attach to your tree. Journal book reviews, publishers' catalogs, and used bookstores may list these family histories. There are also book dealers and Internet sites that locate rare and out-of-print publications. Software reference books and clip-art CDs are also common items in the home collection.

If you are just beginning a home reference library, determine your goals for the collection. Maybe you want to buy all the books on a particular county. If so, buy the book sight unseen. If you are looking for specific subjects or names, you may want to review the preface and introduction before you decide to purchase the book. You may focus on one type of book for a while and another topic after that. That is, you might purchase census-related publications now, followed by court-related books later. As you study each topic, you will become an expert on the subject.

Journals and Newsletters

If you belong to a few genealogical or historical societies, you probably receive a newsletter and journal from each one. Some are easy and quick to read; others are more detailed and take longer to absorb. Most genealogists end up with a stack of unread publications, more arriving before you have time to read each previous issue. Organize a "to-read" basket, placing the new publications on the bottom so that you read them in order of arrival.

After reading the journals and newsletters, you can decide which publications to retain and which you can live without. Often newsletters are throwaway publications with time-specific information. Next year you will not care about the time or place of this month's meeting. Journals usually contain articles that could have long-term value. Some societies combine the two publications. Do not despair if your family is not listed in the journals. By reading journal articles, you learn about the given area and time, and learn new research techniques. The best way to find your ancestors in the journal is to write an article about them. Maybe an unknown second cousin is reading the same journal.

If you have journals to discard, don't just throw them away. First check with your local library or genealogical society to see whether they would like a donation of the publications. Decide how much you should purge. Perhaps you want to keep only the publications for the last five years. Make a photocopy of any special articles and file those copies in your location or topic folders before purging the journals. Sort journals, magazines, newsletters, and pamphlets by placing like items together. Purchase cardboard or Lucite magazine holders to maintain a neat and organized periodical bookshelf.

Other items important to family historians include computer reference books and clip-art CDs. While learning how to use a new software program, the reference book should be at your fingertips. When you have somewhat conquered the program, move the book to an out-of-the-way location where it is still available for reference. When you upgrade to a new version or another program, discard your old reference book.

Clip-art reference books and CDs should be within arm's reach while you are being artistic. CDs can be stored in special CD furniture, containers, or cubbyholes. Make sure the spine label is easy to read for quick retrieval. It is necessary to sort the CDs occasionally, as well. If your current PC operating system is Microsoft XP, will it read those old DOS CDs on your shelf?

Storage

All your resources should be stored or placed on a bookshelf. Determine which reference books should be within arm's reach of your computer and which ones can go on the shelves. If you place the books in logical groupings, as librarians do, they will be easier to locate when needed. Place general reference books together. All books on New England should be together, followed by books on Pennsylvania and Virginia. Place the books in alphabetical order by title or author within the state, perhaps arranging the states from east to west coast. Another method is to place the books you use most often at eye level or waist height on the bookshelves. The less-used books can go on the bottom shelves. Small pamphlets store nicely in a magazine holder, where they remain visible and upright.

If you are moving, pack the books as you want them shelved at the new location. I know one person with so many books that he keeps different subjects in different rooms. Will your books go to an office, a bedroom, or the basement? If you mark each box with the subject matter, you won't have to unpack every box to locate one book. Be sure the movers put them in the room where the bookcases will be located. There is no need for you to carry those heavy boxes farther than necessary.

Home Library Catalog

Have you ever purchased the same book twice? If so, you understand the need for a library inventory. A list of your holdings should eliminate that problem. The inventory allows you to remember what you have, including those small pamphlets. The library inventory also assists you when it is time to downsize or purge part of the collection. Finally, it helps your family to make decisions when the time comes that you cannot speak for yourself.

Once you arrange your books in an orderly manner, make a list of your holdings using the home library catalog worksheet shown in Figure 3.1. Include audiotapes, books, CDs, maps, microfiche, and microfilm. Compile the list using your word-processing program, spreadsheet, database, or card file. This file should contain the basic information about each item, including the title, author's name, and publication information. Include the date of purchase and the price. To help sort the information, establish a code to denote each media type, such as book, CD, fiche, film, or map. The subject category may or may not be obvious by the name of the publication. If the book is about a particular state, list that state in the subject category. If the book is about a topic, such as the census, list the topic in the subject category. Once the file is complete, you can sort by any of these fields.

HOME LIBRARY CATALOG

Title	Author	Publication Information (Place, Publisher, Date)	Date of Purchase	Purchase Price	Media Type	Subject Category	Subject & Description

Figure 3.1 Home library catalog worksheet

You want to include the publication information for two reasons: to use in your source citations and for identification. First, if you purchase a book, you may use it as a source in your family history. By listing the publication information once in the inventory file, you can cut and paste the data the next time you need it. Second, you know which edition you have in case a new edition is published in the future. A good example of this is *The Source: The Guidebook of American Genealogy.* The original edition was published in 1984, edited by Arlene Eakle and Johni Cerny. The revised edition was published in 1997, edited by Loretto Dennis Szucs and Sandra Hargreaves Luebking. Both editions were published by Ancestry. If you tell your relative about an article on page 123, which edition are you referencing? Likewise, when searching a bookstore, do you know which edition of every book you have? I don't. The edition or version of CDs is very important. New versions are so easy to produce that publishers upgrade often. If your inventory states you have a map of Boston, when was it made? An 1800 map of Boston varies greatly from one made in 1900.

Publication Information to Record

The following list includes the basic publication information that should be recorded for all of your references. There may be additional information for some items.

- Title
- Author(s) or editor(s)
- Place of publication (city, state)
- Publisher
- Year of publication
- Edition number
- Volume number

You can make your library catalog as simple or sophisticated as you like. You may want to add the purchase price and date of purchase for each item. Additional information could include the condition of the book and the storage location. One friend has several bookcases that he numbered and identified in his library catalog. By identifying the location of the book, or at least which bookcase it is in, the items should be easier to locate. Of course, you must be disciplined enough to return the item to the same spot after each use. Try using a simple identifier, such as "corner bookcase," "white bookcase," or "bedroom closet shelf."

You may have inherited some old books in your heritage trunk. Add them to your home library catalog inventory, as well. Determine the value of these books by checking various Web sites or used bookstores. Do you have any first editions? Are any of the books autographed? Do they have sentimental or monetary value? Maybe your grandmother used this dictionary in grade school. Add any such information to the item's entry on the inventory.

If you like, you can assign some type of library number to each book, something similar to a library's catalog number, that helps you keep like items together. Another option is to place color-coded tape on the spine of the books. Tape is available in at least a dozen colors. You could use one color for family histories, one color for how-to books, another for state references, and one for software reference books. You can use a different color for each state reference. If you run out of colors, combine two colors. You can decide how much detail you want. If you use a numbering or color system, add this information to the inventory.

This is a project you can accomplish a little at a time. Organize the books, do the basic data entry, then decide whether you want to color-code the spines. If you want to add more columns to the home library catalog worksheet, but find the printed pages won't fit on 8½ x 11-inch paper, purchase a ream of 8½ x 14-inch paper to be used just for this catalog.

Once you have your bookcases organized, photograph them for an overview of the book spines, including titles. Add the photos and home library catalog to your file of important family papers. In addition, you should store a duplicate copy of your library catalog off-site, possibly by e-mailing it to a relative. In case of a disaster, include the list and photos with your insurance claim. The insurance company will appreciate your organization and documentation and the list and photos will support the insurance claim. There is no way you will remember every book in your collection! You should also tuck a copy of your home library catalog into your tote bag, or store the file on your PDA, when attending a genealogical seminar. You can refer to it to avoid making duplicate purchases from the vendors. In addition, the vendors will see from your inventory that you are a book connoisseur and be able to offer you more focused assistance with your search for additional publications.

Although the home library inventory may seem like extra work, we have seen that there are at least three good reasons to compile the list:

🍃   Eliminate duplicate spending.

🍃   Protect yourself in case of a disaster.

🍃   Assist family members when downsizing or disposing of your collection.

If a computer is not available, you can use index cards to inventory your collection. Develop a format that works for you. Include the title, publication information, and any pertinent personal notes or reminders about the book. The cards are not convenient for traveling and off-site storage, but they help organize your collection. You could place four or six cards on the photocopier to duplicate your inventory as a backup.

Maps and Tapes

Audiotapes, videotapes, and maps are accessories found in almost every genealogist's home. The items may be new or used. You may have purchased some items from a society sales shop or a genealogical exhibitor; others may have been gifts. Include all items in the inventory.

Audiotapes

Have you ever thought about how much time you spend in the car? Talk radio and the news get old quickly. Do you like to take walks in the neighborhood? As a family historian, why not spend those hours learning more about research methodology, techniques, and records? Lectures recorded at national genealogical conferences are available for purchase. Since conferences offer multiple lecture sessions each hour, attendees must choose between several good learning opportunities. Purchase the audiotapes for lectures you cannot attend, and listen to them as time permits. The

Genealogical Audiotapes

Repeat Performance offers audiotapes from lectures presented at national genealogical conferences. The company's Web site (www.audiotapes.com) has a complete listing of available tapes.

National Genealogical Conferences

Two organizations, the National Genealogical Society (NGS) and the Federation of Genealogical Societies (FGS), present multiday conferences each year in different locations around the country. National and regional speakers present one-hour lectures on an assortment of topics for beginning to advanced genealogists. Topics include census, computers, ethnic, immigration, Internet, land, migration, military, writing, and special topics on the host region of the conference. NGS also offers a two-day conference concentrating on the combination of genealogy and technology, NGS GENTECH. Conference programs are available online at *www.ngsgenealogy.org* and *www.fgs.org*.

tapes are available even if you could not attend the conference. This is the perfect way to educate yourself at a time and place convenient to you.

You should be sure to clearly label the tapes with the lecture title and speaker's name. Indicate this information on the spine of the containers, as well; then stand the tapes on their side. File the items in alphabetical order by speaker's name, lecture title, or topic, whatever works best for you. When you listen to the lectures, jot down key points and document where the information came from. Once you are finished with the tapes and it is time to purge some items from your library, donate the tapes to the local library or genealogical society.

Conference organizers produce a syllabus that contains printed material for most lectures. Speakers often reference a bibliography or some other information that appears in their syllabus materials. You can usually purchase remaining syllabi after the conference by contacting the conference sponsor. Include the syllabi along with the tape in your catalog.

Videotapes

Your videotapes should be organized like the audiotapes and filed chronologically or alphabetically. Be sure to clearly date and label the tapes so that you do not tape over something important, like your wedding video.

Maps

Maps come in an assortment of sizes and shapes. Some are available on individual sheets and are rolled for good storage. Others are published in bound books. Some atlases are 8½ x 11 inches; others are larger, which is good news and bad news. We like to have large maps that are easy to read, but they can cause a storage problem.

Atlases generally require a special storage spot. Perhaps you can stand them next to the bookcase, slide them under the bed, store them in the closet, or make a special bookshelf for oversized books. But be sure the books are easily accessible. If the spine is not marked, add a label. Large atlases should be stored flat to protect the spine, or the overall weight will damage the binding.

If you have rolled maps on multiple sheets with a rubber band around them, consider a special storage holder. Purchase a gift wrapping paper roll holder to place in your storage area or closet. Instead of using it for wrapping paper, store your rolled maps in this cardboard or plastic container. Chapter 4 discusses special archival containers in which you can store your more valuable maps. But determine a map's value and availability before you invest too much money for storage.

If you roll together several maps the same size, place a label on the outside top of the roll. Provide adequate information so you don't have to unroll the maps to locate the one you seek. If you prefer to keep the maps flat, purchase a large flat zipper portfolio case. Artists and architects use this type of case to transport their work. It has a handle and stands nicely in the closet. Be sure to include the maps in your home library catalog inventory.

Microforms

Microfiche

In the past, many records were published on microfiche, including entire books and endless indexes. A microfiche reader is necessary to view the approximately 4 x 5-inch flat sheet of film. Many of the same records are now available on the Internet or CDs.

The easiest way to store this resource is by standing the fiche in a box or drawer with tab dividers. The fiche usually has a guide at the top of the film indicating the range of records available on that particular fiche, similar to the top of a telephone book page.

Microfilm

Some family historians and genealogical societies purchase microfilm for their areas of interest. This includes census records, deeds, probate, and even family histories. As with the books, you may be interested in one county. Most state archives offer for sale rolls of microfilm for each county in their state. If you are building a microfilm collection, check with the state archives and the National Archives to see what film is available on your county of interest.

The films should be stored in individual boxes—available from library supply vendors—and properly labeled. As you have done with your books, place similar items together in the cabinets or drawers. Depending on the film quantity, use a long, shallow plastic container with a lid available at discount stores. Microfilm should be stored away from light, perhaps in a container in the closet.

A special reader or machine is necessary for microfiche and microfilm; some equipment can display both. Genealogists can purchase new or used equipment from catalog listings or local microfilm dealers. Add microfilm and microfiche to your home library catalog inventory.

Disposition of Resources

As we progress through research, some books, CDs, journals, maps, and other items become obsolete. Place those items in storage, perhaps in an out-of-the-way location, or donate them to your genealogical library or society. Check your local library to be sure you agree with its donation policy. Libraries that receive a large volume of materials may accept the donation, process the needed items, and then donate the other items to a sales table or book fair. The library may have limited space.

Some genealogical societies accept donations from members. If the society has a library, the donated resources may find their way to the shelves. Other items will be placed in the society's sales area.

If your library already has these books in their reference area, ask the librarian whether your donation can go into the circulating collection. Many books are huge volumes, too big to read word for word during limited time at the library. If your books go into circulation, future genealogists will thank you for the ability to check out that book and take it home.

If you are disposing of books after the death of a loved one, ask the librarian whether you can insert a bookplate on the inside cover providing the name of your friend or loved one: "This book was donated in memory of Charlene Fagyal."

No matter what the disposition, the items are out of your house, which means you may be eligible for a tax deduction. Check your home library catalog for the original value of the items you donate. A tax advisor can suggest the donation value. At the same time, delete the donated items from the catalog listing.

Home Library Identification Dots

- **Red:** Do not discard; the family should retain this book.

- **Yellow:** Review this book as it may have some family significance.

- **Green:** Donate this book to a library or genealogical society.

Of course, you should not dispose of your favorite books. However, someday your family will need to divide and dispose of those items. You can help your family by providing some clues to that disposition.

Establish a color-coded system with matching dots on or in the books. The dots can be placed on the inside front cover so they are not confused with any color library tape used for cataloging. Red means stop, do not dispose of the red-dotted books. This could include first editions, autographed books, books written by a family member, books that mention your specific family, or books with special meaning. Yellow means proceed with caution. Since we have to leave something for those family members to do, they can choose which items they want among the yellow-dotted books—whether to keep them within the family or include them with the library donation. Green-dotted books go directly to the donation stack. Leave instructions that green-dotted books should be donated to a research facility. You enjoyed reading and using them in your collection, but it is time to share them with others. List all these books on your home library catalog worksheet, thus providing a monetary value for the family and tax advisor.

All the reference materials mentioned in this chapter should be cared for as they become part of your heritage trunk. Your home library, both paper and electronic, is a valuable asset to you as a genealogist; however, don't let the reference items overwhelm you. As you purchase new items, continue to organize, review, and dispose of unnecessary ones. Photographs and heirlooms are also valuable assets. In the next chapter, learn how to organize, share, store, and inventory these items.

CHAPTER 4

Objects of My Affection

OTHER THAN FAMILY MEMBERS, WHAT WOULD YOU SAVE IF YOU HAD ONLY five minutes before a fire, flood, tornado, hurricane, or some other disaster hit your home? Which items are replaceable? Which are one of a kind? Are they stored together for quick retrieval? You may need to organize the photos and heirlooms that are part of your heritage trunk. This chapter discusses good storage techniques for maintaining your materials over time. As you read this chapter, consider the different means of storage, ways to create and maintain back-up records, and how to prepare your materials in ways that would minimize the loss of valuable information and heirlooms should catastrophe strike. Your heritage trunk runneth over with these items!

Photographs

Photographs are visual records of your life and the lives of your ancestors. They can produce a unique chronology of events and provide a glimpse into the history of a period. Photos capture clothing styles, buildings, types of transportation, and familial features passed from one generation to another. Photographs are a precious asset whose preservation requires your best efforts.

Do you have a photo of your parents' wedding? Maybe you have your grandparents' wedding photo or a picture taken at their fiftieth wedding anniversary, just months before one of them died. These items are priceless. Do you have the original, which is the only copy?

Questions to Ponder

As you gather the treasures from your heritage trunk, ask yourself these questions:

- Where are the family photographs?
- Can you identify all the photos, as well as each person in the photos?
- What family books, journals, or letters have survived and where are they located?
- What family artifacts are available?
- How should you store these items to maximize their lifespan?

For your family and descendants' sakes, don't risk losing any of your photos—make copies. Copying your photos is the same as buying an insurance policy—you ensure that those photos will be available for future generations.

Original photos should be kept in archival boxes in your home. Never take the original on a trip to the library or to a family event. The only trip this original should go on is to the photo duplication studio. Try to find a good-quality photo restoration and duplication studio that will care for your photos as you do. Do they offer while-you-wait service? If so, you can then take the original home with you the same day. Seriously consider whether you want to place your only copy of

What quality are your photos and reprints? Will the photos printed on your home printer last as long as those reproduced by a photographer? Probably not! The lifespan of any photo depends on several conditions, including storage temperature, moisture, and light. Too much light shortens the life of a photo. The quality of the paper is another factor. A professional photographer may ask whether you want the reproduction on paper with a lifespan of twenty-five or one hundred years. So consider lifespan and quality when making decisions about reprints.

Grandpa Harry's photo in the mail, either to a photo studio or a family member. I sure don't!

Current technology allows you to electronically reproduce photos and print them at home. Several computer programs assist with the reproduction process. The life span of those prints is unknown, but most likely it is not as long as a reproduction provided by a professional photographer. Some photos may be worth the extra expense; others are not. Store any digital photos on a CD or DVD. Use this option to share photos, not to archive them, since we do not know the lifespan of the electronic media.

Identify Photographs

Family events such as parties, weddings, family reunions, vacations, and holidays are remembered through photographs. The flowers, music, wrapping paper, and glitter are gone, but the essence of the event is preserved in photographs, movies, or videos.

Do you have an ancestor's photo hanging on the wall in your home or hidden away in the basement or attic? Do you know the date of the photo or anything about that person? It is time to identify, organize, and properly store your photos.

Photos should live where you live. Just like people, they do not like the continually changing temperature and humidity in the attic, basement, or garage. Try to store photos in a closet or some other out-of-the-way place in your living area. The photos will last longer if they are warm in the winter and air-conditioned in the summer, just like people!

Always take a good look at your pictures—and don't hesitate to use a magnifying glass. What do you see in the background? Does a vintage automobile date the photo? Is there a house or other recognizable feature? Your ancestors probably did not take a photo of the farmhouse fifty years ago, but they may have stood in front of the house for a group photo. That may be the only shot of the farmhouse. While analyzing a picture, make some notes about its contents. Who are the people? Where was it taken? Was this a special event? What was the date of the photo?

Sometimes the identification process is easy, and other times it is not. With a wedding photo, the date can usually be determined. Perhaps the groom is wearing his military uniform and the wedding occurred just before he went overseas in one of our nation's conflicts. Those are easy. Other pictures may be more difficult. If a baby is included, determine who it is and find the baby's birth date. A photo may not have any easily visible clues, but look carefully. A family group picture may have been taken on a front porch or in the front yard. Is a house number or a street sign visible? What information can you glean from the photo?

If the photo includes an automobile with a license plate, try using a magnifying glass to determine the state and date of the plate. You may not know whether the person in the picture or the person taking the picture owned the car. However, you have some clues.

My paternal grandmother gave me a family photo of her parents, her five sisters, and one baby brother. Her father, a police officer named Joseph James, was wearing his uniform in the photo. I knew where they lived and recognized that the family was sitting on their front porch. But I did not know the date of the photo, and neither did my grandmother.

What was the story behind the photo? My grandmother was born in 1895. Her father died in September 1910, so we have a fifteen-year window to date the photo. My grandmother looked like a teenager in the photo, so we can narrow that window to perhaps 1905 to 1910. The clothing indicates it was summer.

I had the advantage of talking to my grandmother about the picture, instead of finding it after she died. As we talked about the photo, she pointed to a poster that was in the living room window, which she said was a campaign poster for presidential candidate William Jennings Bryan. Bryan ran for president three times. He ran in 1896 and 1900, both times against William McKinley. Those years were too early because my grandmother would have been a small child. Bryan ran again in 1908 against William Taft. That was just right—she would have been thirteen years old. Bingo!

This picture was the only surviving photo of that family. Just ten years later, six of the eight family members were dead from tuberculosis or the flu. I later found a 1908 baptismal record for the baby, which confirmed the photo date.

Make a list of your old pictures, and record whatever you know about each one: who, what, where, and when. As you visit with other family members, they may be able to add to the story. Take copies of the photos to family picnics, reunions, or holiday gatherings.

You could also make a photo album notebook. Scan the heirloom photos, saving them in family folders on your computer. Use your word-processing program to record the history of each photo, and then add the digitized image to the same file. You may have ten photos or a hundred. Just keep adding the information to the notebook. The notebook can safely go on trips or to family events; it's replaceable if lost or damaged. You can e-mail the file to other family members, asking for their help in identifying people, places, and dates.

Some photos may be images of a business, church, or school in a particular community. If you don't need those photos in your collection, contact the local historical or genealogical society or state archives. Local historians may be able to help you identify the people and places. They may also welcome a photo donation for their collection, particularly if community buildings, parades, or local landscapes are involved. You can donate either the original or a copy.

Share Photographs

Share photos with other family members. Every household has a collection different from any other. Perhaps your sister has the best picture of Grandma and Grandpa, and you would like to have a copy for your collection. You may have a picture that she would like to have. Share copies with each other. Who else might like a copy?

Sometimes we have more than one copy of a particular picture, perhaps a studio picture from the 1920s or a school picture from the 1980s. Share the duplicate with your children, siblings, or cousins. While going through some photos, I found duplicates of my father and uncle as children. My only cousin on that side of the family lost many belongings in Hurricane Andrew. I shared the duplicate family photos with him—purging those same items from my files and making him very happy at the same time.

If you are planning a family reunion, suggest that everyone bring copies of old photos of your ancestors. For safety's sake, a copy of the photo is best; leave the original at home. At the reunion, find a safe place for the photos, and then place a number next to each one. Give everyone a piece of paper and ask the family to identify each photo. This works as a good mixer for cousins from out of town, but you may also learn something new about the family. And you can take orders for duplicate copies of the photos. For more ideas for family reunions, refer to another book in the NGS series, *A Family Affair: How to Plan and Direct the Best Family Reunion Ever*, by Sandra MacLean Clunies.

For a variety of reasons, including natural disasters or movers' mishaps, some families have no photos of their ancestors. Duplicate your photos and distribute them on special occasions. You will be giving your loved ones a wonderful gift.

Label and Organize

Do you have boxes and boxes of photos throughout the house? Are they in any order? Are the labels clear? Accumulate the photos in one spot, organize them into family groups, and then label each photo. There are various methods to label photos. You can place them in a photo album with labels next to the photo. Or write on the back of the photo or on a sticker you attach to the back.

If you choose to write on the photo, archivists suggest that you use only pencils and write only on the back edges so the writing does not go through to the front and ruin the faces. Ink may damage the photo. A photograph archivist recently told me that some catalogs advertise archival adhesives—an oxymoron, since anything with an adhesive could damage the photo.

In the 1950s, photo albums with black pages were popular. Every household probably has at least one album with pictures glued to the pages or attached with photo corners. Sometimes the photo album compilers identified the picture on the black paper. All too often, they did not. The black paper is very acidic and will eventually damage the photos if it has not already. Consider removing the photos attached with photo corners and placing those photos in an archival container. When it comes to removing glued photos, study each one. Removal may be easy for some photos and impossible for others. If you cannot remove the photo, consider its value. Is it worth the cost of a copy? Or is it just a nice photo with no long-term value? Whatever you decide, take care not to damage the photo.

Starting in the 1970s, "magnetic" photo albums became very popular. They were inexpensive, readily available, and inspired many people to organize their photos. Unfortunately, at the time, we just did not know the long-term consequences. Those clear sheets are often PVC (polyvinylchloride), which contains ingredients such as plasticizers that exude from the sheet and can attack your photos. The photos may change color, completely fade, and permanently adhere themselves to the sheets.

Today, polyethylene is on the list of plastics that are safe to use with photos. Pictures can be safely stored in archival safe plastic sleeves or archival boxes.

If you can safely remove the photos from magnetic albums, do so. If the photo is stuck to the paper, try using an Exacto knife to loosen the clear covering from the face of the photo. If that does not work, talk to a professional or just leave it alone.

Photos get bent, broken, and scratched over time. Do not try to glue or tape a photo back together. Glue and tape will damage the original. Tape will discolor over time, so the photo will never look the same. Archivists tell us not to do anything to a photo that you cannot undo. A professional photographer can simulate repairs before making reprints. The original is unchanged and still looks the same. You can make the same repairs with the proper photo enhancement software on your computer. The software allows for scratch and blemish removal, cropping, and other adjustments. But family historians should not use digital capabilities to intentionally alter or falsify an impression. Do not impose George Washington into your most recent family reunion.

Electronic Photo Album

An electronic photo album makes a wonderful gift for a relative's special birthday. Gather photos from your collection, and request photos from other family members. Scan the photos into your computer, saving the scanned images in a source file. If you do not have a scanner, family members can e-mail their photos to you.

You can burn a CD or DVD of your electronic photo albums and then distribute copies to family members. Electronic photo albums can include family photos, captions, and background music. You can arrange the photos chronologically, in family groups, or in random order.

Begin by selecting a software program that helps you produce an electronic photo album. Talk to others who have worked on this type of project; ask them about the program and its capabilities. Demonstrations may be available at an electronics store or from the software Web site.

After installing the program, decide on the focus of the project. You may want to make an album for each child or cousin. A wedding photo album is a great gift for an anniversary party. An assortment of photos on one family is a wonderful present for a seventieth birthday party. The focus or topic can be as general or as specific as you like. Once you have scanned the photos, you can arrange them in numerous albums.

Photo Enhancement Software

Software that allows you to enhance and clean up digitized copies of your photos is improved on a regular basis. To determine which software is best for your needs, check *Consumer Reports* or *PC Magazine* for editorials on these products. Photo enhancement software includes the following:

- Adobe Photoshop
  www.adobe.com

- Adobe Photoshop Elements
  www.adobe.com

- Microsoft Picture It
  www.Microsoft.com

- Ulead Photo Impact 8
  www.ulead.com

Once you scan the photos, analyze each one. Should you crop the picture? Does it have scratches that need to be removed? Does a missing corner need to be repaired? A photo-enhancement program can fix all these problems. Save the repaired photo in your source file.

The source file is a collection of folders within your My Pictures folder, which can be found on most computers. Make a folder under My Pictures labeled with your mother's name. Place all the photos of your mother in that folder. If you later scan a collection on your father, make a folder using his name. Use the folders as the source file to store the photos in an organized fashion so that you can easily retrieve them as needed (see Figure 4.1).

From the source file, select the photos you want to use in an album. You may want to have a theme or just an overall collection about Mom. You must decide the order of the photos—chronological or random. You can add borders or frames electronically to enhance the pictures. You can also add captions to describe the people, place, date, and event for each photo. If you are adding a border or caption, be sure to save the original photo without the border and caption. You may want to use it again for another purpose.

Figure 4.1 Folders for family photos

Children usually have a photo taken every school year, even in college. By placing the photos together in chronological order, you will see the growth from kindergarten to college graduation. Throw in a few baby pictures, holidays, vacations, proms, weddings, and other events, and you have prepared a great photo biography. Add music, if you like, before you create the CD photo album. But if you use commercially produced music, be cautious about copyright infringement. Check with an attorney for clarification.

The CD or DVD album program prompts you to make a disk label and case cover. A photo from the album makes a great cover. Be aware of that big hole in the disk and select a photo that will work around it. You do not want to lose the face of the featured person. Add a title in the text box overlay—and it's finished!

There are benefits to making an album. Tell your family members what you are working on, and request that they share their photos with you long enough for you to scan the needed shots. Most likely, you will come across photos you do not remember or have not seen before.

If any family member has a vision problem, showing the photos enlarged on a television screen might enable that person to see something he's been missing for years. The photos may bring back memories of their parents or siblings, or their own earlier years. Have your pen and paper in hand, ready to record new information.

If you debut the album to a group of family members, it will undoubtedly bring comments from the audience. People will remember when and where the photo was taken or why they were there, and then someone else will chime in with other memories. Maybe the dress someone was wearing was special, or she liked the particular hairstyle. You will be delighted with your audience's emotion and enthusiasm. Have an ample supply of tissues available—everyone will be laughing and crying at the same time.

In addition to basic photos, the albums can incorporate video clips and voice recordings. The only limitation is your imagination. You will probably find yourself making more than one album; they are as addictive as your search for your ancestors. Siblings and cousins will want a copy. After the photo albums are complete, store the photos on a Zip drive, CD, or DVD. They do take up space on the hard drive.

Heirlooms

Do you have one or more family heirlooms in your heritage trunk? Perhaps one ancestor was in the Civil War and his sword has survived. Do you know the background on that soldier and the sword? Maybe you have a 1920 vintage radio. Do you have a first edition book or a book autographed by a famous author? Do you have a quilt handmade by your great-grandmother? Maybe you have a trunk that actually sailed across the ocean with your ancestors 150 years ago!

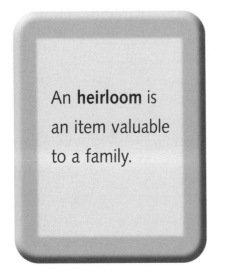

An **heirloom** is an item valuable to a family.

Over the years, you have probably heard a story or two about these heirlooms. Make those stories part of your family history. Record the story as it is known today so that it will not be lost or altered in the future. The history of the heirlooms is just as important as the names and dates of the ancestors. These memories are what bring our ancestors to life in our minds.

Heirlooms include such items as quilts and other needlework, dishes and vases, jewelry, silverware, crystal, furniture, and tools, to name just a few. Perhaps your family saved postcards, political buttons, a baseball card collection, or other sports memorabilia. Do you have an old train you received as a child, dolls that are fifty years old, or maybe your wedding dress? All these items are heirlooms.

Inventory the Heirlooms

We lost our home in a tornado years ago. This was our newly married era, so the heirlooms and valuable items were minimal. (Yes, we were in the house when the tornado hit, but we were not hurt.) Of course, we had not inventoried anything, but our memory was good. Armed with a yellow tablet, we walked down each aisle at the hardware store, saying, "Oh yes, we had one of those, and three of these."

That system worked fine for our general household goods. It would not have helped with antiques or heirlooms. They were literally gone with the wind. A neighbor had a

Grandma's Hoosier Cabinet

In 1980, shortly after his grandmother's death, my husband, Jim, visited his Aunt Betty in Southern Illinois. Betty told Jim and all the other grandchildren they could select one piece of furniture that had belonged to Grandma Snedden. Jim chose a Hoosier cabinet that had been a feature in Grandma Snedden's kitchen for as long as anyone could remember. It still bore the impression and stains from where the water bucket sat, as there had been no running water in the house. The bucket, along with the accompanying dipper, had provided drinking and cooking water. Also visible were small nails forming the initials JR, added by her son, John Robert, when he was a child.

The two-piece all-wood cabinet had many practical features. It contained a tin flour bin and sifter in the top section. The roll-up cover still worked and revealed a storage area for baking ingredients. Above that, a double-door storage area provided room for canned goods. The lower section had a pullout baking board, which served as a countertop or work area. A removable cutting board was stored beneath the baking board. The cabinet had three drawers down the right side with the bottom drawer lined in tin, including a tin sliding cover for the drawer, used to keep bugs out of the bread or baked goods.

Jim brought the cabinet home, and we removed the numerous layers of paint, uncovering nice hardware and rich-looking wood. We left the baking board untouched to preserve the initials and stains and the memories they conjure. This cabinet now stands in our kitchen as a cherished family heirloom.

family heirloom clock that was missing. The insurance company told her it was just an old clock of minimal value without proof of purchase or an appraisal. She had neither!

It's vital that you make a list of your heirlooms. If the item is important to you, add it to the list. Do not forget to look through old trunks, cedar closets, or china cabinets. Ask your family members what items are important to them, as well.

On your heirloom list, try to categorize like items. Maybe you have military memorabilia and a gun collection. Group those items together. One category could be the postcard collection or the sports memorabilia. List some items in sets, others as individual items. Some items could go either way. For example, baseball cards are sold in sets; however, if you have an original Mickey Mantle rookie card, list that one separately.

When you helped clean out a loved one's house, what did you bring home? Perhaps it was your grandmother's special table or maybe a piece of Depression glass. Do you have a set of pillowcases trimmed with Grandma's tatting? Maybe you have special holiday ornaments. Or porcelain figurines brought by the family immigrant from the old country. List all these items.

Then photograph each heirloom. If you want to be able to prove when you had this item, date the photo by including the current day's newspaper. If you have silverware on the list, don't just take a photo of the box or container that you keep it in. Lay out each piece on the table so every item is visible. Along with the photo, write a brief description about the item, including how your family obtained it. You know the item's history today, but will your descendants fifty years from now? Your work makes sure they do.

Some heirlooms have sentimental value only, while others also have monetary value. If you're not sure of the value, visit some antique shops, resale shops, or even museums. Have the valuable items appraised by a jeweler or antiques dealer, and request a written appraisal. You do not want to end up like the woman in the tornado with the missing clock.

You should keep the list of heirlooms, photos, and appraisals in a notebook. Use clear plastic sleeves for the appraisals or some other type of container—do not three-hole punch the important document. Place the notebook in a lockbox or at some other off-site location. You should also keep a copy of this notebook at home to make additions and adjustments as needed. But don't forget to update the off-site copy, as well.

Be sure to scan the appraisals, documents, and photos for every heirloom. Add your written history, and make an electronic file. Include the home library catalog inventory and photos of the library collection mentioned in Chapter 3. Send this file to a relative for safekeeping. Whenever you update the file, just send another copy to your relative. If you send a PDF file, the documents cannot be altered.

Disaster Plan

It is also important for you to prepare a disaster plan. What heirlooms would you save if you had only a few minutes to evacuate your house and you knew your family was safe? Think about the irreplaceable items first and what you could move quickly.

If you store photos and other nonreplaceable items in one location—such as a closet—there is a better chance of saving more items. You wouldn't have to rush throughout the house looking for each item.

Read All about It

You should photocopy important newspaper articles. Include the date, newspaper's name, and page number along with the article. Eventually a newspaper disintegrates. You can prolong its lifespan by placing the newspapers in acid-free folders and boxes. Some boxes are sized to accommodate one or more daily newspapers. Save only those newspapers most important to you personally—the announcement that President Kennedy had been assassinated or, on a lighter note, when Mark McGwire broke Roger Maris's home run record.

Did you save a copy of the newspaper dated the day your child or grandchild was born? Many families do. While you cannot photocopy the entire paper, do copy an assortment of the pages, such as the front page, sports page, stock market, or some advertisements. Make these copies at the library from microfilm. You now have a more permanent copy, as well as the actual newspaper. Store them all safely.

Letters, Journals, and Diaries

Some Civil War ancestors sent letters home from the battlefield. So did World War I soldiers. Perhaps you have love letters from your father to your mother before they married. Preserve the letters in archival sleeves. That way, you can read the letters through the transparent sleeves without touching the actual paper. Transcribe, scan, or photocopy the letters for siblings, cousins, and yourself. If you transcribe the documents, do not change the spelling, wording, or punctuation—they reflect the era and author. Then store the original letters and sleeves in an archival file folder and place it in an archival box. That is about as much as we can do to save those letters!

Diaries and journals are very similar. **Journals** probably have more matter-of-fact daily events and experiences, while **diaries** usually have more personal thoughts about those same events. The words can be and certainly are used interchangeably.

Keeping a journal is not new. Two hundred years ago, Lewis and Clark kept journals of their travels across the Louisiana Purchase territory, documenting their entire trip. Many women in wagon trains traveling from Missouri to California kept diaries as they crossed the prairie, while other people recorded major conflicts. Because of these journals, we have a history of events that were otherwise undocumented.

Then and now, people have their own journaling styles. Some like to gossip about the day's events. Others prefer to record just the facts. Your ancestors cooked, did the laundry, and raised a family. If you have any of their journals, be sure to take notes about the contents. The family recorded its lifestyle, and that record is right in front of you. The day-to-day entries may seem boring, but if you look at the series as a whole, it should be quite interesting.

My maternal grandmother kept a journal from 1925 to the day before she died in 1982. Some years were lost to water damage, but many are extant. Reading the daily entries can be boring; however, her life on the farm with seven children was certainly not. We know how many quarts of tomatoes she canned, when she picked the berries, and what days she did the laundry, sewing, and housework. She told us when she went to church, when she went to town, and when she visited friends. In all those pages, year after year, there is not one line of gossip! That alone tells us something about her character.

Extant records have survived time and still exist.

She mentions attending school graduations, weddings, and other family events pertaining to her seven children, twenty-two grandchildren, and two great-grandchildren. She recorded entries at the time and place of the activities; therefore, the journals serve as firsthand documentation for those events.

What do the journals tell us? They chronicle a family living on a farm through the Depression, the growth of her children, and her husband's death in the early 1950s. She then shares the lifestyle of a single woman trying to make a living before the feminist movement. Journals often reflect life in grassroots America. Heirlooms like this are beyond monetary value and are truly irreplaceable.

Archival Supplies

The archival boxes mentioned previously come in various shapes and sizes. They have a flip-up top and are available in either letter or legal size. There are clamshell boxes for books, journals, and large photos. A larger size is available for newspaper storage, and a still larger size is available for quilts and other such items. Archival boxes come in an assortment of shapes and sizes, such as tubes for maps and charts.

Archival research facilities maintain manuscript collections in archival boxes. The box contents are safe from acid and light, both of which are harmful. Family historians can purchase the same type of boxes to store their valuable papers, photos, and heirlooms, as shown in Figure 4.2.

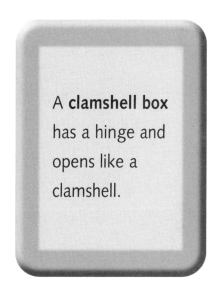

A **clamshell box** has a hinge and opens like a clamshell.

In archival boxes, store old journals and books flat. Because the spines are not strong, standing the books on end will further deteriorate the spines. You can purchase archival boxes that fold to the size needed for each individual book, such as a family Bible.

Photo preservation is important to everyone. It is necessary to analyze the photo's value, both monetarily and historically. If the photo has survived for a hundred years, do nothing that might harm it now. Check with a photographer or camera shop about archival-safe materials.

Smaller boxes, similar to shoeboxes, hold snapshots. Tab dividers easily separate the different events remembered in the photos. All these products are available in archival-quality materials. Determine the size and quantity needed before you place an order.

You should be sure to carefully label each box. If you divide the pictures and memorabilia by family, place a label on the outside of the box with the family name. Then when you want to retrieve a particular photo, you can simply go to that box and there it is. You won't waste time looking through every album to find that one photo. Add the name of the box to your photo inventory.

You can further divide the photos within the boxes by using acid-free file folders. In addition to organizing the photos, these folders also protect the photos from each

Figure 4.2 Archival boxes in an assortment of shapes and sizes (Courtesy of Hollinger Corporation)

other by preventing acid and dirt from one photo to contaminate another. Within the boxes or folders, you could also use clear archival sleeves to protect each photo. It's up to you to decide which photo storage system will work best for you.

Archival-Safe Products

Archival-safe products are available from various companies, such as those listed below. Determine your needs and which company specializes in those products.

- Creative Memories
  www.creativememories.com

- Demco Inc.
  www.demco.com

- Hollinger Corporation
  www.hollingercorp.com

- Light Impressions
  www.lightimpressionsdirect.com

Scrapbooking

Scrapbooking is a popular hobby right now and is certainly a great way to organize your photos. Most people identify, label, and organize scrapbook album photos. What more could a family historian want?

If you are a scrapbook enthusiast, you have probably already organized your photos. Many families store their photos and other memorabilia in plastic bins, maybe one container per child. These are the same organizational skills you should apply to your collection of family history. As you examine each award, report card, and other special item in the bin, take time to write a paragraph or story about the history of that item. Chapter 12 explores the writing of your family's history in further detail.

People often trim scrapbook photos, saving only the focus area. Trimming is good for the design, but not for genealogists. The car in the background is a current model today; someday that "old car" could date the photo. That house on the hill behind the people could be the only photo of the old homestead. Trim carefully!

Scrapbooking and genealogy are very similar. Both serve to preserve the memories of our families and ancestors. **Scrapbooking** specializes in memorabilia and photos. Scrapbooking supplies, instructions, and ideas are available at local stores and at numerous Web sites. To find those Web sites, enter the keyword "scrapbooking" in the window of a search engine such as Google (*www.Google.com*).

Final Resting Place

We all have our favorite photos and heirlooms, but what will happen to these items when we can no longer make decisions for ourselves? Do other family members know the history of these items? Will a family member welcome the genealogical material or will it end up in the trash?

When our family was cleaning out the house of my great-aunt Alean, we found a small purse at the bottom of a cedar chest. Nobody knew what it was. Inside, Alean had left a note explaining that the purse had belonged to her mother, who had purchased it at the 1904 World's Fair in St. Louis, the same year Alean was born. Without that note, the history and possibly the purse would have been lost.

When making your photo and heirloom inventory, record the name of the person to whom you would like to give this item. If children, siblings, nieces, or nephews indicate an interest in an item, record their names next to that item on your inventory. Perhaps you want to donate an item to a historical society or museum. Make those arrangements yourself, and sign any necessary paperwork in advance to ensure that the family follows your wishes. It will save a lot of time and discussion when you cannot speak for yourself.

The office and desk are shaping up, the files are becoming manageable, and the photos are organized. Now we need to talk about that big thing sitting on your desk—the computer! The next chapter helps you organize your data in genealogical software programs, identifies some good Web sites, and provides suggestions for file management. Even if you are not comfortable using the computer, you may want to read this chapter and see what you might be missing.

CHAPTER 5

Digital Direction

MOST FAMILY HISTORIANS USE COMPUTERS IN ONE WAY OR ANOTHER. The convenience of online census access is a tremendous time saver. The ability to take a laptop to a research facility is wonderful. Even if you do not use a computer personally, the authors of the research books in the libraries used technology to produce those publications. Computers help with the organization of family histories. If you do not use a computer, maybe other members of the family research team do. Share this chapter with them.

Genealogical Software Programs

Numerous genealogical software programs are available for your computer. Each program has unique features; however, overall they offer similar capabilities. Before purchasing, visit the Web sites for the various programs of interest to you. Download the sample programs, and review the options. You might test the programs by entering five or ten names with source citations. If possible, enter the same data in each program to compare the screen options using the same information. Print out some of the charts and the written family history.

You should also review the Facts field in each software program. Some programs have just a few preprogrammed facts; others are more plentiful. The program you select should allow you to add facts. What do you want to add? For example, if you have several soldiers in your family, you may want to add a fact that represents each of the major wars instead of an overall military fact. You can add a fact named Colonial Wars, another for the American Revolution, War of 1812, Civil War, and so on. The goal is to customize the software so that it works best for you. After you enter a fact, it remains in the program until you update, alter, or delete it, even if it's wrong. With a sound foundation of facts, your genealogical information will grow as your research progresses. And with a genealogical software program, it is possible to generate a variety of lists based on various facts. Review the list options in the software you choose, and use the custom list option to develop special lists.

Genealogical software offers many features. Before purchasing a program, determine whether it has the features that interest you. Ask yourself the following questions:

- How many individuals does the program allow per database?
- Does the program allow you to enter multiple parents per individual (biological, adopted, or step)?
- Will it convert date formats?
- Are date and Soundex calculators included?
- Does the program accept multimedia sources, including photos, video, and sound?
- Does it produce good reports and charts?
- Will it properly cite sources?
- Is there a place for notes about individuals and families?
- Can you use GEDCOM through the program?
- Does the program help you creates a Web site?

Cyndi's List *(www.cyndislist.com/software.htm)* provides up-to-date information on available genealogical software. Another Web site *(www.mumford.ca/reportcard/)* provides a Genealogical Software Report Card, with information on the special features for most genealogical software programs. You will find a thorough review of

Standards for Use of Technology in Genealogical Research
Recommended by the National Genealogical Society

Mindful that computers are tools, genealogists take full responsibility for their work, and therefore they

- Learn the capabilities and limits of their equipment and software, and use them only when they are the most appropriate tools for a purpose

- Do not accept uncritically the ability of software to format, number, import, modify, check, chart or report their data, and therefore carefully evaluate any resulting product

- Treat compiled information from online sources or digital databases in the same way as other published sources—useful primarily as a guide to locating original records, but not as evidence for a conclusion or assertion

- Accept digital images or enhancements of an original record as a satisfactory substitute for the original only when there is reasonable assurance that the image accurately reproduces the unaltered original

- Cite sources for data obtained online or from digital media with the same care that is appropriate for sources on paper and other traditional media, and enter data into a digital database only when its source can remain associated with it

- Always cite the sources for information or data posted online or sent to others, naming the author of a digital file as its immediate source, while crediting original sources cited within the file

- Preserve the integrity of their own databases by evaluating the reliability of downloaded data before incorporating it into their own files

- Provide, whenever they alter data received in digital form, a description of the change that will accompany the altered data whenever it is shared with others

- Actively oppose the proliferation of error, rumor, and fraud by personally verifying or correcting information, or noting it as unverified, before passing it on to others

- Treat people online as courteously and civilly as they would treat them face-to-face, not separated by networks and anonymity

- Accept that technology has not changed the principles of genealogical research, only some of the procedures

genealogical software programs in another book in the NGS series, *Genealogy 101: How to Trace Your Family's History and Heritage,* by Barbara Renick. Many communities have software user groups that encourage experts to share their knowledge with new users. Genealogical societies often have user groups or knowledgeable people who can assist new genealogical software users.

GEDCOM stands for GEnealogical Data COMmunication and is available with most genealogical software programs. GEDCOM prepares file transfers from one program to another or file sharing from cousin to cousin. However, be aware that some data may be lost in the transfer. *Genealogy 101*, mentioned just above, also reviews GEDCOM features in detail.

Data Entry

In Chapter 2, you thought about organizing and filing all the papers that have been stacking up, thus finding a home for each piece of paper. Was the information contained in those papers recorded anywhere? Probably not. In order to organize the papers quickly, filing was the first step. Now it's time to review each folder and glean all the information you can.

The first and biggest step is for you to systematically enter the data and documentation into your software program. This is a huge job that will take some time to do properly. Before you start, make some decisions about your data entry format. For example, you should select the date format you prefer, and determine how you would like to print the names—in uppercase or standard letters. Additional data entry suggestions are available in Chapter 12.

Depending on the size of the folder, you may be able to enter data for just one folder at a time; the task could take anywhere from a half hour to several hours per folder. Don't go too fast. Take the time to absorb all the information in one folder before progressing to the next.

After you finish the data entry phase, you may want to again review each folder to double check your work and to continue to add research suggestions to your to-do list. You should focus on each piece of paper in the folder, so select a time and location that works well for you. You might prefer to review each folder while sitting in a comfortable chair with your feet propped up. Or you may want to sit at a desk or table where you can spread out the folder contents. If necessary, use sticky notes to make notations on the papers. Have your software program open or printouts available. Be sure to have a note-taking tablet to capture the new research ideas that jump off the page as you review each folder. You'll be surprised how many dates, names, or places you hadn't noticed previously.

Internet and E-mail

The Internet is a blessing and a curse. Genealogists want to find all the records for their ancestors on the Internet, but current funding for institutions and organizations prevents this. Nevertheless, the vast amount of records online today is amazing, and more become available every day.

Vital records for some states are available online. Secondary records, including indexes and family histories compiled by genealogists, are plentiful. Some of the secondary information is documented. Here are a few things to consider about Internet searches and discoveries:

- Not all genealogical records are on the Internet.

- Most items on the Net are not documented.

- Undocumented records on the Net are *clues*, not facts.

You can print Web site pages; however, they quickly add volume to your files. For some sites, a worksheet to record the data is easy to use. The Social Security Death Index (SSDI) database is a good example. Record the names of deceased relatives that you want to locate in the SSDI on the Social Security worksheet (see Figure 5.1). Also include the date of birth or death, if known, to help identify the correct person as there may be several people listed with the same name you are seeking. Remember to use the forms in the same manner as your filing system. Do not mix the Smith and Jones families if you file by surname. The Social Security system updates the online SSDI database every few months. This electronic database began about 1962. Very few deaths prior to that date are available online even though they were reported to the Social Security office and possibly had benefits paid to survivors. Information available online varies based on the date of death; the more recent entries provide the complete death date, but earlier entries show only the month and year. The SSDI is building a national death record. For a nominal fee listed on the Social Security Administration Web site, you can order the Social Security application of the deceased. It contains the signature of the

SOCIAL SECURITY DEATH INDEX WORKSHEET

Name	Birth Date	Death Date	Last Place of Residence	Social Security Number	Request Application	Results

Figure 5.1 Social Security worksheet

deceased, parents' names, address at the time of the application, and in the earlier entries, place of employment. In the past, individuals obtained their Social Security number when they were looking for their first job. Today, parents are required to obtain Social Security numbers for infants. Obviously, the applicant's signature is not included on those applications.

The SSDI is available on several Web sites, each varying the search possibilities. Enter the name of your relative and see what comes up. If your ancestor does not appear, omit some of the information and search again. The database could contain a different date of death or birth, the surname spelled differently, or a nickname in the given name field. Try various combinations.

A fellow genealogist told me that after his wife died he looked at her entry in the SSDI. It listed the wrong date of death, but all the other information was correct. My friend sent a letter to Social Security informing them of the correct date. They made the correction to the death date, but now it says she died in Montana instead of Missouri, which had been correct on the earlier entry. He sent another letter, but they did not correct the entry or respond. There are definitely errors in the system.

As you locate ancestors, you may also be able to track down living relatives. Maybe Uncle Joe moved to Oregon in 1940 and the two families lost touch. If you locate Joe's Social Security record, you may be able to locate additional sources that will lead you to his children or grandchildren.

This book mentions several Web sites. For more information, you can read another book in the NGS series, *Online Roots: How to Discover Your Family's History and Heritage with the Power of the Internet,* by Pamela Boyer Porter and Amy Johnson Crow; it provides excellent insight and details regarding online sources and research for genealogists.

E-mail

Does the large volume of e-mails you receive ever overwhelm you? Once you delete the junk mail, the real correspondence between family and friends comes to the surface. Sometimes you can answer immediately; other times you have a reason to delay the response. You want to save some e-mail, particularly if you are working on a project with other people. However, when you save e-mail, your Inbox gets bigger and bigger.

Creating electronic folders for the correspondence you want to save helps keep your Inbox a manageable size. Make numerous folders—for individual people, family surnames, projects, or one called "I will get to it tomorrow." By moving the e-mail from the Inbox to one of these folders, you will organize similar items and have all correspondence on any one subject together.

You can move files two ways. First, make a new folder in your e-mail system. After that, the simplest method of moving and saving new e-mail is to click and drag the e-mail from the Inbox to the new folder. The other method to move e-mail from the Inbox is to click on Edit, click Move to Folder, then click on the appropriate folder. Either way, the mail now appears under that folder and is out of your Inbox. You can move messages from the Delete and Sent boxes in the same fashion. Do not let those e-mails pile up and prevent you from receiving new mail. This process works in Microsoft Outlook. You can also establish rules in your e-mail so that your new correspondence goes directly into the appropriate folders. Check the Help menu for guidance in your program.

Save e-mail attachments in the proper subject folder. If someone sends you information about a new baby, save it in your word-processing file under that surname. In many cases, attachments and e-mails should be printed and the paper copy filed with your other documents or correspondence.

Bookmark Web Sites

Organize your Web sites by placing a bookmark in the Favorites list on your Internet toolbar. This process allows you to return easily to the same site tomorrow or next week.

When you find an interesting site, click on the Favorites button. Since you may have many favorites, it is advisable to make category folders. If you research in California, make a California folder. Within that folder, add any Web site that applies to that state. You may want to add the California page from Cyndi's List to start. Then include any state or county sites you visit regularly.

Sometimes the Web site has a long official name. Short descriptive names work better in the Favorites list. Adjust the name so that it clearly describes the site.

Word Processing

Several good word-processing programs are available for your computer. Whichever one you select, be sure to use that program to its fullest capability. Transcribe the oral interviews, make list upon list upon list, produce file folder labels, and write your family history.

If you are not familiar with your word-processing program, you can plan to learn a new feature every day or every week, as time permits. A class at the local library, society, or college is another option. The more you use it, the easier the program becomes. As new projects arise, you may need to learn and use additional features. You can use the word-processing program to format your family history, as outlined in Chapter 12. Mastering a software program is a great learning experience, and you will be proud of your finished work.

Use the word processor in conjunction with the Internet. With both programs open, you can switch back and forth to cut and paste important data found on the Internet, adding them to your files. Be sure to include the site name and URL (its address on the Web), and the current date in your documentation so you can find the site again.

Templates

You may want to organize some of your documents by using templates. Save anything that you do repetitively as a template. Perhaps you like to send letters to other family members or government facilities on paper with your letterhead. The name and address information can be as simple or complex as you like. Find a style, and then save the template or form file as "your name letterhead." Then each time you want to write a letter, open the letterhead file and write your letter. After you write the letter,

Templates

To locate templates in Microsoft Word, click on File, New, Word templates, then select the tab that best represents the document you need to develop. Document files are saved as .doc files and available in the template folder.

WordPerfect templates are available by clicking on File, New from Project Expert, then selecting the document that fits your needs. You can develop your own templates or use the preprogrammed files.

save it under the name of the recipient or the subject and use the template extension. The original letterhead file is still the same, ready for use the next time. Do the same for a fax, memo, or any other form that you use regularly. Store the blank templates in a template folder. Most word processors have templates within the program, which you can modify or make your own. Refer to the Help menu in your software program for guidance.

Shortcut Keys

Using shortcut keys is another timesaver. If you use a phrase or symbol frequently, establish a shortcut key so that you do not have to retype the phrase repeatedly. For example, rather than type "National Genealogical Society" every time, you can create a shortcut by using letters and symbols. The shortcut should be something you will remember and something you will not be likely to type by accident—for example, ngs[(three letters and the left square bracket). You can select any combination of letters and symbols that works for you, but focus on convenience. Use lowercase letters and symbols on the keyboard, and use the least number of keystrokes possible to accomplish your goal. Access the AutoCorrect tool or something comparable in your word processor, and enter both the original phrase and the shortcut you selected. Then go back to the normal text area to test your new entry. Type the shortcut keys, press the spacebar, and the longer phrase should appear. Be sure it is correct; you don't want to repeat a typo.

Red Print

As you write your family history, letters, or research reports, sometimes you are missing a number, quote, documentation, or even a name. Type something in that spot even if it is a series of "xxx." Then make those letters or numbers red. The unknown information will jump out at you when you look at your computer screen or printout. You will not forget that you need to fill in that information. This works well for documentation. All too often, one part of the documentation is missing, maybe a page number. Type page "xxx." Place "page" and "xxx" in red to remind you to locate that number. In the beginning, your document may look like the text is bleeding. When the text stops bleeding, you may well be finished with that project.

Editing Options

As mentioned before, family historians often work with cousins or friends. Perhaps together you are writing a story about an ancestor or writing an article for your local genealogical society. You can share the work in progress via e-mail as an attachment. Transmit the word-processing document to the other person. Upon receiving this document, the other person can add to the text or edit the previous text. Several word-processing features allow you to mark any changes or additions.

Between the two of you, identify and organize your editing marks. Perhaps you want to use the highlighter feature to indicate new words or punctuation. Yellow could indicate newly added information. Green could indicate you have a question about that sentence or paragraph. Use the strikethrough feature to suggest deleting material. Save those changes and send the revised copy back to your writing partner. If that person agrees, delete the strikethrough material, remove the highlighting from the good text, and move forward. This editing technique works whether you live across town or across the country. Some word-processing programs have a Track Changes feature that does the same thing automatically. Check your software program.

Databases and Spreadsheets

Databases

Most computers have spreadsheet or database programs, which are helpful to genealogists. Many people use the word "database" when they really mean any program that has a table that can be sorted on various fields. If you are working on a large project for your society, such as a marriage index for an entire county, a real database would be better. Databases allow you to use multiple tables, with a defined data entry screen. A database program has the ability to cross-reference to another related database through a common data element. The major difference is the query option available in the database program. By using a query, you can locate any word or number in the database easily. Databases have the capability to make fancy reports. Genealogical software programs use a database format.

Before starting a project, we need to get organized, establish a plan, and set goals. All too often, we enter data and need to make changes later because of poor planning. Do you want to sort by surname, by year, by cemetery, or some other way? If you want to sort by surname and then by given name, it is best to provide two fields, one for surname and one for given name. If you want to sort by date, do you want the first sort by year? If yes, use three fields—one for the year, one for the month, and one for the day.

Spreadsheets

Recently I used a spreadsheet to compile a list of family burials in a three-county area. I listed the names of potential burials in the focus area, the surname in one column, and the given name in another column. I provided three columns for the death date, three for the birth date, one for the cemetery name, one for the township where the cemeteries are located, and a column for the lot and section numbers. This spreadsheet served as my worksheet while I uncovered new material.

When you are studying one particular county, you often have several lists pertaining to that county. There could be a list of potential marriages to research, a list of cemetery information to locate, and perhaps a list of potential soldiers to research. In your spreadsheet program, you can combine those multiple lists into one workbook under the county name. By using the tabs at the bottom of the screen, put the marriage list on tab one, the cemetery list on tab two, and the military list on tab three. Click on the tab to give it the appropriate name.

You can also use a spreadsheet for its original purpose, accounting. If you want to keep track of your genealogical expenses, a spreadsheet is the tool to use. Divide the sheet into various expense columns. Format the columns for currency with two places after the decimal point. Format the first column for the date of each purchase. Format the last column for text, available for notes to identify each purchase. If any of these expenses are tax deductible, your tax advisor will thank you for this organized file. Just keep the receipts in a folder or large envelope, and you are ready for April 15.

On this spreadsheet, make a column for office supplies such as file folders, labels, paper, envelopes, postage, and ink cartridges for your printer. Another column could be for books and software. Every time you purchase new software that applies to your genealogy or a new reference book, list the expense in that column. List your expenses for dues to various societies and fees for magazine subscriptions in another column. If you travel, add a column for those expenses. Research expenses should include your copy costs at the library or fees for research by others. Do not forget to include those incidental fees from your correspondence log. If you do research for others, add a column for income. Total each column at the bottom, and then make a grand total of all the expenses on the entire sheet. Save this file as (Current year) Expenses. In subsequent years, use the same template; just change the name to include the current year. Of course, whether you choose to keep up with your genealogical expenses is up to you. It's your call.

Serial Numbers and Passwords

Every software program has a serial number, version number, and perhaps other numbers that are important only if the program crashes and you need technical assistance. Where is that number when you need it? Keep a computer file for this important data. The file folder can include all software information or use one folder per program.

When you purchase a new computer, you should record the important information about that hardware. Keep a file on that purchase with a copy of the invoice, warranty, and specifications. The file will help you remember the features included with that hardware. Even CD or DVD drives have serial and model numbers.

A file for the hardware and another file for the software should be the minimum. If you have numerous notes on one item, establish a separate file for that particular item. You cannot have too much information.

It's a good idea to create a spreadsheet that includes information about every program you own. For each program, list the purchase or installation date, serial number, and version number. Record the new version number when downloading a patch. If it requires a login name or word, password, and perhaps a "secret" backup word, such as your mother's maiden name, add that data in pencil after you print out the list. It is not advisable to keep a computer file for your passwords since hackers could obtain that list. Remember, in genealogy, mother's maiden name is not a secret. Establish a word to use instead of your mother's maiden name. The computer will not know the difference. When you need the information, simply go to the paper file and you are ready to proceed. You should also make a printout of this data in case your computer problems block you from getting to the needed file. For security reasons, computer experts discourage password lists. Determine the system that works best for you.

In the same file, you can retain any notes or Web site printouts regarding upgrades or FAQs. If a

FAQs is an abbreviation used for Frequently Asked Questions and is usually associated with computers.

problem recurs, the answer is at your fingertips. Record the current Web site address on the paperwork retained in the file. Take comprehensive notes if there is a conversation with the software or hardware experts. These items should remain in the folder.

Software CDs should be stored in an out-of-the way location, and data CDs should be within arm's reach of your computer. Purchase a container to hold the program CDs. If you have a program upgrade, consider disposing of the older version.

File Management

Computer files, like manila folders in the filing cabinet, need to be organized. There are several ways to organize these files. Again, use the system with which you are comfortable. Whatever system you use, divide the files into folders. You really cannot have too many folders.

The folder name should be descriptive, short, and adequate to identify the purpose and contents. If you are a volunteer for a genealogical society, you probably have files on your computer under that name. If you volunteer for NGS, all files for NGS should begin with the letters NGS. You may have the NGS cemetery project, the NGS marriage project, NGS bylaws, or numerous other types of files. At a glance, you know it pertains to the society. By using a standard format for file names, the files will be easier to locate if you forget the exact name.

File Name Description

A computer file name is similar to a person's given name and surname; the combination of the two is unique (first name.last name). The first name should provide sufficient information to describe the file, and the last name, commonly called an **extension**, tells the computer user the type of file. The program usually assigns the last name.

- **First name:** What information is in this file?
- **Last name:** What program is this file in?

Make as many folders as necessary. Start with a folder, such as My Documents, and then move to the general categories as shown in Figure 5.2. You can continue adding folders inside folders inside folders until you have all like items together. The general categories could divide your various hobbies or interests. Genealogy should be one folder, and others could be antiques, fishing, gardening, or home decorating.

Figure 5.2 Family history folder separated by individual surname folders

How do you want to group your files? Some projects use multiple programs; others use just one type of program, such as word processing. While working on this book, I made a folder under My Documents called Organizing Book; that folder holds all files related to this book. I open Windows Explorer and then open the Organizing Book folder. All files for this project are available regardless of the program used to produce them.

This option works well for volunteer organizations. Make a folder for NGS. Save any documents, spreadsheets, photos, or e-mail under that one header. It is not necessary to go to the word-processing file, then the spreadsheet file, and then the photo file. If you work on several projects for NGS, make separate folders under that main file. Make one folder for publications, one folder for Bible records, and another folder for conferences.

The other filing option is to have a folder for each program with project folders listed below the main folder. Under this plan, My Documents would have one folder for the word-processing program, one for spreadsheets, one for databases, one for genealogical programs, and so forth. Under each folder, you might have an NGS folder. A folder for your family history with a file for each surname in your genealogy would also be appropriate for the word-processing directory.

Both plans work; it just depends on the project or purpose of the documents. Try it both ways to see which works for you. It could be that you like both options, using one format for one type of project and another format for another project.

Backup

Every time you update the data, back up the file. Use a floppy disk or Zip disk, or burn a CD for your backup. Establish a series of disks to use for backups so you don't use the same disk each time. Rotate the storage disks on a regular basis. If one disk fails, you have another, guaranteeing minimal loss of information. Back up the files on a regular basis if not every day. Maybe every Friday works well for you. The scheduling decisions are yours. Some people back up every hour; others once a week. The volume of work and your comfort level help determine your backup schedule.

If all document files are saved somewhere under My Documents, it is easy and efficient to back up the data files without backing up the program files. It is also possible to back up your data files in smaller quantities, perhaps by project.

Once you complete a project, delete any unneeded files. There is no point in cluttering the hard drive with old files if space is a problem. If you do not want to delete the files, save them to a CD or floppy disk for storage. If you have space on your hard drive, make a folder named Archives. Then move any completed projects into this folder. The files will be available but out of the way. If you upgrade your computer, your old files will copy to the new computer, along with the active files.

Establish a system for labeling the backup disks. Always include the file name and backup date. Any additional information is optional. Do you file the disks alphabetically based on the file name? Do you just randomly throw them in a drawer? Establish a filing system that works for you based on your space and storage containers. Otherwise your valuable backup disk will be lost.

Organizing your data, files, books, photos, and computer is now complete. The next task is to organize your research plans. By establishing a research plan, you will be a more effective researcher and have a more successful visit at libraries and courthouses.

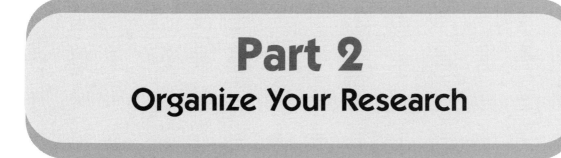

Part 2
Organize Your Research

CHAPTER 6

Tools of the Trade

PLANNING, PLANNING, AND MORE PLANNING ARE THE MOST IMPORTANT elements of researching your family history. You have started organizing your heritage trunk. Now it is time to move to the next step, organizing your research. Some techniques are useful for research at home, and others are more helpful while you are at a library. Additional techniques become important as you find and record online data and information. The following research aids help you with your research:

- To-do list
- Note-taking tablet
- Research notebook
- Research report
- Surname list
- Timeline

Organizing and planning your genealogical research is critical to your success. It is helpful to divide a project into sections. This could be as easy as analyzing your family lines and using geographic divisions. As an example, the New England Historic Genealogical Society would be the place to go if your maternal grandmother came from an old New England family. The Family History Library microfilm collection would be helpful if your paternal great-grandfather's family came from Germany.

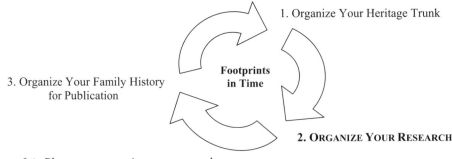

1. Organize Your Heritage Trunk

Footprints in Time

3. Organize Your Family History for Publication

2. ORGANIZE YOUR RESEARCH

Figure 6.1 Phase two, organize your research

Research in different regions of this country, as well as abroad, offers different opportunities and challenges.

In the previous chapters, you organized the items in your heritage trunk—books, documents, files, heirlooms, notes, photos, and other genealogical materials. Now you are moving to phase two, organizing your research by using worksheets and forms (see Figure 6.1).

To-Do List

New family historians find an abundance of information. Data is often available on their parents, siblings, aunts, uncles, grandparents, and great-grandparents. After you enter the data in your genealogical software program, determine the missing pieces of the puzzle.

Begin by printing out family group sheets for your grandparents. Do you have all birth, marriage, and death dates for your grandparents, their children, and the children's spouses? If not, it's time to establish a research plan for this family group.

The best way to begin is to make a to-do list of your questions. You can compile this list in your database, spreadsheet, or word-processing program. The to-do list is a perpetual list of items to research, as shown in Figure 6.2. Some items are easy, others more detailed. When you complete a task, remove the item from the list and add any new questions. This list is just a to-do list, not a place to document your sources. Add the notes, transcription, or documentation to your note-taking tablet or laptop, or make photocopies.

The to-do list should be categorized. You should begin by dividing the questions by country, state, and then by county. If you want to review some family histories at the library, have a separate section for surnames. If you need information regarding a marriage in Ohio, list the state and county, the approximate or known date of the

TO-DO RESEARCH WORKSHEET

State	County	Call or Film Number	Title or Type of Record	Searching for . . .

Figure 6.2 To-do research worksheet (see next page for examples)

TO-DO RESEARCH WORKSHEET

State	County	Call or Film Number	Title or Type of Record	Searching for . . .
Illinois	Saline	FHL 965055	Female marriage index	Julia Anderson marriage to Jeff Lynch ca 1865
	Saline	FHL 965063	Probate index	Thomas Anderson probate record after 1860
	Saline		Census 1870	Jeff Lynch household
	Saline		Census 1860	Beverly Fleming & wife?
Missouri	St. Louis	StL Courthouse	Probate	Samuel James probate packet 1898
	Texas	FHL 931634	Probate	Ozias Upton probate file ca 1870
	Texas	FHL 931629	Marriage	Alphonse James & Eunice Cable marriage ca 1885
Tennessee	Sumner	976.847 v 2	Marriage	Beverly Fleming & Polly Aspley marriage ca 1812
	Sumner	FHL 467512	Deeds – Direct index	Beverly Fleming 1810–1840
	Sumner	FHL 467513	Deed – Reverse index	Beverly Fleming 1810–1840

Figure 6.2, *continued* To-do research worksheet with examples

event, and the bride's and groom's names. When you review a library catalog, list the name of a book or film that you want to review. Enter the resource in the Title field, and add the catalog number if known. Sort the list by state and then by county. Armed with this list, you are now ready to proceed with your research on the Internet or at the library and courthouse.

This list is just a tickler to remind you what holes you need to fill in your family history. Research time in any facility is limited. This list is your plan of attack; it helps you use that limited time most wisely. For example, your to-do list should have all the questions on Virginia grouped together. That way, you can go to the Virginia section of the library and find what is available. You probably won't locate everything on your list. Cross out the items you do find, and move on to another state.

After you visit a library, update the list. There will be items to remove because you answered that question and new questions to add. This list is a continually changing document, with the old version thrown away after you produce a new list. It is important to have the date on each page for easy identification. Do not record any documentation on this paper.

Genealogy is a unique hobby since it does not need constant attention. Sometimes life events prohibit research for weeks, months, or even years. The research to-do list should be maintained and adjusted as your research progresses. It is always ready when you find time and are ready to do research—whether this week, next month, or in the future.

Note-Taking Tablet

Some researchers use a laptop computer while at a research facility; others prefer pencil and paper. Either way, you need a note-taking tablet. Some people use a yellow tablet, others like loose-leaf papers; however, most prefer a spiral tablet because the pages stay in order and nothing can be lost. Use this tablet for anything you write down during your time at the research facility, even what time you are meeting someone for lunch or your locker number. Write down book or film numbers to review, notes taken from a resource, or new ideas that you do not want to forget. This tablet is your memory while you are at a research facility. When you get home, enter the data in your genealogical software program or your word-processing program. After you enter the information into your computer, make a big checkmark next to the data to remind you that information has been processed (see Figure 6.3).

Whatever kind of note-taking tablet you choose, be sure to record your name, home address, e-mail address, and cell phone number on the inside cover, which is easy to do with one of your address stickers. If you lose your tablet in a library, perhaps a fellow genealogist will contact you immediately. Date the tablet, and indicate the research facilities used during that period. Also, date the pages inside. As you fill one tablet, start another. I prefer tablets with a hundred pages or less; larger tablets are too heavy and bulky to carry around. Store the spiral tablets with your file folders in case you need to refer to a citation months or years from now, and keep them in chronological order for easy reference.

Figure 6.3   Note-taking tablet

A **research notebook** contains research outlines, notes, charts, and worksheets that are ready for the next research trip.

Research Notebook

A research notebook is an absolute must for all family historians. It is your best genealogical friend; do not leave home without it. Some people use a laptop as their research notebook. Use whatever method works best for you.

The notebook should include a copy of your current research, worksheets, research reference lists, and checklists. As your research continues, you certainly cannot carry every family group sheet in this notebook. The notebook is helpful whether you are at home, going to a library, or visiting a courthouse. Divide the notebook with tabs similar to your file folders. You could have a tab for each family or a tab for each of the eight great-grandparents. If you summarize information on each family, as in writing your family history, it will fit nicely in a notebook. Again, divide the notebook in the way you think about your genealogy and how you file it. Be sure your name, address, and other contact information are in this notebook.

Worksheets

Worksheets or checklists help you organize similar records. For example, if you are looking for all the marriages in a particular county, prepare a worksheet of the potential marriages in that location.

The worksheet is a "work in progress" or "check-off list," not something that will be completed in one evening. As you gather new information from various sources, fill in the empty spaces on the worksheet, with the goal of filling in every space. The completed worksheet should mean that you have solved all problems and answered all questions related to that form. If you find unique records for your ancestors or region, add new columns. You may use the forms shown here by photocopying them or printing them from the CD, or you can make your own with the appropriate fields. Many genealogical software programs allow you to customize lists of specific records and places.

Remember that these worksheets are throwaway items. They are just finding aids and a way to organize your thoughts. While at the library, do not document your research on these worksheets. Document your research in your note-taking tablet or on your laptop.

The next few chapters provide numerous worksheets. By organizing your research and adding these worksheets to your research notebook, you will be able to quickly search the records when you are at libraries and courthouses.

Laptop and PDA

If you have a laptop or a personal digital assistant (PDA), you may prefer to use one of these at the library instead of a research notebook. Both have advantages and disadvantages.

A laptop can contain every bit of information held in your home file cabinet. It can hold scanned images of documents and maps, all of your text information, and photographs. There is no need for you to carry every piece of paper to the library. The images can be stored on the hard drives, or on CDs or DVDs. If you have organized well, you should be able to pull up every file at a moment's notice.

However, a laptop is expensive. And it requires some set-up time at the library and may limit where you can sit if you need access to a power source. In addition to the laptop, you need a briefcase, extension cords, locking device, and CD holders. If you take a laptop to the library, do you take time to do the data entry while at the library? Do you make photocopies of the resources and complete the data entry when you get home? These can be tough decisions when time is limited at research facilities. Some researchers take a laptop along on research trips but use it only in their hotel room, saving library time for further research. If you travel by air, the airport hassle is another consideration when it comes to laptops.

A PDA is a small handheld device that can hold your genealogical data. A fellow genealogist has a PDA he uses only for genealogy, with a genealogical PDA software program. You can use GEDCOM to transfer the data from your home genealogical software program to the PDA program. Use your home computer as the master; with no entries ever made directly to the PDA. Before traveling or visiting a library, update the PDA file from the master file on your desktop.

Another friend uses her PDA for contacts, e-mail, grocery lists, medical information, calendar, notes, and genealogy. She has a folding keyboard and uses this combination in research facilities to take notes in Pocket Word. She also uses Pocket Excel.

A **personal digital assistant**, otherwise known as a **PDA,** is a computer that fits in the palm of your hand. The touch screen is used with a stylus or your finger. The PDA connects to your desktop or laptop computer to transfer information.

The PDA is small enough to hold in your palm or keep in your pocket. Many libraries have restrictions on notebooks, briefcases, or other materials allowed in the facility. So far, libraries allow PDAs. Imagine having thousands of names, dates, and places available in the palm of your hand. The software may not hold all the text in your notes, but certainly holds the basic data. No doubt, new software versions will hold even more in the near future.

Whether you use a laptop, PDA, or research notebook, organize your research in the way that works best for you. You may need to try a couple of methods to see which you prefer.

Guidelines for Genealogical Self-Improvement and Growth
Recommended by the National Genealogical Society

Faced with ever-growing expectations for genealogical accuracy and reliability, family historians concerned with improving their abilities will on a regular basis

- Study comprehensive texts and narrower-focus articles and recordings covering genealogical methods in general and the historical background and sources available for areas of particular research interest, or to which their research findings have led them

- Interact with other genealogists and historians in person or electronically, mentoring or learning as appropriate to their relative experience levels, and through the shared experience contributing to the genealogical growth of all concerned

- Subscribe to and read regularly at least two genealogical journals that list a number of contributing or consulting editors, or editorial board or committee members, and that require their authors to respond to a critical review of each article before it is published

- Participate in workshops, discussion groups, institutes, conferences, and other structured learning opportunities whenever possible

- Recognize their limitations, undertaking research in new areas or using new technology only after they master any additional knowledge and skill needed and understand how to apply it to the new subject matter or technology

- Analyze critically at least quarterly the reported research findings of another family historian, for whatever lessons may be gleaned through the process

- Join and participate actively in genealogical societies covering countries, localities, and topics where they have research interests, as well as the localities where they reside, increasing the resources available both to themselves and to future researchers

- Review recently published basic texts to renew their understanding of genealogical fundamentals as currently expressed and applied

- Examine and revise their own earlier research in the light of what they have learned through self-improvement activities, as a means for applying their new-found knowledge and for improving the quality of their work-product

Research Report

Now is the time for you to analyze some of your records. Find a comfortable place to sit with pencil and paper in hand. The family group sheet for your grandparents is a good place to begin to analyze the data. Determine what you know and what you do not know. What major question do you have for this couple? Perhaps you want to find Grandma's maiden name. Maybe you want to find the city and state where they were married. As you jot down questions, make them as specific as you can.

Professional genealogists prepare research reports for clients. You should do the same for your family search. Write a report to yourself for each question that is difficult to answer. When you focus on the question at hand, the facts often become clear. Research report examples can be found in the *BCG Genealogical Standards Manual* by the Board for Certification of Genealogists. A research report enables a genealogist to focus on one question at a time. You want to

- Determine known information

- Record the data pertaining to that question

- Outline a research plan

The **Board for Certification of Genealogists** is an internationally recognized independent organization that is a certifying body, not a membership society *(www.bcgcertification.org)*.

As you review the information, write down the known facts, findings, and conclusions, and list your documentation. Analyze the information—what makes sense, and what does not? What do you know, and how do you know it? Maybe one of the sources of information was your grandmother. Perhaps she inadvertently gave you the incorrect date or name. What facts can lead you to other records? For example, if you are looking for the place of marriage, try to determine the state where the first child was born. Often you will find a child's birth state listed on a census,

When and Where Did Charles Blittersdorf Die?

Charles Blittersdorf, my third great-grandfather, was born in Germany and married Charlotta Kappel on 3 November 1852, in Cincinnati, Ohio. The 1860 Hamilton County, Ohio census listed Charles, a confectioner, and his wife Charlotta, also listed as Jeanette on some records, with three children. In 1861, Charles enlisted in Company H of the Twenty-eighth Regiment of the Ohio Volunteer Infantry. This mostly Cincinnati German unit served at the battle of Antietam and other East Coast encounters. They mustered out on 23 July 1864.

After the war, Charles returned to Cincinnati. He is listed as a cake maker in the 1866 and 1867 city directories. The 1868 directory lists Charlotte Blittersdorf as a widow, along with their son Jacob. Presumably, Charles died. I reviewed records including probate, will, and cemetery, but could locate no information on the death of Charles.

What was my next step? What did I know, and which records had not been searched? In this case, Civil War pension files were not searched because I thought Charles died so soon after the war.

But upon searching Civil War pension files, I discovered that Charles had moved to Little Rock, Arkansas, remarried, and had three additional children, all born in Arkansas. Charles died in Little Rock on 8 July 1887, with burial at Oakland Cemetery. As a minor, Louisa, the youngest daughter of Charles and his second wife, Lizzie, received a Civil War pension from Charles's service. I was able to find the date and place of death for Charles Blittersdorf and answer my original question!

1850 or after. If the child was born in Illinois, as were the parents, chances are good that the parents were married in Illinois, maybe a year before the child's birth date. Your research plan should include a search of the Illinois marriage records with an open mind on spelling options.

When preparing a research report, as shown in Figure 6.4, include every search conducted, both positive and negative. The negative results are as important as the positive results. The research plan is a running summary of the research on a particular question. The report could be one paragraph or several pages. Use as much space as you need, but be concise.

RESEARCH REPORT
(Real story with fictitious names and places.)

DATE:	30 December 1995	**SURNAME:**	Jones
FROM:	Self		
TO:	File		

QUESTION: Who was the mother of Susie Jones?

SUMMARY OF KNOWN INFORMATION: Susie Jones, born about 1865, was living in Blue County, Missouri, when she married William Casper in 1885.[1] Susie's birth was unrecorded since Missouri birth certificates were not available until 1910 and Blue County did not keep a local birth register.

The 1880 census shows Susie, age fifteen, living with her grandmother, Rebecca Stone.[2] The 1870 census lists a Susan Lee, age five, living with the same Rebecca Stone.[3] The 1850 census showed Mary, age nine, a probable daughter for John and Rebecca Stone.[4]

Blue County marriages were searched for a marriage between Jones and Stone since Rebecca was Susie's grandmother. No records found. A search was conducted in the surrounding counties of Yellow, Beige, and Purple for the same marriage record. Nothing was found.[5] There was a record for Mary Stone, who married David Lee in 1858.[6]

David and Mary Lee, with one daughter Rebecca, were found in the 1860 Blue County census,[7] but they were not found in the 1870 census. The 1870 Mortality Schedule listed the death of David Lee on 10 August 1869 and the death of Mary on 15 August 1869.[8]

Probate records were searched, finding none for Mary; however, David appointed his father, Harry Lee, as administrator of his estate. David left his entire estate to his only child, Rebecca Lee.[9]

FUTURE RESEARCH:
1. Search for guardianship papers for Rebecca Lee and Susie Jones.
2. Locate an obituary for Susie Jones Casper.
3. Research Rebecca Lee to determine a possible connection with Susie.
4. Search deed records for John Stone and David Lee.

---

[1] Casper-Jones marriage record, Blue County, Missouri, copy of certificate in family papers of Jane Doe.
[2] Rebecca Stone household, 1880 U.S. census, Blue County, Missouri, population schedule, Red Township, ED 4, SD 1, page 12 written, page 202 stamped, dwelling 34, family 34; NARA micropublication M222, roll 25.
[3] Rebecca Stone household, 1870 U.S. census, Blue County, Missouri, population schedule, Red Township, Green post office, page 4 written, page 145 stamped, dwelling 23, family 23; NARA micropublication M111, roll 20.
[4] John Stone household, 1850 U.S. census, Blue County, Missouri, population schedule, Red Township, page 34 written, page 56 stamped, dwelling 42, family 43; NARA micropublication M65, roll 24.
[5] Jane Smith, *Yellow County Marriages* (Mauve, Missouri: XYZ Publisher, 1997). Mary Tulip, *Beige County Marriages* (Cream, Missouri: ABC Printer, 1995). Also, Sharon Rose, *Purple County Marriages* (Black, Missouri: DEF Printer, 1999). No record was found for a Jones-Stone marriage.
[6] Lee-Stone marriage record, Blue County, Missouri, Recorder of Deeds office, Book 2, page 99.
[7] David Lee household, 1860 U.S. census, Blue County, Missouri, population schedule, Red Township, page 10 written, page 45 stamped, dwelling 25, family 25; NARA micropublication M85, roll 16.
[8] David Lee and Mary Lee, 1870 U.S. census, Blue County, Missouri, mortality schedule, Red Township, page 6, original document reviewed Missouri Historical Society, St. Louis, Missouri.
[9] David Lee probate record, Blue County, Missouri, Probate Court record, file no. 589.

Figure 6.4 Sample research report

You do not want to mix your Smith question with your Jones question, so as you develop the research plan, use a different piece of paper for every question. That way, you can file each report in the proper family folder. When you come back to this project, in a few days or next year, you will be able to pick up where you left off. The report will refresh your memory of the completed research, and you can review your own suggestions for future research, without starting all over again.

The research report helps you analyze conflicting evidence. Review the information, and analyze the records. For example, William's family was confused about his birth year. William usually stated he was born in 1896, but some records indicate he was born in 1892. It is not a significant difference, but the family wanted to be accurate. All records had the same day and month, 14 April. In the research report, the family listed the year the record was produced and the type of record, followed by the stated year of birth:

1917	World War I draft card	1892
1919	Marriage record	1896
1920	Census record	1896
1925	Naturalization record	1892
1965	Death certificate	1896

By listing the records in an abbreviated format, the common thread became clear. The marriage record could be an error if William wanted to tell his bride he was a few years younger. The census record could be wrong for the same reason. That was the date William told his family; plus, the census informant is unknown. The death certificate information obviously did not come from William, and the family thought 1896 was correct.

Most likely, the naturalization record data was firsthand information provided by William while in the courtroom. Likewise, William provided his birth date when registering for the World War I draft, while standing before the federal clerk. Do you see the common thread? When William provided firsthand information to the federal government, he gave his birth year as 1892. When he gave the birth year to a less intimidating official, he used the more pleasing 1896. This problem may not have been solved without William's family's writing a research report that focused only on information pertaining to his birth year. That is the theme of this book: Organize your research and analyze your thoughts; positive results will follow.

Surname List

As you locate those special books on your ancestors, check the index and text for all names pertinent to the research. How do you ensure that you remember each name in each book? Use a surname list. An alphabetical surname list is certainly one option. An annotated surname list, which includes the surnames and given names, is another option. Another list can show each surname of interest divided by county and state, with the list stored in your research notebook.

An alphabetical surname list has limited information. This is the list to use when you review indexes so that you don't forget any important surnames. As you expand your research, add new surnames to the list. Maintain this list in your computer so you can add new surnames and easily maintain the alphabetical listing.

The annotated surname list is more detailed; it includes the given name and surname, along with the known birth and death dates for your ancestors. This annotated list is helpful for the more popular names and allows you to

> A **surname list** is a collection of family and collateral surnames. This list could also contain locations and dates.

An **alphabetical surname list** simply lists the surnames in alphabetical order, as in the following example:

> Anderson
>
> Ferguson
>
> Fleming
>
> Lynch
>
> Stucker
>
> Williford

An **annotated surname list** is an alphabetical list that includes surnames, given names, and additional information such as birth and death dates.

Anderson, Thomas	1800–1872
Ferguson, George	1842–1925
Fleming, Beverly	1785–1862
Lynch, Thomas	1845–1896
Stucker, George	1733–1780
Williford, John	1780–1855

A **county-surname list** is divided by state and county, and includes surnames, given names, and birth and death dates.

Illinois	Franklin County	Fleming, Beverly	1787–1863
		Fleming, John	1856–1910
		Fleming, Samuel	1820–1907
		Hathaway, Charles	1832–1880
		Ice, John	1770–1832
	Williamson County	Britton, Kate	1860–1842
		Ferguson, George	1842–1921
		Fleming, John	1856–1910
Missouri	Crawford County	Dorf, Jacob	1878–1965
		Rowland, Andrew	1857–1933
	Jefferson County	Green, James	1770–1842
		Piatt, John	1720–1827
	St. Louis County	Carter, Charles	1860–1910
		James, Samuel	1817–1898
	Texas County	McLaughlin, James	1832–1891
		Upton, Ozias	1800–1871

Collateral families are those that are not your direct line. An aunt, cousin, and in-law are part of your collateral family. Collateral records can be quite helpful when searching a common name, as shown in the following example.

Strubel-Roberts Family

Jane Strubel married John Roberts. A family historian searching for information on the Strubel family uncovered the will of Hiram Hudley Strubel. This previously unknown person listed his sister, Jane Roberts, wife of John Roberts, as the sister of Hiram. The document also listed Hiram's father as John Strubel from New Jersey. The same document listed another sibling as Francis Strubel of Leroy, Kansas, located just a few miles down the railroad tracks from the town where Jane and John Roberts lived in later years.

By searching the siblings and collateral family lines, the family historian discovered further information about Jane Strubel Roberts. Jane apparently left few records of her own. The researcher also identified the name Hudley, as it was a name given to other family members.

select which John Smith fits your ancestor's profile when you find several in the index. However, if all your ancestors have unique surnames, such as Swahlstedt, the alphabetical surname list will work just fine.

The third type of list includes direct and collateral names and dates divided by county and state; it provides a complete review of the names pertinent to each county. This list is quite helpful as you review county-specific publications. The same name may appear on several county listings, indicating the family's migration. This type of list is particularly useful when you are working at a library where the research requires you to jump from one county to another. It is easy to forget one or more names, particularly if you are rushed. Update this surname list as you locate new ancestors, and keep the list in your research notebook.

Timeline

Have you ever been confused about when various family and historical events occurred? I certainly have. A timeline helps resolve this problem. Timelines may be general or very specific.

A timeline may cover the life of an ancestor, starting with the birth date and end-ing with the death date. The chronological list should include all events that occurred during the ancestor's life, plus the place of the events. If you are trying to resolve a question with a short time span, you can be very detailed. This is how I resolved the question mentioned in Chapter 1 about when my hus-band came to St. Louis.

You should list the ancestor's birth, marriage, and death dates, as well as the place of each event. Include the place and dates of birth of his children, adding the death data for those who predeceased him. Additional information may include census listings, church affiliation, military enlist-ment, grantee and grantor records, and any legal docu-ments witnessed by the ancestors. The time and pattern of migration will develop along with the timeline.

A **timeline** is a list of events in chronological order.

You can use timelines in many ways. For example, you might have a timeline for each ancestor or a time-line for a married couple. As you try to prove a point, hone in on the important infor-mation. States also have a timeline. Tennessee was originally part of North Carolina, and Kentucky and West Virginia were part of Virginia. When was the state formed? Was your area part of a territory before statehood? Within the state, each county has a timeline. When was your county formed? What was the parent county? You need to know this important information so that you conduct your research in the correct records. An ancestor may have lived on the same land all her life, but the governing body may have changed numerous times. Since the records usually remain with the old government, it may be necessary to research in Virginia for someone who lived on land in Illinois before the American Revolution.

When you are researching a particular area, you should understand the records. A records timeline within a state or county could be helpful. When did your state officially start keeping vital records? Did the local government, either city or county, keep any vital records before that date? Missouri started keeping vital records in 1910. However, the city and county of St. Louis started keeping vital records as early as 1850. Therefore, if you are looking for a death certificate for a resident of St. Louis before 1910, the local records are the place to go.

You could also add to the records timeline any information about state laws. What

Timeline Suggestions

Timelines are an asset to genealogists. It is necessary to include as much information as possible to see the full picture. If you break down the data by age and by category, the missing links become obvious. Here are some questions to answer in your timeline.

Children five or younger:
- What was the date and place of birth?
- Is a baptismal record available?
- Did the child die from illness during that time?

Children five to late teens:
- Did the child attend school?
- Are any school records or yearbooks available?
- Did the young adult serve an apprenticeship or work for others?
- Did the young adult work outside the home?

Adults:
- *Family information:*
  - Did the adult marry and have children?
  - Did the adult live near other family members?
- *Occupation:*
  - What was the occupation of the ancestor?
  - What were the occupations of other people in the area? (for example, farmers, merchants, coal miners)
- *Transportation:*
  - Did the ancestor arrive in the area by wagon train, railroad, ship, or some other means?
- *Religion:*
  - Was there a predominant religion in the area?
  - Did the ancestor serve as a church elder, clergyman, or deacon?
- *Civic duties:*
  - Did the ancestor serve as a census enumerator, councilman, county clerk, juror, justice of the peace, mayor, road commissioner, or witness?
- *Military:*
  - Did the ancestor serve in the military?
  - Did he receive a military pension or bounty land?
- *End of the road:*
  - Where was the ancestor buried?
  - Do you have a copy of an obituary?
  - Did the ancestor leave a will or probate record?
  - Who were his heirs?

are the names of the various courts in your state, and when were they established? Should you look for divorce or naturalization documents in the Supreme Court records? Did a wife have any right to land owned by her deceased husband? When were women given voting privileges in your state? These timelines are ongoing projects. As you learn a new fact, add the date and information to the timeline. Before long, you will have a wonderful and valuable document. It's also advisable to document your sources of information on a timeline.

Timelines can be very helpful when you are trying to determine the battles in which your Civil War ancestors served. Start with the enlistment and discharge dates, if known. Of course, those dates may be the information you are trying to determine. The Thirty-first Illinois Infantry participated in various battles, including Fort Donaldson, Shiloh, and Atlanta, but not all soldiers participated in all battles. Some soldiers enlisted while forming the unit; others enlisted as the war progressed. If a soldier enlisted in 1864, he did not fight at Shiloh in 1862.

Add historical facts to your family history if the facts relate to the family. If you mention the signing of the Declaration of Independence, someone in the family should have had some connection to that event. Otherwise, it is not pertinent to the story. Just the fact that a child was born on the same day as the signing is not sufficient. There are computer programs that will generate a timeline of historical events that may be helpful in analyzing your data.

Research Project

As you organize your files and make various worksheets and timelines, you should also organize your entire research project. Where are you heading with this project? What are your goals? Are you trying to find your great-grandmother's maiden name? Do you want to research every family line back to the immigrant ancestor? Or to conduct research in the old country? It's time to write down your goals, both short term and long term.

Your goal is the same as a mission statement of an organization or business. If your goal is to join a lineage society, include the basic membership requirements for that society in your project plan. If you plan to compile a family history, list the families to include in the book—maybe a book on your mother and another on your father. Will you start with yourself or one of your parents or great-grandparents? You may have two goals, to write a family history and to trace the family back to the immigrant ancestor. (I hope that writing your family history is always one of your goals.)

If your family arrived in this country about 1900, tracing your family back to the immigrant ancestor is a short-term goal. If you believe your family arrived on the Mayflower or shortly thereafter, tracing your family to the immigrant ancestor is a long-term goal. You will have to accomplish many short-term goals, such as finding your great-grandmother's maiden name, before you reach the long-term goal.

Family members may be willing to help you research or perhaps compile the family history. Just like a baseball team manager, you need to know the strengths and weaknesses of every player. Willie Mays was a great outfielder and hitter, but he probably would not have been a star pitcher. To organize your team, you should begin with some small projects and goals in mind; then select the best people to accomplish those tasks. Some family members like to use the computer; others enjoy library research. Some live in Pennsylvania; others in California. Each person can add something to the projects if the team manager assigns the right tasks.

Whether you work as a team or independently, decide how you want to proceed with your research. Will you research one family line at a time, maybe dividing the task based on your eight great-grandparents? By dividing the research, you can focus on one county or one state at a time. You can learn about the resources available in that county, then migrate with the family to a new location. If you are stuck, work on one of the other lines while you think about the difficult situation in the first line.

The research notebook, containing your data, surname lists, and timelines, is the foundation of organizing your research. Be sure to make use of this vital tool. You don't want to leave home without this notebook.

In this chapter, we've mentioned census records in some of the examples. Census records are a valuable asset that is now available online. The next chapter explains why and how you should organize your census research.

CHAPTER 7

Census: The Records Count

CENSUS RESEARCH SHOULD BE VERY HIGH, IF NOT FIRST, ON THE genealogical job list. You never know what the census will tell you, even though you may think you know everything about an ancestor. Sometimes the census reveals unknown data; other times it provides clues or pointers for further research. By organizing the census records, you will begin to formulate a picture of your ancestor.

Federal census records are available online at subscription Web sites, putting this vital research tool as close as your home computer or local library. If these sites are not available at the library, ask about them and request this service. If you cannot locate your ancestor in the online census, check the book indexes. Published indexes are available for the 1790–1870 census records. The indexes for the 1880–1930 census records are available online. The 1880–1920 online indexes contain only names listed as head of household. An every-name index is available for the 1930 census. Refer to the "Soundex and Miracode Indexes" section in this chapter for further information on census indexing.

Census information is also available in publications, often published by local genealogical societies. These publications are usually available at genealogical libraries or for sale by the society. Census records are available on microfilm at the National Archives, local libraries, and the Family History Library. If you have data that is difficult to read, check a variety of sources for that census—books, online, and microfilm.

All too often, genealogists do not organize their census research. Some genealogists look at indexes without following through to the actual census record. Some researchers record the basic information but not all the details. A systematic plan will open many doors for family historians.

Which ancestors should you research in the census? All of them. In every census! List your ancestors, starting with parents or grandparents who were living in 1930. Then add to the list their siblings, their parents, and grandparents. Review all census years during their lifetimes. Be flexible with the spelling of the surname and given name. The enumerator sometimes recorded an initial for the given name instead of the full name.

Census language can vary. Sometimes the place of birth, county or country, was spelled out; most often it was abbreviated. Be sure you are aware of the abbreviations used at that time. The location column often includes "do," which means ditto. The enumerator simply continued the last location mentioned. It is not a special abbreviation for a state or country. Sometimes what seems to be an obvious abbreviation can cause a problem. In the early years, the abbreviation "Ia" was used for Indiana, but many researchers rightfully confuse this with Iowa. If you see this, you probably assume it means Iowa. A genealogical dictionary may help sort out these abbreviations.

Use a census overview worksheet, as shown in Figure 7.1, listing the ancestor's name. Delete the census years that do not apply to your ancestor's lifetime. For example, if your grandfather was born in 1892, 1900 is the first census on which he is listed. Write an *X* or *N/A* in all previous census years since you do not need to search for that person. As the research progresses, indicate the completed years by marking yes when you locate the ancestor. You could also record the abbreviation for the state in which you located that person.

Federal Census Population Schedules

Once you find the record online, you should print the census page. If you have a printer and paper that accommodates 11 x 17-inch paper, the census will be easy to read. If you only use 8½ x 11-inch paper, the census you print could be difficult to read. Check with your library about the printer and paper available at its facility. Another option is to wait and print the census page when you visit a research facility that has the census on microfilm. Carefully record the state, county, page number, and other identifying numbers so you can easily find the correct line again. Forms for recording the census findings by hand are available in this chapter and on the CD.

CENSUS OVERVIEW WORKSHEET

Name	Female's Married Name	Lifespan	States to Search	1790	1800	1810	1820	1830	1840	1850	1860	1870	1880	1890	1900	1910	1920	1930

Figure 7.1 Census overview worksheet

Timeline of Census Records

Because some census data may be inaccurate, you need to look at the big picture. Joseph Rowland was born in Missouri, and his wife was born in Alabama. However, the place of birth on the 1860 census was listed incorrectly. If a researcher looks only at the 1860 census, he will find Joseph Rowland born in Alabama and Sarah Ferguson born in Missouri. If the researcher reviews the census until Joseph and Sarah died, he will see the correct pattern. You should not base future research on the information in one census year. Find the pattern.

Year of census	Name	Place of Birth Listed on Census
1850	Joseph Rowland	Missouri
1860	Joseph Rowland	Alabama (incorrect)
	Sarah Ferguson Rowland	Missouri (incorrect)
1870	Joseph Rowland	Missouri
	Sarah Ferguson Rowland	Alabama
1880	Joseph Rowland	Missouri

The head of the household, another family member, or even a neighbor may have provided the information recorded on the census. Thus, the information on one census may be erroneous. If you compare the censuses for that person's lifetime, the correct pattern will likely be uncovered. Analyzing the data collectively may keep you from going down the wrong research path.

The enumerators were instructed to take the census as of the official census date. Anyone who died after that date should be included. Any children born after that date should not be included. It often took weeks and months to complete the enumeration.

Some census takers or enumerators must have been unique individuals, for they provided unique information. The government gave enumerators instructions on how to take the census, but some enumerators did not follow the rules. Residents provided oral information to enumerators, so spellings are questionable. Some enumerators listed a city instead of a state or country as a birthplace. Others listed the county of birth if it was within the state of enumeration. Of course, family historians usually appreciate any additional or unique information provided. You should carefully review every census record for each ancestor; you never know what you will find.

Have you ever looked for an ancestor's name in the census records without locating him? Have you located siblings, parents, or grandparents? It may seem as if some ancestors are hiding. When you find an ancestor in the census, continue the search ten pages forward and backward; you may find other relatives. For example, I was searching the 1820 Ohio census for John Tanner and could not find him. Then I looked for his son-in-law, Hiram Palmer. When I found Hiram on the microfilm, guess who was right next door—John Tanner. He was in the index, but under the wrong spelling. John Tanner was listed in the index as John Farmer.

If you continue to have trouble locating someone in the census, look for something other than the name because the name may be spelled incorrectly. If you are looking for a daughter Mary who was eleven years old in the previous census, look for a married female named Mary who is about twenty-one. She may be as close as next door. If your ancestor was born in Scotland, look for other people born in Scotland. I did just that while searching for a family in Schuylkill County, Pennsylvania. The name was Britton, and it was spelled incorrectly. By searching for all couples born in Scotland, I located the family. It was difficult to read, but was probably recorded as Raitton.

Census records usually have a written page number and a stamped page number. To identify which one you are using in your documentation, add the word "written" or "stamped" in front of "page;" then there is no question which page number you are quoting. If you use a census index and cannot locate your family on that page, select another person at random from any page. If you selected Alexander Govan on page 123 at random, look up his name in the index. What page does the index provide for Alexander Govan? By doing this, you can better understand the numbering system that the index used and then find your ancestor.

Census records reveal naturalization clues. The 1820–1840, 1870, and 1900–1930 records provide naturalization information. From 1900 to 1930, a code or abbreviation was used to indicate the stage of the naturalization process.

Each census year provides new or different data, compared to the census taken ten years earlier. Some information is quite informative; other items are merely interesting. The birthplace, provided since 1850, is a great pointer for further

Census Naturalization Abbreviations

- **AL:** Alien
- **NA:** Naturalized
- **PA:** Petitioned

research. Whether the family owned a radio in 1930 is an interesting fact and certainly a family status symbol for that era, but that information will not lead to additional research.

Some census records were taken but are no longer extant; others were lost in disasters. For example, Ohio became a state in 1803, but the first census available is 1820. The 1810 census was taken but lost. Every genealogist would love to see the 1890 census; however, the records for only a few counties survived the fire in a government building in Washington, D.C. Many states took a census at various years, and some survived but others have been lost.

Resources for Census Research

There are several good books on census research. The following two books provide an overview of both the federal and state censuses:

- *State Census Records*, by Ann S. Lainhart (Baltimore: Genealogical Publishing Co., 1994)
- *Your Guide to the Federal Census for Genealogists, Researchers, and Family Historians*, by Kathleen W. Hinckley (Cincinnati, Ohio: Betterway Books, 2002)

Soundex and Miracode Indexes

You can thank WPA workers during the Depression for indexing the census records. The Soundex index system or code was established for the 1880 census. The code, which is still used today by some government agencies, allows for names with various

Using the Soundex

The Soundex is a coded index based on the way a surname sounds, which groups similar names together regardless of spelling. This allows researchers to find like names that are spelled differently, such as Smith, Smyth, or Smythe. Soundex indexes are available for most U.S. census records for the years 1880 and 1900–1930, but not for all states. For more information about the Soundex available for each census year, refer to the National Archives and Records Administration's Web site at *www.archives.gov/publications/microfilm_catalogs/census_schedules/ 1790_1890_federal_population_census_part01.html*.

A Soundex code consists of a letter and three numbers, such as F652. The letter is always the first letter of the surname, and the three digits are determined by the Soundex guide below. Zeroes are added to the end of a Soundex code, if necessary, to produce a four-character code. The basic rules for determining the Soundex code for a surname are shown in the list below. For more details, see NARA's "Soundex Indexing System" article online at *www.archives.gov/research_room/genealogy/ census/soundex.html*.

- **Write** the first letter of the surname.
- **Assign** a number to each letter after the first until the code is four characters long. Number values are assigned to letters as follows.
    - 1 B, F, P, V
    - 2 C, G, J, K, Q, S, X, Z
    - 3 D, T
    - 4 L
    - 5 M, N
    - 6 R
- **Disregard the letters** A, E, I, O, U, H, W, and Y. Some examples:

    Francis = F652 (F, 6 for the R, 5 for the N, 2 for the C)

    Reynolds = R543 (R, 5 for the N, 4 for the L, 3 for the D)

    Law = L000 (L, ignore the A and W, and add three zeroes to create a four-character code)

    Lowe = L000 (L, ignore the O and W and E, and add three zeroes to create a four-character code)

- **Double letters:** If a name contains double letters, treat them as one letter (for example, the double Ts in Litton should be treated as only one T, so the name is coded L350).

- **Side-by-side letters:** If side-by-side letters have the same Soundex code, use the number only once (for example, in the name Jackson, coded as J250, the C, K, and S letters are all represented by the number 2, but only one 2 should be used in the Soundex).

- **Names with prefixes:** If a surname has a prefix, such as Van Cortland, De los Santos, or Le Compte, code the name both with and without the prefix because the surname may be listed under either code. Note, however, that Mc and Mac are not considered prefixes, so their codes begin with M. Example: Van Cortland could be coded as V526 under listings for Van Cortland (V, ignore the A, 5 for N, 2 for C, ignore the O, 6 for R) or C634 under listings for Cortland (C, ignore the O, 6 for R, 3 for T, 4 for L).

- **Consonant separators:** If a vowel (A, E, I, O, U) separates two consonants that have the same Soundex code, the consonant to the right of the vowel is coded. Example: Tymczak is coded as T522 [T, ignore the Y, 5 for the M, 2 for the C, ignore the Z (see side-by-side rule above), 2 for the K]. Since the vowel A separates the Z and K, the K is coded (even though both C and K have the same Soundex code–2).

  If H or W separate two consonants that have the same Soundex code, the consonant to the right of the H or W is *not* coded. Example: Burroughs is coded B620, not B622 [B, ignore the U, 6 for the R, ignore the second R (see double letter rule), ignore the O and U, 2 for G, ignore the H, ignore the S (it's the same code as the G–2—and it's the consonant to the right of the H)].

As you see in the Law and Lowe examples above, similar names are coded the same and grouped together in a Soundex index, allowing you to find names you might not otherwise locate.

Some genealogy database programs have built-in Soundex calculators. You can also access the following free online Soundex calculators:

- JewishGen's JOS Soundex Calculator
  www.jewishgen.org/jos/jossound.htm

- Ancestor Search Surname to Soundex Converter
  www.searchforancestors.com/soundex.html

- RootsWeb's Soundex Converter
  resources.rootsweb.com/cgi-bin/soundexconverter

From *Online Roots: How to Discover Your Family's History and Heritage,* by Pamela Boyer Porter and Amy Johnson Crow; used by permission.

spellings that sound alike to be grouped together. A researcher may not know whether an ancestor spelled his name Meyer or Myer. Those names are listed together in this system. Miracode, used in some states only in 1910, is a variation of the Soundex code; it has had limited use.

The first digit of the Soundex code and the first letter in the surname are the same, even if it is a vowel. The next three digits are numerals based on the spelling. Some letters are dropped, thus not coded. Other letters are assigned a number. When the three numbers are added, the code is complete. If the name is short, zeros are added to the end of the code. The name Lee is coded L000. Similar names are coded the same: James J520, Jones J520.

The Soundex card provides the basic information on each family within a household. If an adult was single and living alone or with a family of a different surname, he has his own individual card. The Soundex is divided alphabetically by state. You need to know only which state to search to locate your ancestor. Within each state, the cards are arranged by the code number, then by given name. If there are numerous men named Joseph James, that section is further arranged alphabetically by the state in which he was born. So Joseph James born in Maryland is listed before Joseph James born in Missouri.

The example in Figure 7.2 is for William Griffith James who was born in Missouri. The James code is J520, and he lived in Missouri. After locating the J520 portion on the film, we naturally go to the William section. He is not there! At the beginning of each letter is a section for people listed only by an initial. William, alias W. Griff, is hiding in that section. If you do not find your ancestor in the obvious location, determine other places to look. On this Soundex card, W. Griff is listed as thirty-seven years old living in St. Ferdinand township of St. Louis County. His wife, Jennie, and their children, Joseph, James, Jessie, and Ann, are also listed on the card. If there were other members of the household, another card would follow. Once you reach this point and find this particular card, do not stop! The next step is to locate the same family on the actual census. The volume, enumeration district, sheet, and line numbers guide you to the exact location of this record.

Many genealogical computer programs can Soundex code a name for you. Several Web sites do the same. While Soundexing one name, why not determine several? List the surname, then add the Soundex code. Add the list of number values and letters (see "Using the Soundex" on pages 121–122) to your research notebook for future reference. Add new names and codes as they become available.

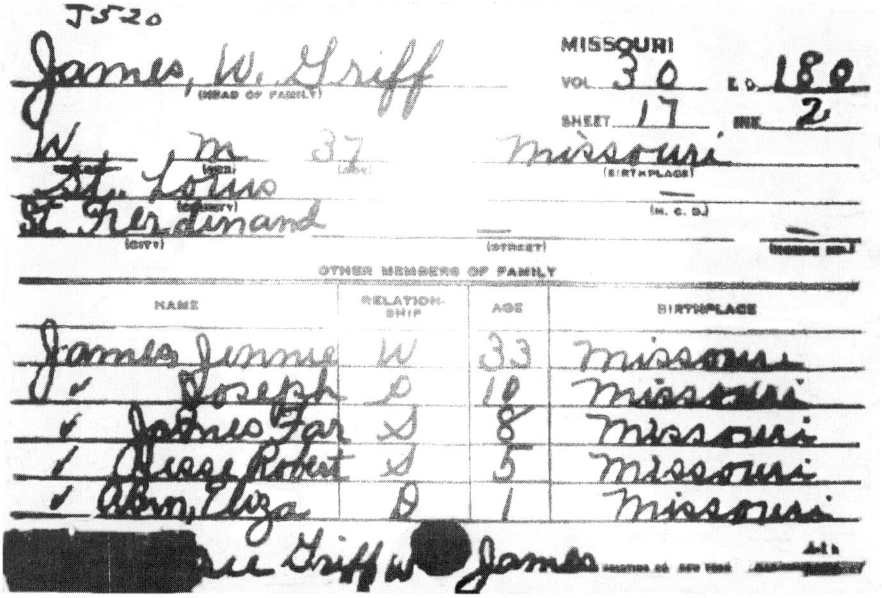

Figure 7.2 Soundex form

The "Using the Soundex" sidebar on pages 121–122 indicates which letters are eliminated and how to identify the other letters. Then you establish the alphanumeric code for your name. With the Soundex code in hand, it is fairly easy to locate ancestors in the Soundex microfilm that leads you to the actual census entry. But do not stop with the Soundex card—it provides only part of the story.

The Soundex includes all households in 1880 that had a child age ten or under. The Soundex is available for the entire 1900 and 1920 censuses. The index covers only twenty-one states for the 1910 census. A combination of Soundex and Miracode systems accomplished this process. Most states used one system or the other, except Louisiana, which used both. The federal government did not make the Soundex available for the remaining states; however, a printed index is available for some counties, thanks to volunteers and their local genealogical societies.

To find your ancestors in the Soundex or Miracode systems, follow the instructions in the "Using the Soundex" sidebar on pages 121–122. Be mindful that both systems use the same codes. When you find the ancestor's name on the computer-generated printout, the Soundex states list the enumerator district and page number. The Miracode states list the enumerator district and family visitation number instead of the page number. Be careful when using the Miracode. All too often ancestors are overlooked when they are actually in the record. The online census is the quickest and easiest way to locate your 1910 ancestors.

Professional genealogist Tony Burroughs had some difficulty finding one of his surnames and inquired about the official Soundex rules. Tony was persistent in his search until he located the original documents. As a result, the December 2001 edition of the *National Genealogical Society Quarterly* contains an article titled "The Original Soundex Instructions."

You should keep in mind that online census research does not require Soundex coding. However, a familiarity with the coding system is necessary in order to understand the options available when doing online research. If you cannot locate your ancestor in online research, you may be more successful in using microfilm, for which you will need to use the Soundex.

1910 Soundex and Miracode States

Soundex

The code provides the enumeration district number and the page number of the correct census page for the following states:

- Alabama
- Georgia
- Louisiana
- Mississippi
- South Carolina
- Tennessee
- Texas

Miracode

The code provides the enumeration district number and the family visitation number for the following states:

- Arkansas
- California
- Florida
- Illinois
- Kansas
- Kentucky
- Louisiana
- Michigan
- Missouri
- North Carolina
- Ohio
- Oklahoma
- Pennsylvania
- Virginia
- West Virginia

1790 Federal Census

The first U.S. census was taken on the first Monday in August 1790 for the states that were in the union in 1790. The government did not provide a regular census form. Enumerators used whatever paper was available. They listed the names of the head of the household, along with an indication of the free white males over sixteen and those under sixteen. Grouped together were all females regardless of age. Today, records are available in print format and online. However, it never hurts to verify your information with the original on microfilm. The census records for Delaware, Georgia, Kentucky, New Jersey, Tennessee, and Virginia were lost. The 1790 Virginia census has been reconstructed from tax lists. Use the form in Figure 7.3 to record your findings.

If you have American Revolution patriots in your background, try to locate them in this census. Add this information to your timeline and research report. Then follow through with a search of other records in the area.

A printed alphabetical index for the entire country appears in a multivolume set available in many genealogical libraries. The printed volumes allow researchers the opportunity to search for names that may be misspelled. The index is also available online at *www.ancestry.com*.

In addition, you can compare census records and tax records to help identify your ancestors.

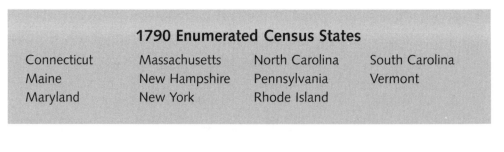

1790 Enumerated Census States

Connecticut	Massachusetts	North Carolina	South Carolina
Maine	New Hampshire	Pennsylvania	Vermont
Maryland	New York	Rhode Island	

1790 United States Census

County _____				Surname _____	
Call Number or URL _____					
Township _____				State _____	

Written page number	Name of head of household	Free white males 16 years & upward including head of household	Free white males under 16 years	Free white females including head of family	All other free persons	Slaves

Figure 7.3 1790 census form

1800 Federal Census

Residents of twelve states were counted in the 1800 census, taken as of the first Monday in August 1800, allowing the enumerators nine months to complete the census. Again the federal government did not provide a census form; however, some states provided their own form. Most enumerated states were situated along the eastern seashore, including residents of the newly formed District of Columbia. Use the form in Figure 7.4 to record your findings.

The data was a little more informative than 1790, listing the free white males and females in age categories. The categories listed children under ten, children ten to under sixteen, young adults sixteen to under twenty-six, adults twenty-six to under forty-five, and mature adults forty-five and over.

The men listed as head of household may have served in the American Revolution. Many of the patriots moved to Kentucky and Tennessee because of land grants. Another place to search are the tax records, which will reveal the same families and perhaps the name of older male sons.

A printed alphabetical index for the entire country appears in a multivolume set available in many genealogical libraries. The index is also available online at *www.ancestry.com.*

1800 Enumerated Census States

Connecticut	Maine	New York	South Carolina
Delaware	Maryland	North Carolina	Vermont
District of Columbia	Massachusetts	Pennsylvania	
	New Hampshire	Rhode Island	

1800 UNITED STATES CENSUS

County _____
Township _____

Call Number or URL _____

Surname _____
State _____

Page number	Head of family	Free white males					Free white females					Number of all other free persons except Indians not taxed	Number of slaves	Remarks
		Under 10	10 & under 16	16 & under 26	26 & under 45	45 & over	Under 10	10 & under 16	16 & under 26	26 & under 45	45 & over			

Figure 7.4 1800 census form

1810 Federal Census

By 1810, sixteen states participated in the third federal census taken on the first Monday in August 1810. The age categories are the same as for the 1800 census. The 1810 census enabled the states to identify taxable members of the household and men eligible for militia service. Census data was available for the first time for the states of Kentucky, Tennessee, and Virginia, plus the territory of Louisiana. Use the form in Figure 7.5 to record your findings.

A printed alphabetical index for the entire country appears in a multivolume set available in many genealogical libraries, and the index is online. If spelling is unclear or questionable, the book format may be more helpful.

If you are trying to locate men who eventually became soldiers in the War of 1812, this could be a good spot to start, since they may have been listed as heads of household in this census. Again, tax records could be helpful companion records. Compare the census records to the tax list to better identify your ancestors.

1810 Enumerated Census States and Territory

Connecticut	Maine	North Carolina	Vermont
Delaware	Maryland	Pennsylvania	Virginia
District of Columbia	Massachusetts	Rhode Island	*Territory:*
	New Hampshire	South Carolina	Louisiana
Kentucky	New York	Tennessee	

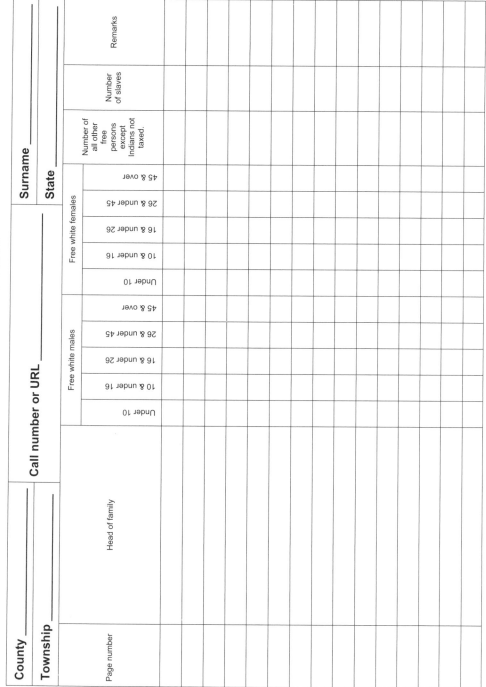

Figure 7.5 1810 census form

1820 Federal Census

The fourth federal census was taken as of the first Monday in August 1820, allowing the enumerators six months to complete the task. The list of states widened to include some interior states such as Illinois, Indiana, and Ohio. The Southern states Louisiana and Mississippi had joined the union by 1820; Georgia was also enumerated. Use the form in Figure 7.6 to record your findings.

An additional category was free white males sixteen to eighteen. Men in that age group were actually counted twice, once in the new category and then in the sixteen to twenty-six category. This census indicates naturalization information for the first time. Foreigners who had not been naturalized were to be noted on the census. Free colored persons were listed in one section of the census, and another category included slaves and servants of color. The final column in the census asked for "all other persons except Indians not taxed."

Residents could be listed in several columns, first for their age and then for agricultural, commerce, and manufacturing. This double listing applied to both free whites and slaves.

While the census lists only the name of the head of household, a researcher can organize other records to try to determine the names of the children in the various age categories.

1820 Enumerated Census States and Territory

Connecticut	Kentucky	New Hampshire	South Carolina
Delaware	Louisiana	New York	Tennessee
District of Columbia	Maine	North Carolina	Vermont
	Maryland	Ohio	Virginia
Georgia	Massachusetts	Pennsylvania	*Territory:*
Illinois	Mississippi	Rhode Island	Michigan
Indiana			

1820 UNITED STATES CENSUS

County _____
Township _____

Call Number or URL _____

Surname _____
State _____

Written page number	Printed page number	Name of head of family	Under 10	10 & under 16	16 to 18	16 to 25	26 to 44	45 & over	Under 10	10 and under 16	16 to 25	26 to 44	45 & over	Foreigners not naturalized	Persons in agricultural	Persons in commerce	Persons in manufacture	Under 14	14 to 25	26 to 44	45 and over	Under 14	14 to 25	26 to 44	45 and over	Under 14	14 to 25	26 to 44	45 and over	Under 14	14 to 25	26 to 44	45 and over	All citizens except Indians not taxed

Column group headers: Free white persons — Free white males / Free white females; Slaves & servants of color — Males / Females; Free colored persons — Males / Females

Figure 7.6 1820 census form

1830 Federal Census

The fifth federal census was taken as of 1 June 1830, with five months to complete the record. This was the first year a federal census form was used by the enumerators. The census added the states of Alabama and Missouri. Arkansas, Florida, and Michigan were enumerated as territories. Use the form in Figure 7.7 to record your findings.

There were three census categories; free white persons, slaves, and free colored persons, all divided by males and females. The age categories for the free whites became more specific with ten-year increment fields for adults over twenty, and five-year increments for children up to age twenty. The slaves and free colored persons categories were divided into age groupings of under ten, ten to under twenty-four, twenty-four to under thirty-six, thirty-six to under fifty-four, fifty-four to under one hundred, and one hundred and upward. The census indicated citizens who were deaf, dumb, and blind, including a cumulative number for whites, free men of color, and slaves. It also asked for the number of aliens in the household, which applied to white males only.

1830 Enumerated Census States and Territories

Alabama	Kentucky	New Jersey	Vermont
Connecticut	Louisiana	New York	Virginia
Delaware	Maine	North Carolina	*Territories:*
District of Columbia	Maryland	Ohio	Arkansas
	Massachusetts	Pennsylvania	Florida
Georgia	Mississippi	Rhode Island	Michigan
Illinois	Missouri	South Carolina	
Indiana	New Hampshire	Tennessee	

1830 UNITED STATES CENSUS — PAGE 1

County _____

Township _____

Call Number or URL _____

Surname _____

State _____

Free white persons (including heads of families)

Written page number	Stamped page number	Name of head of family	Males — Under 5 years	5 to under 10	10 to under 15	15 to under 20	20 to under 30	30 to under 40	40 to under 50	50 to under 60	60 to under 70	70 to under 80	80 to under 90	90 to under 100	100 and upward	Females — Under 5 years	5 to under 10	10 to under 15	15 to under 20	20 to under 30	30 to under 40	40 to under 50	50 to under 60	60 to under 70	70 to under 80	80 to under 90	90 to under 100	100 and upward

Figure 7.7 1830 census form, page 1

1830 UNITED STATES CENSUS – PAGE 2

County _____   Surname _____

Township _____   Call Number or URL _____   State _____

Name of head of family (from page 1)	Slaves												Free colored persons													Total	White persons included in the foregoing who are					Slaves & colored persons included in the foregoing who are		
	Males						Females						Males						Females							Deaf & dumb under 14	Deaf & dumb 14 to under 25	Deaf & dumb 25 & up	Blind	Aliens / foreigners not naturalized	Deaf & dumb under 14	Deaf & dumb 14 to under 25	Deaf & dumb 25 & up
	Under 10	10 to under 24	24 to under 36	36 to under 54	54 to under 100	100 & upward	Under 10	10 to under 24	24 to under 36	36 to under 54	54 to under 100	100 & upward	Under 10	10 to under 24	24 to under 36	36 to under 54	54 to under 100	100 & upward	Under 10	10 to under 24	24 to under 36	36 to under 54	54 to under 100	100 & upward									

Figure 7.7, *continued* 1830 census form, page 2

1840 Federal Census

The sixth federal census was taken as of 1 June 1840, with four months to finish. Arkansas and Michigan were new states in the census, as were the territories of Iowa and Wisconsin. Use the form in Figure 7.8 to record your findings.

The census enumerated males and females in the same age categories as in 1830. It is usually possible to identify the various members of a family with the more specific age groups.

State and county names were listed across the top of the sheet. The township was often listed along the side of the page next to the names of the head of household. The census inquired about employment, asking if the head of household worked in one of these fields: mining; agriculture; commerce; manufacturing; navigation and ocean; canal, lake, river; or learned professional and engineer. It also inquired about aliens.

The 1840 census was the first to list military information. This census indicates all surviving military pensioners or widows within a household by name. This often, but not always, applies to American Revolution patriots or their widows. A publication available at most libraries, *A Census of Pensioners for Revolutionary or Military Service as Returned under the Act for Taking the Sixth Census in 1840,* is an index of the military pensioners listed on the 1840 census.

1840 Enumerated Census States and Territories

Alabama	Indiana	Missouri	South Carolina
Arkansas	Kentucky	New Hampshire	Tennessee
Connecticut	Louisiana	New Jersey	Vermont
Delaware	Maine	New York	Virginia
District of Columbia	Maryland	North Carolina	*Territories:*
	Massachusetts	Ohio	Florida
Georgia	Michigan	Pennsylvania	Iowa
Illinois	Mississippi	Rhode Island	Wisconsin

1840 UNITED STATES CENSUS — PAGE 1

County _____
Township _____

Call Number or URL _____

Surname _____
State _____

Written page number	Stamped page number	Name of head of family	Free white persons (including heads of families)																																											
			Males																	Females																						
			Under 5 years	5 to under 10	10 to under 15	15 to under 20	20 to under 30	30 to under 40	40 to under 50	50 to under 60	60 to under 70	70 to under 80	80 to under 90	90 to under 100	100 and upward	Under 5 years	5 to under 10	10 to under 15	15 to under 20	20 to under 30	30 to under 40	40 to under 50	50 to under 60	60 to under 70	70 to under 80	80 to under 90	90 to under 100	100 and upward																	

Figure 7.8 1840 census form, page 1

Figure 7.8, *continued* 1840 census form, page 2

1850 Federal Census

This was the seventh federal census, with enumeration starting 1 June 1850 with four months to complete. The new states of California, Florida, Iowa, Texas, and Wisconsin were counted, as were the territories of Minnesota, New Mexico, Oregon, and Utah. Use the form in Figure 7.9 to record your findings.

This is the first census to have dwelling and family numbers and to name everyone in the household. The enumerator's instructions stated to list the head of household first, then spouse, then children in chronological order. Other household members were listed after the children. The relationships are not recorded, but some theories can be formed. This census also listed the age and birthplace for every person. The census listed the occupation for those over fifteen, along with the value of real property, both of which can lead to other records. Enumerators asked all persons twenty and over if they were able to read and write. They also asked whether a person was deaf and dumb, insane, an idiot, a pauper, or a convict.

Because the 1850 census is more sophisticated, it is necessary to record all numbers relating to your ancestor. Record the page, dwelling, and family numbers in your documentation. That enables you or others to easily return to the correct page.

1850 Enumerated Census States and Territories

Alabama	Indiana	New Hampshire	Vermont
Arkansas	Iowa	New Jersey	Virginia
California	Kentucky	New York	Wisconsin
Connecticut	Louisiana	North Carolina	*Territories:*
Delaware	Maine	Ohio	Minnesota
District of Columbia	Maryland	Pennsylvania	New Mexico
	Massachusetts	Rhode Island	Oregon
Florida	Michigan	South Carolina	Utah
Georgia	Mississippi	Tennessee	
Illinois	Missouri	Texas	

1850 UNITED STATES CENSUS

County _____

Township _____

Call Number or URL _____

Surname _____

State _____

Written page number	Stamped page number	Dwelling house number in order of visitation	Families in order of visitation	Name of every person whose usual place of abode on 1 June 1850 was with this family	Age	Sex	Color	Profession, occupation, or trade of each male over 15	Value of real estate owned	Place of birth naming state, territory, or country	Married within the year	Attended school within the year	Persons over 20 unable to read & write	If deaf & dumb, blind, insane, idiot, pauper, or convict

Figure 7.9   1850 census form

1860 Federal Census

The eighth federal census was taken on 1 June 1860. This census included an enumeration for the Dakota, Kansas, Nebraska, Nevada, New Mexico, Utah, and Washington territories, plus the new states of Minnesota and Oregon. Use the form in Figure 7.10 to record your findings. Just as in 1850, people over twenty were asked whether they could read and write. Males over fifteen were asked their occupations. Again, society identified the deaf and dumb, blind, insane, idiots, paupers, and convicts. Previously, the census listed real property value; now the personal property value was also included. The personal property total for slave owners included the value of slaves. If your ancestors were slave owners, compare the personal property value in the 1860 and 1870 census before and after the abolishment of slavery.

1860 Enumerated Census States and Territories

Alabama	Iowa	New Jersey	Virginia
Arkansas	Kentucky	New York	Wisconsin
California	Louisiana	North Carolina	*Territories:*
Connecticut	Maine	Ohio	Dakota
Delaware	Maryland	Oregon	Kansas
District of Columbia	Massachusetts	Pennsylvania	Nebraska
	Michigan	Rhode Island	Nevada
Florida	Minnesota	South Carolina	New Mexico
Georgia	Mississippi	Tennessee	Utah
Illinois	Missouri	Texas	Washington
Indiana	New Hampshire	Vermont	

1860 UNITED STATES CENSUS

County _____
Township _____

Call Number or URL _____

Surname _____
State _____

Written page number	Stamped page number	Dwelling house number in order of visitation	Families in order of visitation	Name of every person whose usual place of abode on 1 June 1860 was with this family	Description			Profession, occupation, or trade of each male over 15	Value of real estate owned	Value of personal estate owned	Place of birth naming state, territory, or country	Married within the year	Attended school within the year	Persons over 20 unable to read & write	If deaf & dumb, blind, insane, idiot, pauper, or convict
					Age	Sex	Color								

Figure 7.10 1860 census form

1870 Federal Census

As of 1 June 1870, the ninth federal census was taken, with three and one-half months to finish. It included the new states of Kansas, Nebraska, Nevada, and West Virginia, and territories of Arizona, Colorado, Dakota, Idaho, Montana, New Mexico, Utah, Washington, and Wyoming. Use the form in Figure 7.11 to record your findings.

The questions asked in the 1870 census were similar to those of the 1860 census, with just a few notable additions. The 1870 census was the first to ask whether a person's parents were foreign born. The census asked whether males over twenty-one were eligible to vote. It also asked whether males twenty-one and over were not eligible to vote. Some people were denied the right to vote due to a crime; this varied by state laws. If a foreign-born person answered that he was eligible to vote, he must have been naturalized. Likewise, if he said no, then he probably was not naturalized. These questions could help you find naturalization records.

If a child was born within the year of the census, the month of birth was supposed to be listed. The same applies to newlywed couples, who provided the month of the marriage. The only options listed for race were white, black, or mulatto. The enumerators asked whether everyone over ten could read or write.

1870 Enumerated Census States and Territories

Alabama	Kentucky	New York	*Territories:*
Arkansas	Louisiana	North Carolina	Arizona
California	Maine	Ohio	Colorado
Connecticut	Maryland	Oregon	Dakota
Delaware	Massachusetts	Pennsylvania	Idaho
District of Columbia	Michigan	Rhode Island	Montana
	Minnesota	South Carolina	New Mexico
Florida	Mississippi	Tennessee	Utah
Georgia	Missouri	Texas	Washington
Illinois	Nebraska	Vermont	Wyoming
Indiana	Nevada	Virginia	
Iowa	New Hampshire	West Virginia	
Kansas	New Jersey	Wisconsin	

1870 UNITED STATES CENSUS

County _____

Township _____

Call Number or URL _____

Surname _____

State _____

Written page number	Stamped page number	Dwelling house number in order of visitation	Families in order of visitation	Name of every person whose usual place of abode on 1 June 1870 was with this family	Age	Sex	Color	Profession, occupation, or trade of each male over 15	Value of real estate owned	Value of personal estate owned	Place of birth naming state, territory of U.S., or the country of foreign birth	Father foreign born	Mother foreign born	If born within the year, month	Married within the year, month	Attended school within the year	Cannot read	Cannot write	Deaf & dumb, blind, insane, or idiotic	Male citizen of U.S. of 21 years of age & upwards	Male citizen of U.S. of 21 years of age & upwards, right to vote denied

Figure 7.11 1870 census form

1880 Federal Census

The ground-breaking tenth federal census was taken on 1 June 1880. All previously existing states, plus the state of Colorado, and the territories of Arizona, Dakota, Idaho, Montana, New Mexico, Utah, Washington, and Wyoming, were enumerated. Use the form in Figure 7.12 to record your findings.

The census listed the relationship to the head of household for every person, along with the birthplace for the residents. It also listed the birthplace for each person's father and mother.

This was the first census to provide the house number and street name of the residence. This information helps researchers locate those people who are difficult to find. For example, you first find the family and its address in the city directory. You locate the census page(s) listing that street, and then find the correct address. Most likely your ancestor will appear.

This census asked whether a person had any disease on the day the census was taken. It also asked about the blind, deaf and dumb, idiotic, and insane.

The Soundex debuted with the 1880 census; however, it was used only for households containing children ten or younger. The 1880 census is now available online at a free Web site *(www.familysearch.org)*.

Remember, most of the 1890 census was lost due to a fire.

1880 Enumerated Census States and Territories

Alabama	Kansas	New Jersey	Wisconsin
Arkansas	Kentucky	New York	*Territories:*
California	Louisiana	North Carolina	Arizona
Colorado	Maine	Ohio	Dakota
Connecticut	Maryland	Oregon	Idaho
Delaware	Massachusetts	Pennsylvania	Montana
District of	Michigan	Rhode Island	New Mexico
Columbia	Minnesota	South Carolina	Utah
Florida	Mississippi	Tennessee	Washington
Georgia	Missouri	Texas	Wyoming
Illinois	Nebraska	Vermont	
Indiana	Nevada	Virginia	
Iowa	New Hampshire	West Virginia	

1880 UNITED STATES CENSUS

Surname _____

State _____

Sup Dist _____ **Enum Dist** _____

Sheet _____ **Page** _____

County _____

Township _____

City _____

Ward _____

Call Number or URL _____

In cities			Personal description						Civil condition				Occupation		Health						Education			Nativity		
Written page number	Stamped page number	Name of street	House number	Dwelling house number	Families in order of visitation	The name of each person whose place of abode on 1 June 1880 was in this family	Color	Sex	Age	Month born if during census year	Relationship to head of household	Single	Married	Widowed / divorced	Married during census year	Profession, occupation, or trade of each person, male or female	Months unemployed this year	Currently ill on day of enumeration? If so, specify.	Blind.	Deaf and dumb	Idiotic	Insane	Maimed, crippled, or disabled	Attended school within the census year	Cannot read	Cannot write	Place of birth of this person, naming state or territory of U.S., or the country if of foreign birth	Place of birth of the father of this person, naming state or territory of U.S., or the country if of foreign birth	Place of birth of the mother of this person, naming state or territory of U.S., or the country if of foreign birth

Figure 7.12 1880 census form

1900 Federal Census

The twelfth federal census was taken on 1 June 1900 with one month to complete. The states of Idaho, Montana, North Dakota, South Dakota, Utah, Washington, and Wyoming had joined the union since 1880, and the territories of Alaska, Arizona, Hawaii, Indian Territory, New Mexico, and Oklahoma were all included in the enumeration. Use the form in Figure 7.13 to record your findings.

This census lists the month and year of birth plus the age on the resident's last birthday. Since most states had not started vital records programs, this census information is significant. Sometimes this is the only document that provides a birth date. The census also provides the number of years each couple was married. The census asked about the person's occupation and how many months that person was unemployed, if applicable. Citizenship information included the year of immigration, the number of years in the United States, and the citizenship status of foreign men over twenty-one. The Soundex is available for every state, and the census is available online.

Each woman who was a mother listed the number of children born to her and how many of those children were still living. While you review this census record, compare the information to your family group sheets. If the mother said she had ten children, do you list ten children on the group sheet? If not, the family probably had a child who died young. Cemetery or church records may reveal the name of the deceased child.

1900 Enumerated Census States and Territories

Alabama	Kentucky	North Carolina	Wisconsin
Arkansas	Louisiana	North Dakota	Wyoming
California	Maine	Ohio	*Territories:*
Colorado	Maryland	Oregon	Alaska
Connecticut	Massachusetts	Pennsylvania	Arizona
Delaware	Michigan	Rhode Island	Hawaii
District of	Minnesota	South Carolina	Indian Territory
Columbia	Mississippi	South Dakota	New Mexico
Florida	Missouri	Tennessee	Oklahoma
Georgia	Montana	Texas	
Idaho	Nebraska	Utah	
Illinois	Nevada	Vermont	
Indiana	New Hampshire	Virginia	
Iowa	New Jersey	Washington	
Kansas	New York	West Virginia	

1900 UNITED STATES CENSUS

County _____

Township _____

City _____

Ward _____

Call Number or URL _____

Surname _____

State _____

Sup Dist _____ Enum Dist _____

Sheet _____ Page _____

Location				Name & relationship		Personal description										Nativity			Citizenship			Occupation		Education					Home ownership				
Name of street	House number	Dwelling house number	Families in order of visitation	Name of each person whose place of abode on 1 June 1900 was in this family	Relationship to head of family	Color or race	Sex	Month	Year	Whether single, married, widowed, or divorced	Number of years of present marriage	Mother of how many children	Number of these children living	Place of birth of this person	Place of birth of father of this person	Place of birth of mother of this person	Year of immigration to the U.S.	Number of years in the U.S.	Naturalization	Occupation	Months not employed	Attended school within the census year	Can read	Can write	Can speak English	Owned or rented	Owned free or mortgaged	Farm or house	Number of farm schedule

Figure 7.13 1900 census form

1910 Federal Census

The thirteenth federal census was dated 15 April 1910, with one month to complete. It included the new state of Oklahoma and the territories of Alaska, Arizona, Hawaii, New Mexico, and Puerto Rico. Use the form in Figure 7.14 to record your findings.

The questions were similar to those in the 1900 census; however, the birth month and year question was removed. Citizens were asked how long they had been married. The enumerator wrote down M1 to indicate the first marriage and M2 for the second marriage. Employment questions included the employer's name, whether the person was currently out of work, and the number of weeks he'd been out of work in 1909. This plus the home ownership questions provide a social background of the family.

The enumerators asked all males over fifty or immigrants in the U.S. before 1865 whether they served in the Civil War. The Union army veterans are listed as UA and the Union navy as UN. The Confederate army veterans are listed as CA and the Confederate navy as CN.

Twenty-one states had an index using the Soundex or Miracode system, with the balance of the states unindexed. The Soundex and Miracode microfilm for 1910 looks like a computer-generated printout, not the handwritten cards as in other years. Remember, there is only one small difference between Soundex and Miracode. The Soundex lists the census page number, and Miracode lists the family visitation number. The census for all states is available online.

1910 Enumerated Census States and Territories

Alabama	Kansas	New Jersey	Vermont
Arkansas	Kentucky	New York	Virginia
California	Louisiana	North Carolina	Washington
Colorado	Maine	North Dakota	West Virginia
Connecticut	Maryland	Ohio	Wisconsin
Delaware	Massachusetts	Oklahoma	Wyoming
District of	Michigan	Oregon	*Territories:*
Columbia	Minnesota	Pennsylvania	Alaska
Florida	Mississippi	Rhode Island	Arizona
Georgia	Missouri	South Carolina	Hawaii
Idaho	Montana	South Dakota	New Mexico
Illinois	Nebraska	Tennessee	Puerto Rico
Indiana	Nevada	Texas	
Iowa	New Hampshire	Utah	

1910 UNITED STATES CENSUS

Call Number or URL _____

County _____
Township _____
City _____
Ward _____

Surname _____
State _____
Sup Dist _____ Enum Dist _____
Sheet _____ Page _____

Location				Name	Personal description									Nativity			Citizenship			Occupation					Education			Ownership of home						
Name of street	House number	Dwelling house number	Families in order of visitation	Name of each person whose place of abode on 15 April 1910 was in this family	Relationship to head of family	Sex	Color or race	Age at last birthday	Single, married, widowed, or divorced	Number of years of present marriage	Number of children born to this mother	Number of these children living	Place of birth of this person	Place of birth of father of this person	Place of birth of mother of this person	Year of immigration to the U.S.	Naturalized citizen /alien	Speak English? If not, give name of language.	Trade or occupation	Nature of business	Employer of wage earner	Out of work 15 April 1910	Number of weeks out of work in 1909	Whether able to read	Whether able to write	Attended school since 1 September 1909	Owned or rented	Owned free or mortgaged	Farm or house	Number of farm schedule	Whether survivor of Union or Confederate	Whether blind in both eyes	Whether deaf and dumb

Figure 7.14 1910 census form

1920 Federal Census

The 1920 census was the only census taken on 1 January. Therefore, no one born in 1920 was listed on the census, unless they were born on 1 January. Likewise, if a couple married in 1920, they should be listed on this census as single people living at home with their parents or elsewhere. By 1920, all forty-eight contiguous states were enumerated, including the new states of Arizona and New Mexico, along with the territories of Alaska, American Samoa, Canal Zone, Guam, Hawaii, Puerto Rico, and the Virgin Islands. Use the form in Figure 7.15 to record your findings.

Citizenship information expanded to include the year of naturalization, a tremendous help to genealogists. The enumerator asked the mother tongue of the resident and his or her parents, and whether the resident spoke English. It also asked whether a person had attended school since September 1919.

If you have unanswered questions about an immigrant, prepare a timeline based on the immigration and naturalization information in the census of 1920 and other years. Include the naturalization status, the year of immigration, and the place of birth for the person enumerated and his or her parents. By combining and organizing this information, you may be able to locate the naturalization records.

1920 Enumerated Census States and Territories

Alabama	Kansas	New Mexico	Virginia
Arizona	Kentucky	New York	Washington
Arkansas	Louisiana	North Carolina	West Virginia
California	Maine	North Dakota	Wisconsin
Colorado	Maryland	Ohio	Wyoming
Connecticut	Massachusetts	Oklahoma	*Territories:*
Delaware	Michigan	Oregon	Alaska
District of Columbia	Minnesota	Pennsylvania	American Samoa
	Mississippi	Rhode Island	
Florida	Missouri	South Carolina	Canal Zone
Georgia	Montana	South Dakota	Guam
Idaho	Nebraska	Tennessee	Hawaii
Illinois	Nevada	Texas	Puerto Rico
Indiana	New Hampshire	Utah	Virgin Islands
Iowa	New Jersey	Vermont	

1920 UNITED STATES CENSUS

County _____

Township _____

City _____

Ward _____

Call Number or URL _____

Surname _____

State _____

Sup Dist _____ Enum Dist _____

Sheet _____ Page _____

Place of abode				Name	Home data			Personal description				Citizenship			Education			Nativity and mother tongue							Occupation			
Name of street	House number	Dwelling house number	Families in order of visitation	Name of each person whose place of abode on 1 January 1920 was in this family	Relationship to head of family	Home owned or rented	If owned, free or mortgaged	Sex	Color or race	Age at last birthday	Single, married, widowed, or divorced	Year of immigration to U.S.	Naturalized or alien	If naturalized, year of naturalization	Attended school since 1 September 1919	Whether able to read	Whether able to write	Person's place of birth	Person's mother tongue	Father's place of birth	Father's mother tongue	Mother's place of birth	Mother's mother tongue	Able to speak English	Trade, profession, or particular kind of work done	Industry, business, or establishment in which at work	Employer, salary, or wage worker	Number of farm schedule

Figure 7.15 1920 census form

1930 Federal Census

The fifteenth census was taken on 1 April 1930 with the same states and territories as in 1920. The basic questions are included, plus a person's age at the time of his or her first marriage, the value of the home, whether the home included a radio, and whether the males twenty-one and over were veterans. Use the form in Figure 7.16 to record your findings.

Two columns provide answers to employment questions: "Did the resident work yesterday, or the last day of work?" and "What is his line number for unemployment?" These are interesting questions, considering the Depression. Enumerators were instructed to use specific occupations, not general statements such as laborer or mechanic.

The online census index includes every name, not just the name of the head of household. Twelve southern states were Soundexed. If you use those microfilmed cards, please note that the cards are printed with 1910, not 1930, on them. Researchers must document this as a 1930 card.

Two columns in this census provide a nativity and occupation code that was added by the census office.

April 2012 is the scheduled release date for the 1940 census.

1930 Enumerated Census States and Territories

Alabama	Kansas	New Mexico	Virginia
Arizona	Kentucky	New York	Washington
Arkansas	Louisiana	North Carolina	West Virginia
California	Maine	North Dakota	Wisconsin
Colorado	Maryland	Ohio	Wyoming
Connecticut	Massachusetts	Oklahoma	*Territories:*
Delaware	Michigan	Oregon	Alaska
District of Columbia	Minnesota	Pennsylvania	American Samoa and Guam
	Mississippi	Rhode Island	
Florida	Missouri	South Carolina	
Georgia	Montana	South Dakota	Hawaii
Idaho	Nebraska	Tennessee	Panama Canal
Illinois	Nevada	Texas	Puerto Rico
Indiana	New Hampshire	Utah	Virgin Islands
Iowa	New Jersey	Vermont	

1930 UNITED STATES CENSUS

County _____

Township _____

City _____

Ward _____

Call Number or URL _____

Surname _____

State _____

Sup Dist _____ Enum Dist _____

Sheet _____ Page _____

Place of abode				Name	Home data					Personal description						Education		Nativity and mother tongue													Employment						Veteran			
Name of street	House number	Dwelling house number	Families in order of visitation	Name of each person whose place of abode on 1 April 1930 was in this family	Relationship to head of family	Home owned or rented	Value of home, if owned, or monthly rental if rented	Radio set	Does this family live on a farm?	Sex	Color or race	Age at last birthday	Marital condition	Age at first marriage	Attended school or college since 1 September 1929	Whether able to read & write	Place of birth of person	Place of birth of person's father	Place of birth of person's mother	Language spoken in home before coming to the U.S.	State or M.T.	Country	Nativity	Year of immigration to the United States	Naturalized or alien	Able to speak English	Trade, profession, or particular kind of work done	Industry or business	Code and class of worker	Whether actually at work yesterday	Line number of unemployed	Whether a veteran of the U.S. military or naval forces mobilized for any war or expedition	What war or expedition	Number of farm schedule

Office code (Nativity and mother tongue)

Figure 7.16 1930 census form

1850 Enumerated Slave States

Alabama	Louisiana	North Carolina
Arkansas	Maryland	South Carolina
Florida	Mississippi	Tennessee
Georgia	Missouri	Texas
Kentucky	New Jersey	Virginia

Special Census Schedules

Slave Census Schedule

Genealogists often overlook numerous special federal census schedules, including slave schedules for some states in 1850 and 1860. The slave census listed the name of the slave owner along with the number of slaves, and the sex, color, and age for each slave. It also asked whether the slave was a fugitive from the state, and the number of manumitted, deaf and dumb, blind, insane, and idiotic slaves. The 1860 census asked the same questions plus the number of slave houses.

1860 Enumerated Slave States

Alabama	Georgia	North Carolina
Arkansas	Kentucky	South Carolina
Delaware	Louisiana	Tennessee
District of Columbia	Maryland	Texas
	Mississippi	Virginia
Florida	Missouri	

1890 Union Veterans and Widows Schedule

A special Union veterans and widows census was taken in 1890, but only part of it has survived. The surviving state schedules include part of Kentucky and the remaining states in alphabetical order. The states starting with *A* through Kansas and part of Kentucky were lost. When adding this resource to your to-do research list, remember that veterans were enumerated in the state where they lived in 1890, not the state for which they had served.

The intent of the 1890 military census was to identify and list all Union veterans; however, you will often find the name of Confederate veterans, usually with a line drawn through their names. Apparently, some enumerators asked whether a person served in the Civil War. If yes, the name was recorded before the enumerator determined this was a Confederate soldier. Then the name was crossed out.

The schedule includes the township, county, state, and house and family number. The rank, company, and name of the regiment or vessel are also included. The veteran provided his dates of enlistment and discharge, and length of service. He also provided information about any disability.

Mortality Schedules

Mortality schedules were compiled for the 1850, 1860, 1870, and 1880 censuses. Some have survived; others are lost. This schedule should include the name of every person who died in the twelve months before the official date of the census. The schedule records the name of the deceased and the date and cause of death. Deceased slaves were listed by name in the 1850 and 1860 schedules. Ironically, their surviving family members were not listed by name in the slave schedule. After checking its availability, add the mortality census schedule to your research to-do list.

Agricultural Schedules

From 1840 to 1910, the census included agricultural schedules. Once again, their availability is limited because many were lost. Moreover, many of the surviving schedules are unindexed and some are not even microfilmed. When available, the schedules provide information about the crops, livestock, and farms owned by our ancestors. The schedules may tell you how many acres of property a person owned, how many chickens he sold, how much corn he grew, and how many horses, cows, and pigs he owned. Add this to your research to-do list—this information is interesting and helpful.

State Censuses

In some nonfederal census years, states periodically took a census within their borders. Some state censuses have survived; others have not. Within a state, census schedules may be available for some counties and not others. Do not overlook this valuable resource. Determine whether your state of interest has any extant census records and where they are located. Then, on your research to-do list, record the names of ancestors living in the state at that time. Search the state census for those people.

For example, the 1925 Iowa state census is very informative. The census includes the basic data plus information about each person's parents, including mother's maiden name, place of birth, and place of marriage. It also provides information on church affiliation, real estate, and military service. Other state census records are not this complete.

Census research is necessary for family historians. The census records provide vital clues and pointers toward other records. However, we do not know who provided the information on each census. Household members or even neighbors may have provided erroneous information, thus accounting for variances in the records. As a test, ask your children how old you are and where you were born. Ask your children the same questions about your next-door neighbor. You may be surprised with the answers.

Despite the limitations of census records, once you analyze them over the lifetime of your ancestor, a clear picture develops. Now that you are familiar with census records, let's examine the federal, state, and local government documents that are valuable to genealogists.

CHAPTER 8

Required by Law

IN THE TWENTY-FIRST CENTURY, NOT ALL LEGAL DOCUMENTS ARE maintained in the courthouse. An annex or off-site facility may house some records. When planning a research trip, it's necessary to organize your research based on the location of the records and record type. Vital records may be located in one building, but coroner's records may be stored at the medical examiner's office and the voter registration records housed at the board of election commissioner's office. Naturalization records may be in the county and federal courthouse. State archives, historical societies, or universities could be the custodians of the older records—and that means they may be in a different city. Do your homework. Determine which records are available on microfilm, which are published, and which are available only in the original format.

Most likely, your ancestor stood in the courthouse to transact his legal business. His marriage, land, and probate records are probably available. Many other records stored in the courthouse can provide additional details about your ancestor. Before visiting the courthouse, plan how best to accomplish your objectives for that visit. The literature search, described in Chapter 11, will reveal the published records, including microfilm and indexes.

After determining the type of records available for the county, make a list of the surnames that apply to each record type. Obviously, the list will be longer for marriage and land records than for military discharge papers. However, each record is important, and you never know what new information each document will provide. Add this list to your research notebook.

159

Courthouse Etiquette

"Have dust, will share" is the unofficial motto of many old courthouses. Wear washable clothes, and take waterless hand cleaner, tissues, and possibly allergy medication. Any inconvenience due to the dust is usually worth the opportunity to see and use the original documents.

Sometimes you need to work at a courthouse all day and the staff is continually helpful when you need copies or have questions. To be polite, give the staff a small gift to show your appreciation—cookies or a box of candy works well. Remember the courthouse is a place of business for the staff, title companies, and attorneys. You should dress in an appropriate manner for a place of business, not in shorts and a tank top. Try to be inconspicuous, considerate, and quiet and to generally stay out of the way of the daily business transactions.

A courthouse plan should include a visit to the marriage license office, the probate office, and the land records office, preferably in that order. Make a list of ancestors to research in each office. A helper with an extra pair of hands and another set of eyes is always welcome when you're doing courthouse research. Perhaps by the end of the day you will uncover additional ancestors and know whom they married, the names of their children, where their land was located, and where the family migrated when moving across the country.

Courthouses and their records, just like people, have a genealogy. Before going to the courthouse, try to review the types of courts available and what records are housed in those courts. In Pennsylvania, the Orphan's Court is the keeper of the marriage licenses. Would you think to look in the Orphan's Court records for marriages? In another state, an early divorce record that today is filed in the circuit court office may be hiding in the state supreme court records. What court holds the naturalization records in your area? Before 1906, the answer could be any court. Study the court system to understand where the records should be located. It may be helpful to create and keep in your research notebook a flow chart or diagram of what court begat what court.

Fires, tornadoes, or even varmints have destroyed some records. We cannot restore the lost records; we can only work around them. Burned courthouses are always a challenge, but not impossible. Some courthouse records may be lost, while other records are available. If there was a courthouse fire, be sure to ask whether everything was lost and whether any records have been reconstructed. You may find that some records were never kept in the courthouse. Or that some records survived because they were not in the normal location when the fire occurred. County officials may have tried to reconstruct records right after the fire. Most often when this happened, it concerned deeds, because being able to prove land ownership was so important to our ancestors. Understand what each record is saying—and what it is not saying. Persevere!

Courthouse Fire

Many courthouses across the country have been damaged or destroyed by fire. In a small southern Missouri community, in about 1861, a group of three civic leaders decided to take matters into their own hands. The three men, accompanied by a young lad, moved the court records to a cave in anticipation of the Civil War and the likely damage to their courthouse. The boy served as their insurance package—if the three men did not survive, somebody would know where the records where hidden. Indeed, the courthouse burned during the war, but the records were saved. Because of the quick thinking of those civic leaders, today's genealogists have access to its deeds and other records.

Vital Records

Birth and Death Records

When did your state start keeping vital records? The vital records office probably maintains those records in the state capital. The county may house birth and death registers for the years before the state vital records office opened. The early county-level registration was probably optional, so compliance was voluntary. Some early birth and death records have been published in book form or on the Internet. For example, early vital records for many New England towns are available in book form. Some states have early birth databases online.

A vital records Web site *(www.vitalrec.com)* lists the availability of records in every state and includes the date the records began. It also provides the office address, hours, and fees for each state.

Some states provide a list of vital records on a Web site. By using the vital records worksheet in Figure 8.1, you can move from site to site searching for information. This worksheet reminds you what data is missing and what you should look for in

VITAL RECORDS WORKSHEET

Name	Spouse	Birth Date	Location	Marriage Date	Location	Death Date	Location

Figure 8.1 Vital records worksheet

each state. For example, Illinois has a database for deaths from 1916 to 1950. The worksheet helps you go to that site and quickly locate the ancestors in whom you are interested.

Use the vital records worksheet to summarize your information. List the ancestors for whom you are searching and what information you know about them.

Marriage Records

Most ancestors married at their local church, courthouse, or home with the clergy or justice of the peace recording the marriage at the local courthouse. Those records are easy to find. The ancestors who married in another county or state are more difficult to locate.

Using the marriage worksheet in Figure 8.2 will help you establish a list of married ancestors. Record what information you know about the marriage, including names and dates. List the county or state where you think the marriage took place. It may be necessary to expand the scope of your search to adjoining counties. This list becomes the foundation of your marriage research.

Now that you have a worksheet, you are ready to visit the local library or courthouse. Compare the information on your worksheet against the marriage indexes, locating as many potential marriages as possible. A county marriage index may reveal unknown daughters, grandchildren, or cousins. Don't stop at the index. Review the actual marriage certificate to confirm that this is the correct couple, the marriage date, the clergy's name, and perhaps the marriage location. The name of the clergy may take you to a specific church, which may uncover additional records. Marriage records may have the clergy's name followed by "M.G.," which stands for Minister of the Gospel. "M.G." does not represent a specific religion, just that he was a member of the clergy. Also, note the marriage witnesses. When possible, you should always review the original record.

Whenever you refer to married couples in your to-do list or research report, be consistent in the order you use to list the couple's surnames. In the example used in Chapter 1, Rudd-Anderson, the groom's surname is first, then the bride's. Follow this style whenever you need to list both names.

It becomes quite expensive to obtain copies of all marriage certificates relating to your ancestors, so determine whether the records are available on microfilm. Usually the microfilm print cost is ten to fifty cents at a library photocopier, compared to several dollars for an official document from a courthouse. Transcribe the information

MARRIAGE RECORDS WORKSHEET

Bride's Name	Groom's Name	Country	State	County	Date	Notes

Figure 8.2 Marriage records worksheet

Possible Marriage Record Information

Marriage records could provide some or all of the following information:

- Name of bride and groom
- Date of application and marriage
- Age at the time of marriage
- Place of marriage and residence before marriage
- Name of clergy and witnesses

carefully so that you don't have to photocopy every document. As you locate the marriages, fill in the worksheet and add the documented information to the genealogical computer program. Be sure to document each entry—list the name of the book, page number, and location of the record. Marriage records can lead to new direct and collateral lines.

In the later part of the nineteenth century, some states and counties required the bride and groom to fill out a marriage license application. Determine the exact date this form was required in your area of interest. The application may be extant today and could provide new family clues. The application could include the current place of residences of the bride and groom, date and place of birth, and perhaps the name of the parents. Any prior marriage could also be listed on the form. Ask the county clerk if this record is available. Indicate on the worksheet if this application is available for each couple.

Some marriage records are available online. Chapter 1 refers to the marriages of Julia Anderson. That particular marriage index is now available on the Illinois Secretary of State Web site (see Figure 8.3). When we enter the name of the groom and bride, Rudd-Anderson, the potential listing appears (see Figure 8.4). James Rudd, husband of Julia Anderson Rudd, left for the war and was never heard from again. After the war, Julia married Jeff Lynch. When we enter the groom's name, Lynch, and the bride's first married name, Rudd, two listings appear (see Figure 8.5). One listing is for Thomas Jefferson Lynch and Julia Anderson Rudd. That's it!

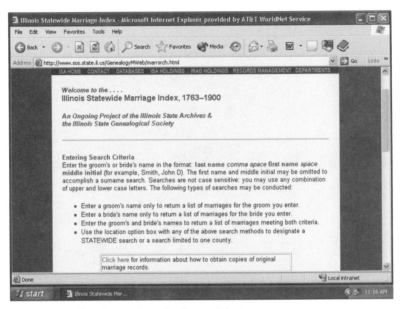

Figure 8.3 Illinois marriage database Web site

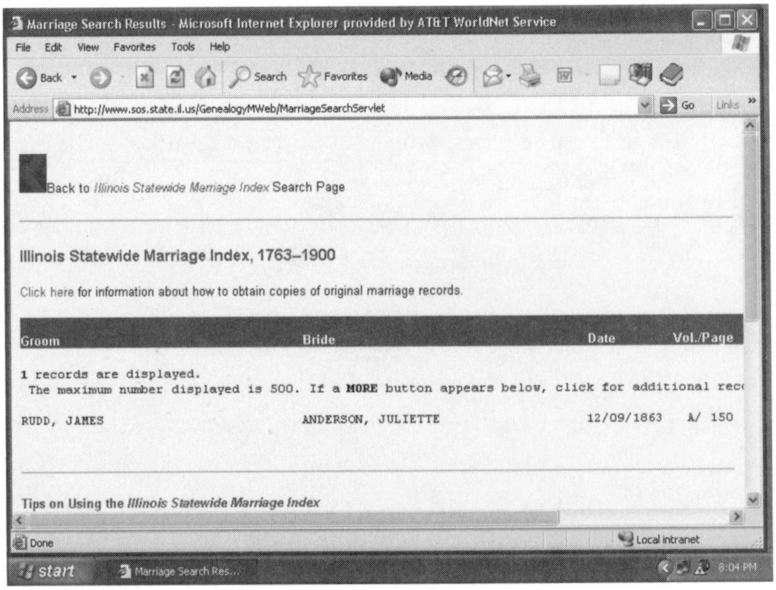

Figure 8.4 Illinois marriage database, Rudd-Anderson

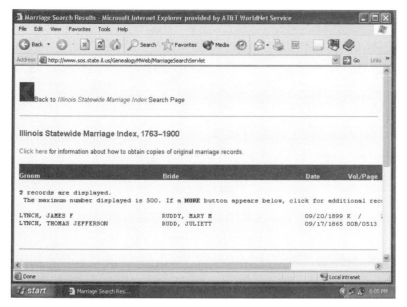

Figure 8.5 Illinois marriage database, Lynch-Rudd

Wills and Probate Records

Wills and probate records are usually located in the county probate office or registrar of wills. Some ancestors did not leave wills or probate records, but other ancestors provided a great deal of information. In many cases, the will was written or dictated shortly before that person died. Friends or relatives usually signed the document as witnesses. Photocopy, transcribe, or abstract this document, and be sure you don't leave out any facts.

A will abstract worksheet (see Figure 8.6) helps to remind you of the key points usually found in wills. If you use the worksheet, be sure you do not change the meaning of the will by omitting or changing the wording. If a will provides a list of children, do not add or omit any commas in that list. For example, if the transcriber omitted a comma from the line "I leave to my children John Henry and Mary Sue," it is no longer clear whether there were two sons, John and Henry, and two daughters, Mary and Sue; two sons, John and Henry, and one daughter, Mary Sue; or two children, son John Henry and daughter Mary Sue. You must take time to review the documents carefully and be sure you transcribe the information accurately.

Paper was not readily available in boxes or reams at the office supply stores one

WILL ABSTRACT WORKSHEET

Surname			Date Abstracted	
Source of Information			Repository	
Country	State	County	Will Book	Page
Testator			Residence	
Executor			Residence	
Date Signed			Date Proved	
Bequests				
Witnesses			Residence	
Signature(s) or Mark(s)				

Figure 8.6 Will abstract worksheet

hundred or two hundred years ago. Therefore, documents used the paper to its fullest capacity. Words often started on one line and continued on another line without a hyphen. Other words were abbreviated. Some letters were written in a style different from today's style. For example, the double *s* in Mississippi often looks like a double *f*. Before you jump into the court documents, review the handwriting style. You can look at words in the document with which you are familiar to learn how the writer made a *T,* compared to an *F.* It's also useful to become familiar with some of the legal phrases used in the wills of that time.

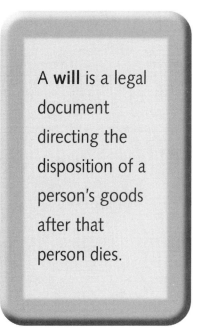

A **will** is a legal document directing the disposition of a person's goods after that person dies.

Probate packets or portfolios usually yield a wealth of information—not just the name of the children. Information may lead to other records, such as deeds, marriage, and military. The probate record may tell you how long the family lived in the county, what property its members owned, whether the deceased was literate, and what children were living at the time.

You should photocopy the probate papers, abstract the documents (see Figure 8.7), or transcribe them. The probate packet may be small and straight-

forward, but it can also be large and complex. It's a good idea to photocopy at least the key documents so you can study them at home. Did all the children except one receive the father's land? Why? Were his children and their spouses listed in the pro-bate file? Review the state statutes in effect when the will was probated. Some children may have received their inheritance previously, so they may not have been listed in the will. It is important to understand the laws and customs of both the area and the era.

If minor children were involved, a probate file may have remained open for many years or until those children were of age. If the estate paid the tuition, this packet may provide the name of the school the children attended. It may also indicate the yearly yield from the farm or give clues to the hometown of the children who moved away. The underage child may be referred to as an orphan. In many cases, "orphan" simply meant that the father of the underage child had died. The mother may still have been living. That same minor child may be listed as an infant. The term

PROBATE ABSTRACT WORKSHEET

Name of Deceased			Date Abstracted	
Source of Information			Repository	
Country	State	County	File Number	
Executor or Administrator			Residence	
Date Filed			Date Closed	
Heirs, Relationship to Deceased, & Residency				
Inventory				
Witnesses			Residence	
Signature(s) or Mark(s)				

Figure 8.7 Probate abstract worksheet

"infant" was often used in place of "minor"; it doesn't necessarily refer to a baby.

If the deceased did not have any direct-line heirs, you may be able to locate nieces or nephews who were living at that time, perhaps cousins to you. Such was the case with Thomas Rosen (a real example using a fictitious name), who was born in 1878 in Augustow, Powland (as spelled in the documents), and died in 1962. The probate record states that next of kin and heirs-at-law of Rosen are descendants of his deceased brothers and sisters, the closest relatives being nephews, nieces, and descendants of deceased nephews and nieces.

Rosen's file lists the names of his parents and his nine brothers and sisters, all of whom were deceased. The heirs of each of those deceased siblings are named—most often the children, but sometimes the grandchildren. The fifteen heirs, thirteen nieces or nephews, and two grandnephews divided Rosen's estate. All heirs are named in the file, along with their addresses in the 1960s. The Rosen family documented four generations of its members just by researching this probate package—which was merely a record for a collateral family member.

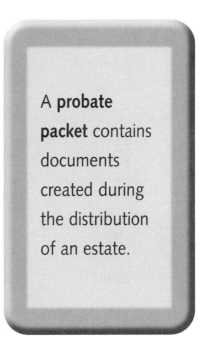

A **probate packet** contains documents created during the distribution of an estate.

Deed Records

Land records or deeds are usually a gold mine for family researchers. The deed obviously provides information on the land transaction. It may also provide the names of spouses and children, as well as the county of residence for the grantor and grantee, and provide clues to other land transactions.

Depending on the laws of the land and time, a deceased man could leave his property to his wife and children. The wife was probably entitled to her dower right or one-third share of the property, with the balance divided among the children. The children were usually listed along with their spouses. In fact, couples would sign the document when they sold the land.

Deed records are like bookends; there should be a set for every parcel of land. The first transaction took place at the time of purchase when your ancestor was the grantee

Resources for Land Research

Interpreting land records can be a challenge. The following books can give you a better understanding of how to do land research:

- *Land and Property Research in the United States*, by E. Wade Hone (Salt Lake City: Ancestry Inc., 1997)
- *Locating Your Roots: Discover Your Ancestors Using Land Records*, by Patricia Law Hatcher (Cincinnati, Ohio: Betterway Books, 2003)
- *Map Guide to the U.S. Federal Censuses 1790–1920*, by William Thorndale and William Dollarhide (Baltimore: Genealogical Publishing Co., Inc., 1987)

or buyer. The second transaction took place when the land was sold and your ancestor was the grantor or seller. Recorded land transactions usually took place about the time of the event, but sometimes the recording took place many years later. Family historians need to locate both sides of the set.

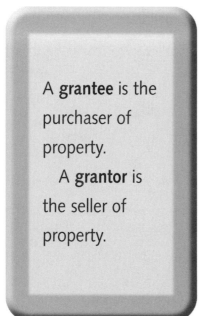

A **grantee** is the purchaser of property.

A **grantor** is the seller of property.

You can capture the information you know or discover by filling out a worksheet for deed transactions (see Figure 8.8). Record the name of the grantee and grantor, the dates of the transactions, and the property location. After recording the known data, you can see what information is missing. Develop your research plan to uncover the missing information.

To help identify transactions for the same property, enter a matching code or symbol on the worksheet. For example, place the symbol * next to the transaction when Samuel James was the grantee for 640 acres in St. Louis County. He sold 320 acres of that same property a few years later. Place another * on the worksheet line representing that transaction. When he sold the final 320 acres, another * designates the last portion of that transaction. You can now see the transaction for the purchase and sale (whether one or

DEED RECORDS WORKSHEET

Code	State	County	Book	Page	Name(s) Grantee	Date Sold	Date Recorded	Name(s) Grantor	Abbreviated Land Description	Quantity of Property

Figure 8.8 Deed records worksheet

numerous transactions) at a glance. If the same person purchased other tracts of land, use a different symbol to indicate that property.

Some transactions may be missing or difficult to find. Titles sometimes passed from generation to generation via wills or handshakes without the parties' recording the transaction. Some property was obtained through grants that may not be filed with the normal county deed transactions. Separate books on the state or national level may contain this information. Be sure to check those transactions. Review state guides to locate the grant and patent transactions for that state. The records are probably available through the Family History Library or the state archives.

Once you locate the land record, you should photocopy, transcribe, or abstract the document (see Figure 8.9). Be careful to record the data accurately—the slightest alteration could change the meaning of the document. It's a good idea to read deed books ten pages before and after your ancestor's deed. He may have recorded another deed or served as a witness for a friend or family member that same day. In some parts of the country, early deed records may be recorded in French or Spanish. Check with a translator if necessary.

You should not assume that the signature from the deed book is that of your ancestor. Usually it is not. Your ancestor signed a copy of the deed and then took the original home. The clerk copied the deed into the deed book and duplicated, in his own handwriting, the signatures on the document.

Your next step is to locate the property on a state or county map. Who lived next door or down the road? Use a township map to diagram the property. The township worksheet (see Figure 8.10) will help you plot the property. Then look at a map to determine the location of rivers, streams, and mountains. Record the land descriptions on the township worksheet. Use a pencil to diagram the property owned by your ancestors. You may determine that your ancestors owned property adjacent to in-laws or other relatives.

Some original grants and patents may be found on the Bureau of Land Management (BLM) Web site *(www.blm.gov)*. Check the site to see whether your state and ancestor are included in this massive ongoing database project.

If you are searching for a parcel of land in a state that uses metes and bounds descriptions, use the maps known as 7.5 minute U.S. Geological Survey (USGS) maps to locate and track your ancestors' properties. Maps are available from the USGS office for the entire country. The land description is usually available in the deed. Either by

DEED ABSTRACT WORKSHEET

Surname		Date Abstracted	
Source of Information		Repository	
State	County	Deed Book	Page
Grantor		Residence	
Grantee		Residence	
Date of Deed		Date Recorded	
Consideration		Quantity of Land	
Land Description			
Witnesses		Residence	
Signature(s) or Mark(s)			

Figure 8.9 Deed abstract worksheet

TOWNSHIP AND RANGE WORKSHEET

Townships usually consist of thirty-six sections numbered in the order shown below, each section containing 640 acres. After locating the deed records, plot the land description on a grid. The property may overflow from one section to another and into the next township or county.

Township _____ Range _____ Principal Meridian_____

6	5	4	3	2	1
7	8	9	10	11	12
18	17	16	15	14	13
19	20	21	22	23	24
30	29	28	27	26	25
31	32	33	34	35	36

LAND DESCRIPTIONS

Deed 1 _____

Deed 2 _____

Deed 3 _____

Deed 4 _____

Figure 8.10 Township and range worksheet

U.S. Geological Survey

The USGS provides a Web site *(geonames.usgs.gov/gnisform.html)* that enables researchers to find the exact location of a cemetery, city, town, or village listed in a family history. This government agency also produces and distributes the 7.5 minute maps that are helpful to genealogists.

hand or with the assistance of a deed software program, plat the land description. Some software programs produce printouts the same scale as the USGS maps. Therefore, you can overlay your plat drawing onto the prepared map, trying to match a stream or other identifiable landmark. Property lines often follow a current road.

Maps are valuable assets and should be put to work for you. Find a map of your county, then make an 8½ x 11-inch copy of it. If your family lived in a particular area in 1850, try to copy a map of that vintage since boundaries have likely changed. It's also useful to be able to see the township boundaries. You can also draw a map or print a computer-generated map.

Using the photocopy or printout, mark where your family lived, went to church, and was buried. Outline the property that your ancestor purchased and sold. When you locate a deed with your ancestor as the grantee, outline the property in green. Then after you find the deed when he was the grantor, draw a red line around the property or diagonal lines. By using two colors (any two colors), you can clearly indicate both sides of the transaction.

If your ancestor overlapped into the adjoining county, copy both county maps and tape them together. My husband's families all came through Southern Illinois. By tracking and marking the direct and collateral lines, I have a map of nine counties. I was able to find maps of similar proportions and taped them all together. You can imagine the precarious set of papers I had. I went directly to a photocopy store that had a blueprint copier. For about three dollars, they copied this fragile, makeshift map onto one piece of paper. The map includes the principal meridian, township, range, and section numbers. It is a research aid for my use only. If I find a township listed in a record, a quick review of the map tells me where the property is located. It is now color coded by surname so that I can keep track of who lived where. I add cemetery and church locations as they become available. When I fold the map carefully, it fits into my research notebook—and of course, it includes my name, address, and phone number, just in case!

Immigration and Naturalization Records

Genealogists have a desire to find their immigrant ancestor's passenger list and naturalization record. What was the immigrant's hometown? From what port did he embark? On what date and at which port did he arrive in America? Did the immigrant become a naturalized citizen? If yes, where and when? You'll find answers to these questions once you organize the data you already know and then extend your research.

Many people want to start immigration research in the old country, when in fact the place to start is in the immigrant's hometown in the United States. Clues are available in an assortment of records. Did the immigrant travel with any relatives, friends, or neighbors? Some census records provide clues to the year of immigration and naturalization. You should research records for direct and collateral relatives and friends since they may provide clues about your ancestor.

What are the immigration possibilities? Baltimore, Boston, New Orleans, New York, and Philadelphia were the five largest ports in this country, but there were numerous other ports in the United States and Canada. Be sure you don't overlook any port in your search. For example, it was less expensive to sail to Canada than to New York. Many immigrants had limited means, so anything was possible—despite family

Naturalization Research Guidelines

Your naturalization research plan should include the following steps:

- Establish timeline.
- Search published records.
- Check available indexes to original records.
- Locate census records.

Resources for Immigration and Naturalization Research

The following resources provide an overview of immigration and naturalization records:

- *American Naturalization Records 1790–1990: What They Are and How to Use Them*, by John J. Newman (Bountiful, Utah: Heritage Quest, 1998)

- *Guide to Genealogical Research in the National Archives of the United States*, by the National Archives and Records Administration (Washington, DC: National Archives and Records Administration, 2000)

- *They Came in Ships: A Guide to Finding Your Immigrant Ancestor's Arrival Record* 3rd edition, by John P. Colletta, Ph.D. (Orem, Utah: Ancestry Publishing, 2002)

- *They Became Americans: Finding Naturalization Records and Ethnic Origins*, by Loretto Dennis Szucs (Salt Lake City, Utah: Ancestry Inc., 1998)

stories that say they came through Ellis Island. Remember that Ellis Island did not open until 1892. Immigrants who arrived before that date did not arrive at Ellis Island.

You should fill out a naturalization worksheet (see Figure 8.11) for every immigrant ancestor in your family. List what you know—and, in the source field, how you know it. As this worksheet develops, analyze the locations and dates. Where was this person at major events in his life? Is there a pattern based on the locations? If the source is family lore as told to you by Aunt Minnie, then it may or may not be accurate. If the information came from documents or legal sources, the accuracy rate is better. This worksheet helps you see what information you have, how you know it, and what is missing.

You can look for the immigrant in census, deed, military, and naturalization records. Also include local records, such as city directories, church records, and voter registrations. Were there witnesses to any recorded events? Do you know who they are? Perhaps the witnesses worked for the court, but they may have been relatives or friends. Make a timeline showing every record you find. It may be necessary to research other family members, friends, or neighbors to find that elusive hometown in the old country.

Naturalization records usually come in two parts—the first papers (or petition) and

NATURALIZATION WORKSHEET

IMMIGRANT'S NAME _____

Naturalization Events	Location	Date	Mode of Transportation	Source of Information
Departs old country				
Arrives in America				
Residence				
First papers (petition) filed				
Final papers (naturalization) filed				
Other Life Events				
Birth				
Marriage				
Death				
Obituary				

Research Suggestions:

Census

City directories

Church records

Homestead records

Military records

Passenger lists

Probate records

Voter registration

Figures 8.11 Naturalization worksheet

the second (or final) papers. Several years after the immigrant arrived, he filed first papers. They may provide clues to the place of origin, family members, and place of residence. The final papers could be as simple as an oath of allegiance to the United States renouncing citizenship from the old country. Final papers post-1890 should contain additional information, including the name of the immigrant's spouse, children, and their birth dates. You might also find the name of the ship, date of immigration, and place of birth. What information you find varies greatly based on the date of naturalization and how much information a particular court required.

Naturalization papers could be filed in any court of record before 1906. After September 1906, the naturalization process was supposed to take place in the federal court and be recorded at the federal level. The Immigration and Naturalization Service may have a record on your ancestor. Many federal records are microfilmed and available at the National Archives or the Family History Library, but some were missed during the filming. National Archives regional facilities house many of the original ledger books. Some indexes are available for those records. You can transcribe the information available there.

You have now organized your research in legal records; the next chapter helps you organize your military research. Unbeknownst to many family historians, their ancestors served in the military. You can discover your family's soldiers by learning about the unique records for the various wars and focusing your research on the correct records for the times and places your ancestors may have served.

CHAPTER 9

Veterans' Affairs

DO YOU HAVE ANY VETERANS IN YOUR FAMILY? THROUGHOUT THE years, men, and now women, have served their country in military conflicts. The American Revolution patriots accepted the challenge of change, formed a new government, defended their beliefs, and established a lifestyle of freedom for their families. This military heroism continued with the War of 1812 to the Vietnam conflict and the present day. You, as a family historian, can find a wealth of information in military pension files, bounty land records, draft registration cards, and discharge papers. Many early veterans received rewards of inexpensive land on the frontier. By organizing your information by military conflict, you can more efficiently use the records.

Some veterans, their widows, or minor children received pensions. The pension files often contain affidavits from family and friends, usually overflowing with genealogical information. The collateral ancestor's files may be as important as those from the direct-line ancestors. Maybe your direct ancestor wrote and signed an affidavit for his brother, brother-in-law, neighbor, or friend.

Today families share stories of known American Revolution patriots or Civil War soldiers, but there may be other veterans to be uncovered. A list of the major American conflicts and dates usually provides clues to new veterans.

There is a vast amount of information, including books, Internet sites, and microfilm, on conflicts from the Colonial Wars to Vietnam. Records are available to help you review your family's participation in any military conflict.

Resources for Military Research

Military records vary from one war to the next. The following resources provide information on what data is available and where it is housed:

- *Uncle, We Are Ready! Registering America's Men 1917–1918*, by John J. Newman (Salt Lake City: Heritage Quest, 2001)
- *U.S. Military Records: A Guide to Federal and State Sources*, by James C. Neagles (Salt Lake City: Ancestry Inc., 1994)

Military Overview

A military overview worksheet (see Figure 9.1) helps you organize your search for direct and collateral male ancestors who may have participated in a military conflict. Today women serve in the military; however, some women participated in heroic events and are patriots from earlier conflicts. For example, during the American Revolution some women supported the troops by carrying water from the streams to the forts while under siege; those women are patriots approved by the National Society Daughters of the American Revolution (DAR).

If you think you have only a few soldiers in your background, you can use the military overview worksheet to list all your ancestor veterans. On that worksheet, you should list all potential veterans, both direct and collateral lines, and indicate their birth dates and the military conflict in which they likely served. Since each war had different types of records, it may be easier to use the separate worksheets provided later in this chapter for the American Revolution, Civil War, and World War I. Often researchers do not think they have any military veterans in their background, but with some research, they find that they do. Do not dismiss this possibility.

The chart of the major military conflicts in Figure 9.2 provides the timeframe of the war and the estimated birth years for participants in that conflict. The military timeline worksheet (see Figure 9.3) will provide clues for further research. The range of birth years covers both the oldest and the youngest participants. Most soldiers' birth years fall in the middle.

MILITARY OVERVIEW WORKSHEET

Name	War	State	Unit	Pension	Bounty Land	Notes

Figure 9.1 Military overview worksheet

Battle	Conflict Date	Birth Years Range
American Revolution	1775–1783	1720–1774
War of 1812	1812–1815	1762–1800
Indian Wars	1817–1898	1767–1885
Mexican War	1846–1848	1796–1835
Civil War	1861–1865	1810–1852
Spanish-American War	1898–1899	1848–1887
Philippine Insurrection	1899–1902	1849–1889
World War I	1917–1918	1871–1899
World War II	1940–1947	1890–1930
Korean War	1950–1955	1900–1938
Vietnam	1964–1975	1914–1956

Figure 9.2 Estimated birth year range for participants in military conflicts

The 1930 census provides research clues for veterans of that era. Men were asked whether they were veterans. To answer yes, the veteran had to be in the service during wartime. If he participated in the military during peacetime, the appropriate answer was no. If the answer was yes, column thirty-one included an abbreviation of the war. The 1930 census war abbreviations are

- **Box:** Boxer Rebellion
- **Civ:** Civil War
- **Mex:** Mexican Expedition
- **Phil:** Philippine Insurrection
- **WarSp:** Spanish-American
- **WW:** World War

Include all potential veterans on your military timeline and worksheet. One by one, you can prove whether that ancestor did or did not serve in the military. If he did not serve, so indicate on the worksheet. If he did serve, pursue the vast number of records available for that particular war.

MILITARY TIMELINE WORKSHEET

		Name
		1620
		1630
		1640
		1650
		1660
	Colonial Wars	1670
		1680
		1690
		1700
		1710
		1720
		1730
		1740
		1750
American Revolution		1760
		1770
		1780
		1790
		1800
War of 1812		1810
		1820
		1830
Mexican War	Indian Wars	1840
		1850
Civil War		1860
		1870
		1880
Spanish-American		1890
Philippine & Boxer		1900
World War I		1910
		1920
		1930
World War II		1940
Korean War		1950
		1960
Vietnam War		1970
		1980
		1990
Gulf & Mid-east Wars		2000

Place an X in the decade of birth and death for each potential veteran. Based on his age at the time of the war, determine the conflicts in which your ancestor may have participated.

Figure 9.3 Military timeline worksheet

Military Conflicts

1620–1774

Colonial Wars

Numerous conflicts occurred during the formative years of this country. Any battle that occurred before the American Revolution was classified as part of the Colonial Wars. Some of these battles were local conflicts in a specific city or area. Others were much broader. If your ancestors lived in the United States before 1775, they may have participated in one or more battles. A state or county history will provide information about battles in that specific area. Publications and records from the Society of Colonial Wars provide further information about the battles of the time.

1775–1860

American Revolution

The American Revolution took place from 1775 to 1783. Young boys, perhaps only ten to fourteen years old, served as musicians. Men of any age may have participated in the battles, sold food to the troops, or otherwise supported the patriots. By using a wide age range, theoretically anyone born between 1720 and 1774 *could* have participated in the American Revolution. Do you have any ancestors born in that period who were living in the colonies between 1775 and 1783? The potential patriots may have been born in the colonies, but many were recent immigrants.

The federal records available for the American Revolution include pension and bounty records and compiled service records. Similar records may be available for patriots who participated in their state's militia. Both the National Society Daughters of the American Revolution (DAR) and the Sons of the American Revolution (SAR) have extensive lineage records.

You may want to start an American Revolution research worksheet (see Figure 9.4) by listing in your database all males born between 1720 and 1774. Include men in your direct line and collateral lines; these are your potential patriots. Search for each of these men, to prove or disprove their participation in the Revolution.

The easy-to-find patriots are those with a federal pension listed in published indexes. If you find your ancestor in these indexes, the records have been microfilmed and are available at many libraries. The patriot often wrote a letter stating the name

AMERICAN REVOLUTION RESEARCH WORKSHEET

Soldier's Name	State	Unit(s) & Battles	Enlisted Date	Discharge Date	Pension: Federal or State	DAR SAR	Bounty Land	Notes

Figure 9.4 American Revolution research worksheet

of his captain or the name of the unit with which he served. When checking this index, just like any other, be broadminded about the spelling of his name. He may be there hiding from you under a different spelling.

American Revolution pensions did not start until 1818; therefore, your ancestor may have served, but the patriot and his widow may have died before the pension program was initiated.

Some soldiers served as representatives of their states and did not join the federal troops. Each state has a listing of patriots. This could include a roster of units from a county or region, payroll lists, or known American Revolution burials in an area. County and state histories may also provide information on the early settlers of an area and record their participation in the Revolution.

The DAR and SAR records are another good source of information. But keep in mind that those records are ongoing; patriots continue to be discovered and documented. My mother, daughter, and I all joined DAR several years ago. My mother and I joined on previously proven patriots; however, my daughter went into DAR on a new patriot. There was no question that he was a patriot, but no one had previously submitted an application in his name. That same situation could apply to one of your patriots. Even if your patriot is not listed in DAR or SAR records, he may still have served.

Many patriots received bounty land as payment for their service. Some sold their rights to land speculators. The 1840 federal census identified men and women who were receiving pensions at the time. Those listed may have been American Revolution patriots, War of 1812 soldiers, or their widows. If your ancestor was living in 1840, that census may give you a clue.

If you still have not located your ancestor, determine where he was living at the time of the Revolution. Where did the men in that area serve? In what battles was he involved? Sometimes the service was for only a few weeks, not a few years. If you think your ancestor served in a particular battle, check for a Web site describing the event and possibly listing the soldiers. There may even be a National Park on the site. For example, Valley Forge has a Web site *(www.nps.gov/vafo/mropening.htm)* that lists all the patriots who served that cold winter. By carefully reviewing all available records and recording the findings on the worksheet, you will see a clear picture emerge. Follow up on any information you know or discover—you never know where it will take you.

War of 1812

The War of 1812 actually lasted until 1815. There were regular army soldiers and a lot of state militia soldiers. Some county histories provide lists of soldiers from their areas. These soldiers received bounty land grants, and some eventually received pensions. A compiled service record, microfilmed by the National Archives, should be available for all soldiers, whether regular army or state volunteer. Those records are arranged alphabetically by state or territory. Some records contain limited information, but others are more complete. The folder of one of my ancestors stated that he lived eleven miles from his enlistment location and fifteen miles from the discharge location. It also listed the dates of service and the name of his captain. With that combination, I could clearly identify this soldier as the one I was seeking. Include the War of 1812 veterans on the military overview worksheet.

Indian Wars

Like the Colonial Wars, the Indian Wars stretched over several decades, from the 1810s to the 1890s, and had numerous names. In the 1830s, some men from Tennessee traveled to Florida to fight in the Seminole Wars. Illinois had the Black Hawk War, and there were Indian wars in other parts of the country. If he was in the right age range, your ancestor may have participated in any of these wars.

On the military timeline worksheet, you should indicate the timeframe in which your ancestor may have participated in an Indian War. The ancestor who fought in the Black Hawk War in the 1830s probably did not fight in the Indian Wars after the 1870s. Be sure to also include these veterans on the military overview worksheet.

Mexican War

The Mexican War took place from 1846 to 1848. Young men from about twenty-four states traveled from the United States down to Mexico for this encounter. The Mexican pension files index is available on microfilm. Many of these soldiers received bounty land. Some of the soldiers also fought in the Civil War. Microfilmed compiled service records are arranged alphabetically by state or territory. This often overlooked war provides great records. Include these veterans on the military overview worksheet.

1861–1916

Civil War

Did you have any Civil War soldier ancestors? List all your male ancestors, direct and collateral, who were the correct age to serve in this event. Remember that very young boys often participated as drummers or in other capacities. Older men who served in the Mexican War may have served in the Civil War, as well. Use the Civil War research worksheet (see Figure 9.5) to identify your potential soldiers.

Where did the soldier live before or during the war? That state might not be the state where he lived after the war. Was the soldier loyal to the North or South? Don't assume anything. Residents in a state could have served on either side. Arkansas had many Confederate soldiers and some Union soldiers. The same was true for Illinois; most served for the Union, but some migrated south to serve for the Confederacy. Missouri was a border state with residents joining both sides. Brothers and cousins may have joined on opposite sides; in many cases, you must research records on both sides.

Union federal pension records are housed at the National Archives in Washington, D.C. They have not been microfilmed, but a microfilmed card index is available and online at *www.ancestry.com.* Be sure to check both; I have found names on the microfilm that did not appear online. If the name appears and you want a copy of the pension file, contact a private researcher, submit NARA form 85 to the National Archives, or go to Washington. Of course, the last option is the most intriguing, but it is expensive and time-consuming.

Confederate soldiers did not receive a pension from the federal government because they did not fight for the federal government. Confederate pensions, which were provided at the state level, were not as numerous as Union pensions. Southern and border states provided a pension for Confederate veterans living in their states after the war. Most of these records are indexed and available on microfilm or published in an abstract format. Check with the appropriate state archives or adjutant general's office.

Military histories for each state and most units are available at various libraries. Allen County Public Library in Fort Wayne, Indiana, has a great collection. The National Park Service battlefields have a copy of the histories for most units that participated in that particular battle. An abbreviated edition or excerpts from a history may be available on the Internet.

CIVIL WAR RESEARCH WORKSHEET

Soldier's Name	State	North or South	Unit(s) & Battles	Enlisted Date	Discharge Date	Pension: Federal or State	CWSS Web Site	GAR Register

Figure 9.5 Civil War research worksheet

When reading the history of the Civil War, be mindful that many battles have two names. The North provided one name and the South another. The battles of Manassas and Bull Run are the same. Antietam and Sharpsburg are the same. Be aware that histories may indicate the loyalty of the author. The National Park Service has publications on each of the major battles that explain both names.

When the war was over and the troops returned home, many soldiers made a stop at the courthouse to submit their discharge papers for recording. The original records may be in the courthouse, state archives, or other repository. Microfilmed records are available for many counties.

After the war, soldiers formed a bond. The Grand Army of the Republic (GAR) was organized by Union veterans, with records of their membership still existing in some areas. The membership logs list the name of the veteran, the unit in which he served, and his death date. Some GAR records have been indexed and are available in print. For example, a recent publication, *Grand Army of the Republic, Department of Illinois: Transcription of the Death Rolls, 1879–1947*, by Dennis Northcott and Thomas Brooks (St. Louis: The author, 2003) lists approximately thirty-two thousand soldiers who lived in Illinois after the war. If the soldier died in 1875, his name most likely will not appear on the GAR death list since the organization did not start until about 1879.

The National Park Service Civil War Soldiers and Sailors System (CWSS) Web site (*www.itd.nps.gov/cwss/*) lists participants in the Civil War (see Figure 9.6). Thanks to thousands of volunteers across the country who provided untold data entry hours, this information is available to us. But it is secondary source material, so be sure to verify the data through other sources.

The CWSS Web site provides a searchable database of the soldiers, both Union and Confederate. Enter the name of the potential soldier, as shown in Figure 9.7. If the name does not appear on your first search, try using various spellings. A list of soldiers with that name will then appear; the example search shown on Figure 9.8 uses a surname unusual enough that only one name appears. The screen lists the soldier's military unit; by clicking on the unit name, an abbreviated unit history appears, as shown in Figure 9.9.

To uncover further information on the veteran, you should research cemeteries, census records, county and military histories, newspaper articles or obituaries, and probate or will records. Cemetery records may help determine a death date. Lists in the *Card Records of Headstones Provided for Deceased Union Civil War Veterans, ca. 1879–ca. 1903* (National Archives–M1845) may also provide the death date. Obituaries for the average person were limited in the late nineteenth century, while

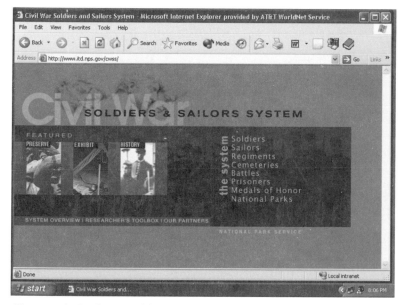

Figure 9.6 Civil War Soldiers and Sailors System Web site

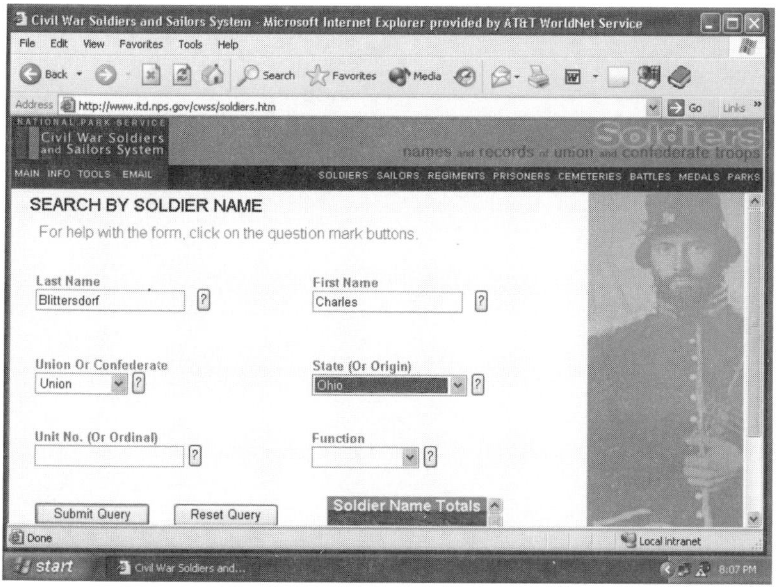

Figure 9.7 CWSS search screen for Charles Blittersdorf

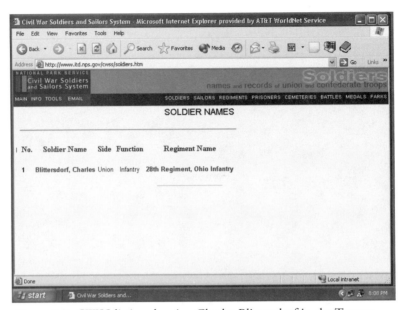

Figure 9.8 CWSS listing showing Charles Blittersdorf in the Twenty-eighth Ohio

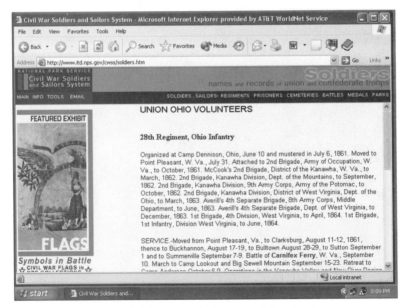

Figure 9.9 CWSS unit history of the Twenty-eighth Ohio

National Park Service

National Park Service rangers or historians will assist family historians visiting the parks. Most Civil War battlefield parks house a staff-only library with unit histories that include lists of the battle participants. By asking brief, specific questions, genealogists can often find information about their Civil War ancestors and their units. Histories and maps of that particular engagement are available at each park's gift shop. Scheduled guided walking tours of the battlefield are usually available every day.

articles about the death of a military hero or old veteran may have been front-page news. County histories also contain lists of soldiers and the military units in which they participated.

When working with military records, you should consider the collateral records that may guide you to pertinent sources. Some collateral records certainly apply to other areas of interest, as well. If the soldier died in 1875, he probably did not receive a pension, although his widow may have. If the widow remarried, she did not receive a widow's pension, although the soldier's minor children may have.

Collateral families are important in all research. Researchers may find their direct-line ancestors mentioned in the pension records of a brother-in-law, neighbor, or fellow soldier. The ancestor may have written a letter that contains information, along with his signature, about life before or after the war. In one such family, five men served in the war; three died in battle. The four brothers and their father were listed in the pension files. The soldiers, widow, or mother received a pension. By compiling all the data, the researcher confirmed and documented that family unit. The pension files stated the names of the brothers, and the names of their mother and father. It provided the age and place of birth for this African-American family—information that may not have been available elsewhere.

Your Civil War research worksheet, and all others, should contain enlistment and discharge dates. The worksheet should also include the name of the unit(s) in which the soldier served. You should use the worksheet as a finding aid to lead you to other records. It also helps you organize and analyze the data. Genealogists can determine the battles in which their ancestors served and get an overview of what life was like at that time.

Spanish-American War

Regular army soldiers and volunteers from various states and territories fought in the Spanish-American War from 1898 to 1899. Many of these soldiers received pensions. Their records are available at the National Archives. These veterans were eligible for pensions after 1916. Include these soldiers on your military overview worksheet.

Philippine Insurrection

Soldiers who fought in the Philippine Insurrection from 1899 to 1902 joined federal regiments. In addition to compiled service records, the National Archives has a name index for these veterans and some personal papers. Pensions were available after 1916. Your military overview worksheet will help you determine whether any of your ancestors participated in this event.

Boxer Rebellion

From 1900 to 1901, the joint forces of France, Germany, Great Britain, Italy, Japan, Russia, the United States, and others defeated the Boxers, a secret Chinese society. This alliance soon deteriorated to fight among themselves in World War I. The veterans of the Boxer Rebellion were eligible for a pension after 1916. Include these veterans on your military overview worksheet.

1917–Present

World War I

Several types of World War I records are available for family historians as outlined on the World War I research worksheet (see Figure 9.10). The most obvious is the World War I draft card, which is actually a civilian record to determine the pool of men for potential service. Every man between the age of eighteen and forty-five who was not in the military at the time of registration was obligated to register. This does not mean he served in the military—he just registered. That registration took place at his local draft board in his home county unless he was out of town. If out of town, the man registered on the designated day wherever he was and the record was supposed to be transferred to his local draft board.

A rural county usually had one draft board, thus one set of indexed cards. Large cities often had multiple draft boards, each indexed separately. If you are searching for

WORLD WAR I RESEARCH WORKSHEET

Soldier's Name	State	Unit(s) & Battles	Draft Board	WWI Draft Card	Enlisted Date	Discharge Date	Discharge Papers	NARA Records	Web Site

Figure 9.10 World War I research worksheet

a city ancestor, locate his address about 1916 or 1917. Then determine his home area draft board.

Within the county the records are filmed alphabetically, with a few variations. Be sure to look at the entire roll—some clerks did not understand the meaning of "alphabetically." Transcribe the data from these cards to your family history. Some newspapers published maps and lists of registration sites just before the sign-up dates. The National Archives has a microfilm of various cities' draft boards marked on maps, and some maps are available on the Internet. Voter registration maps can also help with this process.

These records serve as a substitute for birth certificates because the registrant stood in front of the clerk and provided firsthand information and then signed the document. He provided a physical description, date of birth, usually next of kin, and occupation. There were three registrations, and the information requested varied with each one.

The original draft registration cards are housed at the National Archives, Southeast Region facility, in the Atlanta area. All the records have been microfilmed; the film is available at the National Archives, Family History Library, or Allen County Public Library. Local or state facilities often have records for their area.

State archives and other local facilities have records for those who served in World War I. The record may indicate the dates of enlistment and discharge. It may also provide the place of service in the United States or abroad. Some states have the index online. One important item is the soldier's service number. Many veterans recorded their discharge papers with the clerk in their home counties. Review all records that may give you clues about the men who lived during this period.

With service number in hand, request a copy of the soldier's service record from the National Military Personnel Records Center in St. Louis. This facility stores mil-

The National Military Personnel Records Center will assist family historians only through e-mail or postal mail requests. The soldier's or his next-of-kin's signature must appear on the request form. When you submit a request, provide as much information as possible, including the soldier's military service number, to facilitate the search. The reply may take from a few weeks to six months or more. Further information about this facility is available at *www.archives.gov/research_room/vetrecs/*.

itary records for those who served after the Spanish-American War. Unfortunately, a 1973 fire destroyed part of this building and many records. So it's possible your ancestor's record is missing. By including the service number with your application, you have a better chance of locating the record if it still exists. Indicate the service number on your request on form SF 180, which is available on their Web site *(www.archives.gov/research_room/obtain_copies/veterans_service_records.html#order2).*

World War II

Records for World War II are becoming available. A few draft cards are open to the public, with others soon to follow. You can contact the National Military Personnel Records Center to see whether your ancestor's record survived the 1973 fire. If your veteran is still living, you should glean as much information as possible from him. Did he serve in Europe or the Pacific theater? Was he in the submarine service or the infantry? Did he land at Normandy Beach on D-Day? If he doesn't want to talk about the war, you may be able to glean some information if you take him to a vintage plane air show, a museum, or anything that might be related to the war. Don't forget the women who served. They, too, have stories to tell and memories to share. Include these veterans on your military overview worksheet.

Korean War

Many soldiers participated in the Korean War, and as with other wars, some did not come home. An online database lists those who gave their lives in this conflict *(www.familysearch.org).* To uncover some of the history of these veterans, you should conduct an oral interview with each living relative who served in Korea. Obtain a map of Korea, and ask your loved one where he served. Ask how he got there and how he was sent home. Any little question might spur some memories and conversation. Include these veterans on your military overview worksheet.

Vietnam War

The soldiers who lost their lives in the Vietnam War are also listed on the same database as the Korean War casualties *(www.familysearch.org).* Of course, the Vietnam Veterans Memorial Wall in Washington, D.C., is also a listing of those same people. Ask the Vietnam veterans in your family about their experiences so you can record their memories of this war. New online databases are becoming available from the National Archives *(www.archives.gov/research_room/genealogy)* and other organizations. Cyndi's

List *(www.cyndislist.com)* includes directions to the most recent Vietnam veterans' Web sites and records.

Military Personnel

Many people are veterans but did not serve during the time of a major conflict. Perhaps your loved one was in Germany or Japan in the 1950s. Maybe he was in a submarine or on a ship during the Cuban Missile Crisis. All these veterans have service records, as well, and stories to tell, so be sure to interview them. Then add their stories to your family history.

Military Academies

Did one of your ancestors attend a military academy? If so, request a copy of his or her record. That person may have later participated in a major conflict. If the student did not graduate, he may not have been in the military; however, he still has a file at the academy.

One of my collateral ancestors attended West Point starting in 1846. His record provides information and copies of certificates on his appointment, his report cards, and some information on his father. It also explains that he was asked to leave on 30 June 1848 due to "deficiencies in mathematics and French." Nevertheless, it is a unique record for him and provides some in-depth information on this person and his family.

By organizing your ancestor's military information on a worksheet, you are prepared to analyze your data, seek new sources, and fill in the blanks as the research progresses. Use these worksheets as a reminder of what records are available, what you have reviewed, and what needs to be completed.

Cities, towns, and villages produce their own records, and those, too, need to be organized. Cemetery, church, newspaper, and school records provide further documents and clues about your family. These resources are outlined in the next chapter.

CHAPTER 10

Around the Town

THERE ARE MANY LOCAL RECORDS AVAILABLE TO GENEALOGISTS. ANY OF them could contain the answers to your research questions. Local records include burial, cemetery, church, funeral home, and school records; city directories; and newspapers. Since there are many steps to this type of research, a worksheet helps you organize your search. Keep in mind, though, that worksheets should be used only as a guide, not a place to record your findings and documentation. Record the data in your genealogical software program, and file the documents in your folders.

Church Research

Many immigrants came to this country for religious freedom. Some ancestors formed religious splinter groups, which left records in the community. Other religious leaders traveled with their flocks from the old country to this country and established churches at various locations across the United States. Perhaps the entire original congregation came from the same hamlet in the old country.

You should start by determining the background of the religious congregation. Is it Protestant, Catholic, Jewish, or something else? What is unique about that congregation, compared to other churches of the same faith? Did the original leader come from England, Ireland, Germany, or other parts of Europe, bringing with him a custom from the old country? What was the migration path of other church members? Did your ancestor follow that same path by ship, wagon train, or railroad?

So what can church records tell us? They often provide original records and clues for birth, baptism, marriage, death, and cemetery information. Church records are frequently used in place of civil vital records, and they often contain more information about an event than civil records do. Prepare a church research worksheet (see Figure 10.1) to use as a finding aid.

Resources for Migration

Pioneers followed basic migration paths. The following books provide an overview of migration to and within the United States:

- *Albion's Seed*, by David Hackett Fischer (New York: Oxford University Press, 1989)
- *Map Guide to American Migration Routes, 1735–1815*, by William Dollarhide (Bountiful, Utah: AGLL Genealogical Services, 1997)
- *Magellan Geographix United States History Atlas* (Santa Barbara, California: Magellan, 2000)

If you are looking at Catholic records, you may be very happy. The baptismal records dating back to the 1700s, and perhaps before, list the name of the child, parents, and godparents. The records may be recorded in Latin, German, Italian, Spanish, Polish, English, or other native languages, depending on the time and the community. Chapter 11 describes how to obtain from the Family History Library a translation list of important words. Marriage records usually include the name of the bride and groom, the name of each set of parents, and the place of baptism for the bride and groom.

You may find some religious records open to the public and others closed; that depends on the governing body of that church. In some cities, Catholic church records are open, but they are closed in other areas. The same applies to Protestant denominations.

Protestant records are often helpful. Keep in mind that the name of the church or denomination may have changed over the years. A timeline of that church's history

CHURCH RESEARCH WORKSHEET

Name	Church Name & Location	Baptized	Confirmed	Marriage	Death	Original Member	Church Directory	Church History

Figure 10.1 Church research worksheet

will help you verify that you are tracking the correct congregation. Quakers (the Society of Friends) have thorough records, which include the signatures of all the guests at a wedding—a great document for genealogists. All these records offer clues for further research.

City Directory Research

You may think city directories are an urban twentieth-century record; in fact, some were published in the 1700s. Some county directories are also available. Since most of the books are old and many are fragile, numerous research facilities permit use of microfilm copies only. Many directories prior to 1936 are available on microfilm. Do not overlook the possibility of this valuable asset.

You will find that city directory information varies from year to year, so you should review all directories for the period your ancestor lived in that area. One year the given and surname are listed, then a few years later the middle initial may be provided. Some years include the spouse's name. You may be able to determine the era that a person moved into town, when he left town, or even the approximate time of his death. Be mindful of the directory publication date. If

City Directory Documentation

Even though many city directories have extremely long names, you should include the complete name in your documentation, plus the page number on which your ancestor's name appears. Here is an example of a complete city directory name and publication data:

Polk's St. Louis County (Missouri) Directory 1949: Containing an Alphabetical Directory of Business Firms and Private Citizens in St. Louis County Which Embraces the Territory Immediately Surrounding the City of St. Louis; a Directory of Households, Occupants of Office Buildings and Other Business Places, Including a Complete Street and Avenue Guide also a Buyers Guide and a Complete Classified Business Directory (St. Louis: R. L. Polk & Co., 1949), page 112

it is dated April 1881, then any event that occurred after that date won't appear until the next year.

One way to begin your search is to list on the city directory research worksheet the names of the ancestors you want to search for when you locate those directories (see Figure 10.2). Indicate the year or range of years you want to include in the search. One facility may not have all the publications you need. Keep this worksheet in your research notebook, and it will be ready when you locate the city directories.

If you are uncertain about the given name of your ancestor, it may be necessary to research all the people with that surname. Copy the data and start analyzing it. By reviewing each year, you will find clues. When a person disappears from the record and a widow appears, check the death record and obituaries. Maybe your ancestor was listed as a child of the deceased. Also, list all the people who lived in the same house. While working, unmarried children or siblings usually lived with relatives, so it is easy to see possible family groups. Further research will uncover exact relationships.

The list below is the result of a search through city directories. It indicates that the Swahlstedt family probably did not live in that particular area until 1881 or 1882. Frank Swahlstedt died about 1905. We think his middle initial was A. and his widow was named Emma. The next step in this search is to examine the death registers for Frank about 1905 or 1906, cemetery records probably for both Frank and Emma, and census records for the Swahlstedt family in 1900.

1881	No Swahlstedt listing
1882–1883	Frank Swahlstedt
1884	Frank A. Swahlstedt
1885–1905	Frank Swahlstedt
1906	Emma Swahlstedt (wid of Frank)

Some city directories are called reverse directories. They are indexed by the address and then list the occupant of the home. With map in hand, you will find this a great way to review the neighborhood. If your ancestors lived on Madison Street and Lincoln Street, which was the adjacent street, you will have to look in two sections of the reverse directory. Let the map be your guide.

CITY DIRECTORY RESEARCH WORKSHEET

CITY _____ COUNTY _____ STATE _____

Name	Year	Page	Residence Address	Occupation	Business Address	Notes

Figure 10.2 City directory research worksheet

Death-Related Research

Cemetery Records

Have you ever walked a cemetery seeking an elusive ancestor? Then after returning home, you discover that yet another elusive ancestor was buried in that same cemetery. Your visit to the cemetery will be more productive with a little preparation and organization. Let your cemetery research worksheet be your guide (see Figure 10.3).

Your ancestors may have lived in one county or community over many years and generations. Your direct and collateral families may have used several cemeteries during those years. A cemetery research worksheet in your research notebook helps you keep the compiled data in one place.

Cemeteries

There are various types of cemeteries in most communities. You should determine which type best identifies your ancestors.

- **Religious:** Many religious facilities have a cemetery near their building. But if the religious facility has moved, the old cemetery may be elsewhere. So it's worthwhile to first review the history of the church. If your ancestor is buried in a cemetery maintained by a religious facility, the family may be mentioned in the church records.

- **Public:** Most municipalities have a local cemetery, sometimes referred to as Potter's Field.

- **Veteran:** National cemeteries for veterans and their family are maintained across the country. If you're looking for a soldier, be sure to review the records at the national cemeteries near the battlefield he fought on.

- **Commercial:** Commercial cemeteries developed in the twentieth century and remain popular today. These nonsectarian facilities are owned by an individual, corporation, or conglomerate.

- **Family:** The family burial ground, usually found on the old farm, is almost a thing of the past. Historical and genealogical societies, as well as veterans' organizations, continue to discover and preserve small family cemeteries. All too often, they are moved to make way for highways or land development.

CEMETERY RESEARCH WORKSHEET

Name	Born	Died	Cemetery	County	Township	City	Section	Lot	Tombstone (Yes or No) & Notes

Figure 10.3 Cemetery research worksheet

Begin this search by gathering the names of the family members in the focus area, including the names of the founding couple, their children and their children's spouses, plus the next generation. Assuming some of the children were female, there will be several surnames on your list. Next, add the dates of birth and death, if known. This process helps you identify people with the same name, possibly from different generations.

If your county or area has a cemetery index, review the publication, looking for the names listed on your worksheet. If your family lived near the county border, it may be necessary to review cemetery indexes for more than one county. The title, introduction, or other listings in the book indicate the dates covered by that index. Did the compiler record all tombstones before 1950? Did your ancestor die in 1952? Is every cemetery included in the index? Make notations on your worksheet so that you remember this important information.

Have you checked with the local genealogical or historical society? More and more genealogical societies are publishing cemetery indexes in book form, on CD-ROMs, or online.

When you find your ancestor's name in the index, record the cemetery name, section and lot number, birth and death dates, and any additional information included in that publication. More often than not, published indexes omit data since it is difficult to include everything. There may be notations on the back of the tombstone, inscriptions such as "Dear Mother," or dates missed by the transcriber or simply not included in the index. If you find an ancestor in the index, try to locate the original records; they'll probably provide additional information.

Did you find every name on the worksheet when you searched the index? Probably not. That means it's time to expand the cemetery search.

You should try to obtain a county map showing the townships. On the map, mark the cemetery locations, then list a number or code with the name of each cemetery. This legend will both serve as a reminder to you and help your family understand the project. On the same map, outline the property owned by your ancestors. Burials probably occurred close to that property, not all the way across the county. Let the map point you in the right direction.

Once you complete the map, it is time to visit the cemeteries. Sort the worksheet on two levels, first by the cemetery name and then alphabetically by surname. Walk each cemetery with your list in hand. If someone is helping you, provide a worksheet for your assistant, as well. Also, have your note-taking tablet handy to record new information from the tombstones you find there. Some researchers also like to use a clipboard when researching in a cemetery. While walking the cemetery, try to accomplish the following tasks:

- Verify the data on your list.
- Add new information.
- Review the neighboring tombstones.
- Take photos of the tombstones.

You will probably leave the cemetery with new names, dates, and clues. Since the time the index was compiled, new burials have taken place. Additional information is probably on the tombstones, sometimes overlooked during the index recording. You should also review the tombstones to correct any transcription errors that appear in the index.

If the cemetery has an onsite office, talk to the cemetery sexton about the burial records. Some cemeteries have card files that provide additional information. If the office is not onsite or is not open, contact the caretaker by phone or letter.

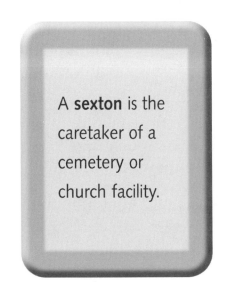

A **sexton** is the caretaker of a cemetery or church facility.

As your research continues, other types of records may reveal additional information for your cemetery research worksheet. Obituaries, county histories, news articles, death certificates, and coroner records are all helpful death-related resources.

Online cemetery indexes are available in some counties. If an index is not available, you may be able to locate a researcher who will do a lookup within that county. A few local researchers will actually visit the cemetery for you, but do not count on that generosity, particularly if you have numerous names to research.

You can send a letter to cemeteries outside your area inquiring about your surname of interest. The cemetery may be able to provide burial information that identifies family relationships. This process may require several letters if numerous cemeteries are involved. Be careful that you don't request too much information in one letter. That one may not be answered.

To assist with cemetery research or death information overall, you should customize your cemetery research worksheet. Perhaps you want to record obituaries, burial records, coroner records, death certificates or registers, or probate records there; add as many columns as you need. Once you do that, your worksheet becomes an overview of many death-related records.

After you research the available records, determine whether any additional records are available at the Family History Library, Allen County Public Library, or any other research facility that is not immediately available to you. Keep the worksheet in your notebook until you have a chance to visit those facilities.

Burial Records

In some large cities, you may find burial records at the courthouse or on microfilm. These records served as a death certificate. In many places the same kind of information was recorded—the date of death, the cemetery and funeral home names, and possibly the name of the deceased parents, along with other information related to the death. If you have numerous entries to research, add a column to the cemetery research worksheet for burial records. Determine the timeframe covered by the burial records; they usually start in the late 1800s. Write *N/A* in the box to indicate the names that are not available in burial records. These records probably don't cover a person who died in 1820. This preparation means that your research time will be more efficient since you won't be looking for records that do not exist.

Funeral Home Records

Do you know which funeral home your family usually used? Which funeral home was close to your ancestor's home? Funeral homes keep files. Since those files may contain private information, some facilities share the file only with direct family members. You'll find that some funeral home records are available at archival facilities. Others are indexed and available on microfilm. For example, the Historical Society of Pennsylvania has the original records of several local Philadelphia funeral homes. Make a list of ancestors who died in a particular town and check the index for available records. Determine which funeral home records are available and where they are located.

Once you obtain as many death-related records as possible, you'll have a clear picture of the events at the end of your ancestor's life. Those records may provide answers to many questions—and clues for further research.

Home Sources Research

You have filed those items from your heritage trunk, but did you analyze the information? In your home or that of a parent, sibling, or cousin, there may be some great source documents. Do you have a birth announcement for a niece or nephew, or even great-niece or nephew? That is a document. It provides the baby's birth date, full name, and the name of the parents. Do you have an invitation to a baptism or confirmation? Do you have an invitation to a graduation party; maybe high school or college? Do you have any ribbons, certificates, or awards received by a family member? Those provide you with a place and date, not to mention activities in which the family member participated. Maybe you have a first-grade photo that is dated and includes the name of the school.

Other family members may have memorabilia in a heritage trunk, as well, that provides similar information. Ask them! If your aunt doesn't want to look through her goodies, tell her you will be happy to do it. With her permission, photocopy anything you need and then return everything when you are finished.

Medical Records Research

Our heritage trunks contain many wonderful memories left to us by our forebears. However, your family medical history may not be so positive. If you want to sort out your family's health history, you need to collect as much information as possible. Have you ever wondered about the cause of death for Aunt Minnie? Do one or more diseases seem to run in your family? Maybe high blood pressure or cholesterol, cancer, diabetes, or heart disease are prevalent and appear often as a cause of death. There are factors that activate some medical situations, such as eating habits, exercise, and weight. If breast or prostate cancer runs in the family, you need to know that. Maybe nobody has ever analyzed the big picture.

Because medical records are private, you won't be able to obtain very many complete records. Start by obtaining a copy of your own medical record. Then review your family's death certificates from the last fifty years. What cause of death is listed? You are interested in the underlying health problem; however, that may not be what is listed as the cause of death. Next you need to talk to surviving family members about the individual's health issues before death.

If the coroner or medical examiner, rather than the family physician, signed the death certificate, another record should be available. Coroners' records are open to the public; medical examiners' records are not. Only the next-of-kin may obtain records from the medical examiner. That could be a spouse, parent, oldest child, or sibling. These records are considered part of your medical records and are, therefore, private.

Coroners' records are older, usually pre-1970s, and open to the public. You can obtain a copy, if they still exist. This record should give you details about the cause of death and perhaps any known conditions at the time of death.

Then talk to your current family members about genetic traits and medical conditions—parents, grandparents, siblings, cousins, or aunts and uncles. This could be a touchy subject, so tread lightly. When you start the conversation, ask for their permission to add this information to your chart, which will be shared with other family members. If there is any doubt or hesitation, ask them to sign a simple agreement. You are looking for simple features, such as the color of their eyes and their height, as well as medical conditions such as arthritis or asthma. You may learn who has blue, green, or gray eyes. You are also looking for unusual situations, such as an extra toe or finger.

Does your family want to take a proactive role in health issues? Have you ever provided a medical history for a loved one? You certainly want to provide available and accurate information. To easily organize this information, you may want to purchase a computer program that generates family charts. Check the Web site for Geneweaver *(www.Geneweaver.com)*. Is that the type of program you need? You can easily transfer data from your genealogical software program to the new program. Then enter the medical information as it becomes available. The charts will display each family member, indicating male or female, any current disease, or death-related health problems.

Newspaper Research

Did your grandmother tell you how she won the spelling bee or the handwriting contest in eighth grade? When you were a child, was there a train accident in your hometown that killed Uncle Sam? Have you been able to confirm any of these stories? Newspaper records may be the answer.

Newspapers, daily or weekly, are part of most communities today, just as they were in years past. Some newspapers specialize in legal matters, some are ethnically oriented, and others serve a special area. Your ancestors had the same experiences. Germans, Italians, Swedes, and others each had their own native-language newspapers. Fortunately, many older newspapers have survived, at least on microfilm. State archives, libraries, and historical societies usually maintain newspaper collections.

The easiest way to begin is by locating a newspaper collection in the city or state of your focus area. Most states have one major collection, then smaller collections housed in other facilities within the state. Use a search engine, or check your state archives or libraries for the library repository in your area. Local libraries usually maintain a local or regional newspaper microfilm collection. You can take advantage of the libraries' finding aids, which provide researchers with in-depth information on large collections. The finding aid for the newspaper microfilm collection may include the name of the publications, the dates of available holdings, film numbers, and descriptions of the records.

Once you locate the newspaper collection, determine how it is organized. The State Historical Society of Missouri in Columbia files its microfilm alphabetically by city, not county. However, most finding aids are divided by county, then subdivided by cities, followed by available dates for each newspaper within that city. You can organize the search list on your newspaper research worksheet (see Figure 10.4) according to that same filing method or customize the worksheet to fit your requirements. If you have research in more than one state, use a separate worksheet for each state.

Armed with several forms, you are ready to review your family history and list all events that newspapers normally report—births, marriages, deaths, or any other news items. Small-town newspapers usually have a column that reports out-of-town visitors, trips for town residents, and small special events. They also have historical

Newspaper Documentation

Newspaper documentation should include the following information: the name of the person referenced, the type of article, the name of the newspaper, its city of publication and date, the page and column numbers where the article appears. For example:

Sam Jones obituary, *Free Press*, Cuba, Missouri, 1 December 1904, page 2, column 1.

NEWSPAPER RESEARCH WORKSHEET

Name	Newspaper Name & Notes	Date	State	County	City	Birth	Marriage	Obituary	News Article	Legal	Other

Figure 10.4 Newspaper research worksheet

columns that reveal what happened in that town ten, twenty-five, or fifty years ago. All these articles are of interest to genealogists and could contain the name of your ancestor.

Sometimes we know only that a person died in 1898—no month or date is available. If the ancestor lived in a small town, the task of finding a news article about his death or an obituary is not as daunting as it is if he lived in a large city. Many small-town newspapers have weekly editions, so you have only fifty-two issues to review for each year. Those same newspapers are commonly six to eight pages. Newspapers tend to have a similar format. The important articles are on the front page, religious articles appear together on another page, and articles about town events (often, the gossip column) are on a different page. Obituaries may be on the front page or page two. They may have the name of the deceased in bold centered on the column. The particular newspaper style will be apparent once you review two or three issues, and that will help streamline your research. One German paper in St. Louis used two bold lines the width of the column with the name of the deceased between the lines, thus making it easy to spot obituaries, even if you don't read German.

During the three World War I draft registrations, many newspapers printed a list of the men who registered. It was a public disgrace not to register, and some papers listed those who did not register, as well. Your ancestor may be on one of those lists. You may find similar lists for those who registered for the draft during World War II.

While reviewing the newspapers, look for clubs or societies to which your ancestor may have belonged. A member of your family may have belonged to the Masons or been a Shriner. Perhaps your ancestor belonged to a lineage society, such as the DAR, SAR, or Mayflower Society. Ethnic groups had local societies. A man may have belonged to a veterans' organization, such as the GAR. Newspapers often list new officers, meetings, and other society events. The clubs or societies were outside activities that served as social events, ways to share news of the community and to meet new people. If the organization was affiliated with another group, such as a religious facility or school, you can broaden your research. Make a list of these possible areas for future research.

Did your family have any hobbies? Did the men like to hunt or fish? Did the women sew or quilt? Someone may have won first prize at the state fair for the best apple pie or the award-winning calf in the 4-H category. The local high school baseball team may have become state champions. Stories with the names of the participants were written about these events and are often accompanied by photographs.

By using the newspaper research worksheet and recording the participant's name, the type of event, and the exact or approximate date, you will find your newspaper research quite rewarding. Remember that this worksheet, just like the others, is a finding aid, not a place to document your sources.

School Research

School records are available at all levels, from elementary schools to universities. These records are worth the time you expend to locate them. If an ancestor does not have a birth certificate or you do not know his parents' names, school records may contain the answer. Some records are open; others are available only to the former student or his direct-line ancestors.

You may find several types of school records—school censuses, report cards, photographs, graduation rolls, student signatures, and yearbooks. You may need to visit several repositories to locate all these resources. Begin by preparing a school records research worksheet (see Figure 10.5). Once you list the name of the students and the schools on your worksheet, you can check card catalogs or Web sites to determine where the school records are stored.

It wasn't just students who produced records; the teachers and school officials did, as well. Board members signed various documents, as did teachers and administrators. Graduates and alumni records and directories are often available. Check with the caretakers at the school archives, libraries, and school buildings to determine where the records can be found.

You may find additional student information in old newspaper articles. Who won first place in the baseball league in 1960? Who was the prom queen? Small local newspapers usually feature students and their good deeds. The members of the honor society and scholarship award winners are usually listed in the newspaper. Today, news articles advertise upcoming class reunions. The high school in Cuba, Missouri, invites all its alumni to each reunion in the spring. The class celebrating its fiftieth reunion is featured each year; however, alumni from other classes also attend. My aunt is planning to attend her seventy-fifth high school reunion in 2005! Tag along—it's a great place to learn more about the high school days of your parents, grandparents, or siblings.

School Records Research Worksheet

Name	Grade School Name	High School Name	College Name	Report Cards	School Photos	Yearbooks	Diploma	Notes

Figure 10.5 School records research worksheet

Organize your plans, use available records, and analyze the research. All too often researchers think they have reviewed all the records, but most likely they have not.

The last step in organizing your research is to plan a research trip. You have gathered, listed, and sorted all the information available at this time. Get ready, get set, let's go on a research trip!

CHAPTER 11

Ancestors' Research Road Show

THE LAST FOUR CHAPTERS INTRODUCED RESEARCH WORKSHEETS. NOW that you have organized your files and prepared worksheets of your information, it is time to take a research trip. This trip can be as close as your local library or as far as your family hometown in another state. The trip can take you to a research facility across the country or around the world. A pre-trip checklist can ensure that you have what you need and increase your chances of a successful outcome.

Although the thought of doing all your family history research from the comfort of your home is tempting, it is not possible. Besides, it wouldn't be any fun. When planning a research trip, include a stop at your ancestor's local courthouse, church, school, and cemetery. If your ancestor's former home is still standing, drive by and take a photo.

The Family History Library, the state archives, or a local organization may have microfilmed or indexed some of the original records. These records may be available through lending opportunities at the local library or the Family History Center in your city. Other libraries may have the records you need onsite.

A few genealogical libraries offer resources via interlibrary loan. The National Genealogical Society (NGS) book loan collection housed at St. Louis County Library in St. Louis, Missouri, is available to all genealogists via interlibrary loan. Check the NGS catalog Web site *(www.ngsgenealogy.org)* and the St. Louis County Library catalog Web site *(www.slcl.lib.mo.us/slcl/sc/sc-genealogy.htm)* for a list of available books. Your library can contact St. Louis County Library for further details on interlibrary loan. Mid-Continent Library in Independence, Missouri *(www.mcpl.lib.mo.us/ge/)*, **223**

The **Family History Library** in Salt Lake City, Utah, is the largest genealogical library in the world. It's maintained by the Church of Jesus Christ of Latter-day Saints. A catalog of its holdings is online *(www.familysearch.org)* and available on a CD-ROM. Microfilm records are available through a rental program at local Family History Centers and at participating local lending libraries.

also has an interlibrary loan program available to the public. New England Historic Genealogical Society *(www.newenglandancetors.org)* has an interlibrary loan program available to members only, as does the Ohio Genealogical Society *(www.ogs.org)*. Bookmark the Web sites for future use.

It's always useful to take blank ancestor charts and family group sheets on the road with you in case you locate a book or an article about your surname. Understanding your place in the family is often easier if you chart the family while you're in the library. You should start the chart with the known ancestor, then record that person's ancestors. Add this data to your notebook or computer, as well.

Now is the time to use one of those project folders, mentioned in Chapter 2, to gather your travel documents. The folder should include your map, airline ticket, hotel reservation, library photocopy card, and any other papers you need to take with you. Gather the items in advance to avoid that last-minute rush.

Your research trip will be less frustrating and more efficient if you first organize it. Begin by visiting the Web site for every facility you plan to visit. Learn about the facility, as well as its resources. Is the building handicapped-accessible? Is there a parking

Photocopy cards are kind of a debit card available at numerous libraries. Each library has its own card, and they are not interchangeable from library to library. The cards can be used repeatedly each time you visit a facility, so it's a good idea to keep each card in a project folder designated for each facility. Write your name on the back of the card, in case you lose it. Researchers are very good about returning lost cards to the staff.

lot, or do you need to have change for a meter? Does the facility have restaurants nearby? Is there a nearby hotel? When is the facility open? Will it be closed for any special event or holiday during your visit? If you are driving, obtain a detailed map from AAA or a similar company. If you can accumulate this information before departing on a research trip, you and your traveling companion will be much happier.

After gathering your data and before you leave, make a list of phone numbers you may need while traveling. Take one copy with you and leave a duplicate list with your loved ones at home. That way, they'll have the names of the facilities, addresses, and phone numbers where you can be reached during this trip, in case of an emergency, since cell phones are sometimes out of range.

Checklists for Success

For any research trip, you need basic office supplies, perhaps packed in a lightweight container that is easy to carry. A clear plastic pencil holder with a zipper, often used

Basic Research Supplies

Your library or courthouse research will be enhanced if you bring along the following basic supplies:

- Highlighters
- Magnifying glass
- Manila file folders or project folders
- Paper clips
- Pens in a variety of colors
- Regular or mechanical pencil with extra lead
- Scissors
- Spiral tablet
- Staples, stapler, and staple remover
- Sticky notes

by children, works well. Identify your briefcase with your name and address on a luggage tag. Add the same information to all items in your briefcase, including your note-taking spiral tablet and research notebook. Your name should be included in the footer of any worksheet or list.

Researching out of town requires a larger travel bag or briefcase. Of course, your mode of transportation will determine how extensive your supply bag can be—a road trip is more flexible than a flight. Your carryall for all trips should include your research data, basic office supplies, a to-do list, and a note-taking tablet.

A laptop computer increases the items on your checklist. The laptop needs a good battery, electrical cord, floppy disks, and CD-Rs to back up your work. A security cord and lock are beneficial in many research facilities. If space allows, take a small portable printer, an additional ink cartridge, and paper. These items will fit in a briefcase, whether a shoulder bag or rolling computer bag.

If you are taking a computer, you might as well take some CDs to help with your research. CDs may include a software mapping program, the Family History Library Catalog, the Periodical Source Index (PERSI), indexes, and perhaps your own research.

With or without a computer, a note-taking tablet is a good tool to use in the library. Everybody needs a place to take notes of any kind, make comments, or transcribe a

Before Departing on a Research Trip

A pre-trip checklist helps researchers get ready. Add your own details to the following list:

- Label all accessories with your name and address.
- Pack lightly and take comfortable shoes.
- Check current airline luggage policy.
- Notify travel companions of any medical conditions.
- Provide your family with a travel itinerary.
- Share emergency phone numbers with your travel companions.
- Take necessary medicine, eyeglasses, and other daily accessories.

document. The tablet is the place. Your note-taking tablet is your research history, so be sure to write your name in it—you do not want to lose it.

A few personal items should travel with you. If you wear glasses, take an extra pair in case you misplace or break the first pair. Pack an ample supply of prescription medicine. Also, take any over-the-counter items that you use regularly, including medication for headaches, eyestrain, and dry hands.

Researchers need to have their hands free. Women should think about what kind of purse to take—a fanny pack, shoulder strap wallet bag, or perhaps no purse. A briefcase, tote bag, or other type of container for your notebook, paper, pens, and other items is essential. Some libraries do not allow bags in their facilities, but they provide lockers for your valuable items.

This trip is not a fashion show. Take comfortable clothes and shoes that mix and match. Remember that hotels usually offer washers and dryers, so you may be able to wear items more than once. Plan which clothes and shoes to wear each day so you don't overpack. Keep in mind that libraries and perfume do not go together, so leave the fragrances at home. Space is often limited, with researchers sitting close to each other. Strong perfume may offend the other patrons or cause an allergic reaction.

Research trips usually consist of brief stops at various destinations, not just libraries, so be sure to pack a camera, along with the genealogical supplies you need for research. While in town, will you attend the church of your ancestor—perhaps even sit in the same pew? You should certainly plan to visit the local genealogical or historical society while you're there; it's sure to have valuable resources. But keep in mind that its hours may be limited. Before you leave on a research trip, try to schedule as many appointments there as possible so that you develop an understanding of the town and its history.

Will your trip include a cemetery stop? Do you want a tombstone rubbing? While visiting a cemetery, it's important that you be respectful of the tombstones. A camera is your best tool. Take a photo of each side of the tombstone that contains an inscription. Take a photo of the group of family tombstones, as well as an overview of the cemetery with a point of reference, such as a building or road. Look at the tombstone neighborhood. Are other family members in the same cemetery? Should you photograph or transcribe those tombstones, as well? Of course!

Cemeteries are often home to bugs and other varmints. If the cemetery is well maintained, walking shouldn't be a problem. However, if it's in the middle of a field or farm, it may be necessary to walk through the tall weeds, climb a fence, and

Cemetery Supply List

Family historians often enjoy a trip to a family cemetery. The visit will be more successful with a little preparation and the following supplies:

- Soft rag or brush to remove the dirt
- Flour to enhance the letters on the stone
- Paper and pencils for tracing
- Tablet and pen to transcribe the information
- Garden tools to clean away debris around the tombstone
- Water in spray bottle to clean tombstone
- Camera

probably step in some holes before you get there. You may need to include insect repellent or allergy medication with your travel gear.

Do you plan to work on records that are written in a foreign language? If so, take an example of the alphabet in that language and an English translation of a list of words often found in genealogical documents. For example, a sheet displaying German gothic letters in upper- and lowercase is helpful for those attempting to read German records. So is a list of German words you are likely to find in the documents, such as "born," "married," and "died," as well as months, numbers, and other words that tend to appear in wills, church records, and deeds. It's also helpful to compile a list of alternate spellings for the names you intend to research. Well-organized researchers are more successful simply because they have more time to devote to the research. After all, you don't want to spend your time looking up words.

If you plan to research German records, you may want to download the eighty-three-page PDF file titled *Genealogical Handbook of German Research* available at *www.familysearch.org*. When the main screen appears, select Search, then Research Helps; select G on the alphabet toolbar, then scroll down to the location, Germany, and click on the title listed above. Additional publications are also available at that Web site. Your research will be more rewarding if you prepare for it by reading such finding aids before you leave. Similar guides are available for other countries. *The Family History Source Guide* CD can be purchased from the Family History Library. That CD has most of the resource guides listed on the Web site.

Literature Search

When you start a genealogical project, you should conduct a literature search online for each county and state in which you plan to research. That way, you can locate the available published records, microfilm, and microfiche. Armed with the findings from your search, you are ready to formulate a master research plan.

The records you are interested in may be available at the local library; your state archives; the Family History Library in Salt Lake City, Utah; the Allen County Public Library in Fort Wayne, Indiana; or any other library across the country. As you locate interesting records, determine the best way for you to make use of those sources. You may need to make a short trip to a local library, take a trip to a major resource center, or use interlibrary loan.

Your literature search should begin with the county where your family lived. Determine when your family lived in that county, adding a few years on each side to be sure you cover the entire period. For example, the Ferguson family moved to Gallatin County, Illinois, about 1820. Gallatin County split into two counties in 1847, with the Ferguson family then living in Saline County because of the boundary changes. To complete this search, it is necessary to search Gallatin County records from 1820 to 1847 and Saline County records from 1847 to 1900.

The next step in your literature search is to check the library catalogs previously mentioned. Also, check local and state libraries. In the Illinois example, the Illinois Secretary of State statewide databases *(www.sos.state.il.us)* include a marriage index to 1900, an assortment of military databases, and land records.

You can customize your research list by opening your word processor and Internet catalog at the same time and using the cut-and-paste feature to copy titles from the catalog to your research list. From the library catalogs, select and copy the titles and authors of books in which you are interested. Then switch back to the word processor and paste those titles into your research list. Continue to toggle back and forth between the catalog and word processor. Organize the titles by state and county. This compiled list of publications will serve as the foundation of your research. A list of research sites follows in alphabetical order. Note that another book in this NGS series,

Literature Search Web Sites

A literature search starts with your home computer. To determine the availability of research materials, visit any or all of these Web sites:

- Family History Library
  www.familysearch.org/eng/Library/FHLC/frameset_fhlc.asp
- Allen County Public Library
  catalog.acpl.lib.in.us/uhtbin/cgisirsi/
- Cincinnati Public Library
  www.cincinnatilibrary.org/catalog
- Dallas Public Library
  catalog.dallaslibrary.org
- Daughters of the American Revolution Library
  www.dar.org/library/default.html
- Denver Public Library
  www.denver.lib.co.us/catalog/catalog.html
- Library of Congress
  www.loc.gov
- Los Angeles Public Library
  catalog1.lapl.org/
- National Archives
  www.archives.gov/research_room/genealogy
- National Genealogical Society
  www.ngsgenealogy.org/libprecat.htm
- New England Historic Genealogical Society
  www.newenglandancestors.org/rs0/libraries/sydneyplus.asp
- New York Public Library
  www.nypl.org/catalogs/index.html
- Newberry Library
  www.newberry.org/nl/collections/collectionshome.html
- St. Louis County Library
  www.slcl.lib.mo.us/slcl/sc/sc-genpg.htm

Genealogy of a County or State

Just as people do, counties and states have a family tree. If a person purchased property before 1818 in what is today Crawford County, Missouri, that land was legally part of four counties before 1830. Therefore, you should review the records of all four counties:

- St. Louis County (original county)
- Franklin County, formed 1818
- Gasconade County, formed 1820
- Crawford County, formed 1829

Online Roots: How to Discover Your Family's History and Heritage with the Power of the Internet, by Pamela Boyer Porter and Amy Johnson Crow, provides detailed information on how to use Internet resources.

Allen County Public Library Catalog

You may want to plan a visit to the Allen County Pubic Library, the second-largest genealogical library in the country. Its collection is extensive, and its online catalog (see Figure 11.1) is easy to use *(www.acpl.lib.in.us)*. On a recent trip to Fort Wayne, I found seventy-two printed publications about one county. The Allen County Public Library and the Family History Library collections complement each other—be sure to check both!

Historical and Genealogical Societies

Your literature search should continue with state and local historical and genealogical societies, which publish records on a regular basis. Newspapers on microfilm, maps, gazetteers, and county histories are resources usually included in their collections. Society volunteers assemble and publish data on their counties for the benefit of genealogists across the country.

If your ancestor was an early settler in a particular state or community, you may be able to find a *First Families* lineage organization sponsored by a local society, which

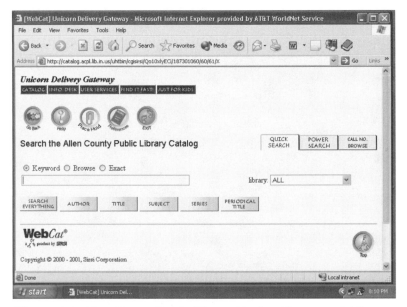

Figure 11.1 Allen County Public Library Catalog (Courtesy of Allen County Public Library)

provides records on the early pioneers in the area. For example, microfilm records for the First Families of Ohio are available at the Ohio Genealogical Society Library and the Family History Library. Societies usually have lists of members and the surnames they are searching. This type of information may be available online or through the societies. Add the society publications to your to-do list.

Library of Congress

The Library of Congress is a treasure trove of information, and its Web site *(www.loc.gov)* is as close as your computer. If you are looking for a book on a specific subject or title, this might be the place to search. You can also browse the catalog by author. The Web site is available to anyone.

National Archives

Your ancestor left local, state, and federal records. The federal records should not be overlooked; you'll find them at the National Archives (NARA) in Washington, D.C.; NARA's regional branches; the Family History Library; or local libraries. Federal records

Join a Genealogical Society

Family historians should join at least one and preferably three genealogical societies. Join your local society to keep abreast of genealogical events, meetings, seminars, and new publications. Join a national society, such as NGS, for educational opportunities and useful publications, including the *National Genealogical Society Quarterly* with methodology and case studies literature. Join a society in your research area to submit queries and learn about local research opportunities. All of the societies will provide publications, probably a newsletter, and journals.

Join your local society even if your family did not come from that area. You want to be informed of educational opportunities such as annual conferences, monthly lectures, or special events. Your local society may have an event with a featured speaker on a subject of interest to you. Maybe Cyndi Howells, creator of Cyndi's List, will be the featured speaker and you'll be able to learn more about using the Internet. For a nominal fee, you can enjoy a day with other family historians, talk genealogy, and learn something new right in your hometown.

If you join a society, consider becoming a volunteer. Societies have numerous projects and are always in need of more helpers. Perhaps a team of volunteers plans to walk a cemetery to record the tombstones, or alphabetize a stack of naturalization cards. Even though you know that your ancestors are not included in these records, volunteer anyway. A similar group of volunteers may have prepared indexes and finding aids that have helped in your research elsewhere. Genealogists can give back to the community and help future researchers. Whatever time you give will be rewarding. You'll learn something new every day just in casual conversation with other volunteers. You'll also learn how societies work and be more knowledgeable as you visit other facilities on your research trips. You'll be able to proudly say that you, too, are a society volunteer.

include federal censuses, post-1906 naturalization records, passenger lists, and bounty land and military records. Determine how your ancestor interacted with the federal government and where those records are stored. The National Archives Web site *(www.archives.gov)* should help you find the type of records available and their locations.

NARA Identification Card

Before genealogists are allowed to use the National Archives, they must register and obtain a NARA photo identification card. A photo ID is required to obtain the new NARA card, which is good for two years.

WorldCat

WorldCat (see Figure 11.2) is an electronic world cataloging system available to most libraries. Some libraries make this electronic catalog available to their patrons. My local library not only makes it available, but also allows me to access WorldCat from my home computer by using my library card number as a password. This is a great service. Check with your local library for availability in your area.

WorldCat is like other search engines. You enter keywords, such as *Swahlstedt family history*, and a list of publications containing those words appears on your screen.

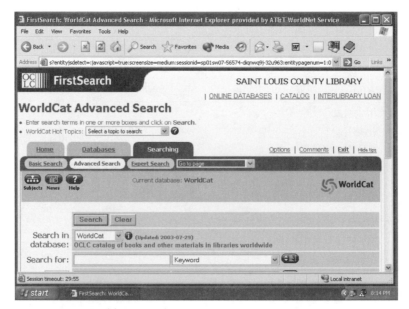

Figure 11.2 WorldCat search

National Archives Web Sites

The National Archives is based in Washington, D.C., and has numerous branches. Determine the branch that can assist with your research by using the following list:

- NARA's Pacific Alaska Region (Anchorage)
  www.archives.gov/facilities/ak/anchorage.html

- NARA's Pacific Region (Seattle)
  www.archives.gov/facilities/wa/seattle.html

- NARA's Pacific Region (Laguna Niguel)
  www.archives.gov/facilities/ca/laguna_niguel.html

- NARA's Pacific Region (San Francisco)
  www.archives.gov/facilities/ca/san_francisco.html

- NARA's Rocky Mountain Region (Denver)
  www.archives.gov/facilities/co/denver.html

- NARA's District of Columbia (Washington D.C.)
  www.archives.gov/facilities/dc/archives_1.html

- NARA's District of Columbia (College Park, Maryland)
  www.archives.gov/facilities/md/archives_2.html

- NARA's Southeast Region (Atlanta)
  www.archives.gov/facilities/ga/atlanta.html

- NARA's Great Lakes Region (Chicago)
  www.archives.gov/facilities/il/chicago.html

- NARA's Northeast Region (Boston)
  www.archives.gov/facilities/ma/boston.html

- NARA's Northeast Region (New York City)
  www.archives.gov/facilities/ny/new_york_city.html

- NARA's Northeast Region (Pittsfield)
  www.archives.gov/facilities/ma/pittsfield.html

- NARA's Central Plains Region (Kansas City)
  www.archives.gov/facilities/mo/kansas_city.html

- NARA's Mid Atlantic Region (Philadelphia)
  www.archives.gov/facilities/pa/philadelphia_center_city.html
  www.archives.gov/facilities/pa/philadelphia_northeast.html

- NARA's Southwest Region (Fort Worth)
  www.archives.gov/facilities/tx/fort_worth.html

Guidelines for Using Records, Repositories, and Libraries
Recommended by the National Genealogical Society

Recognizing that how they use unique original records and fragile publications will affect other users, both current and future, family history researchers habitually

- Are courteous to research facility personnel and other researchers, and respect the staff's other daily tasks, not expecting the records custodian to listen to their family histories nor provide constant or immediate attention
- Dress appropriately, converse with others in a low voice, and supervise children appropriately
- Do their homework in advance, know what is available and what they need, and avoid ever asking for "everything" on their ancestors
- Use only designated workspace areas and equipment, like readers and computers intended for patron use; respect off-limits areas; and ask for assistance if needed
- Treat original records at all times with great respect and work with only a few records at a time, recognizing that they are irreplaceable and that each user must help preserve them for future use
- Treat books with care, never forcing their spines, and handle photographs properly, preferably wearing archival gloves
- Never mark, mutilate, rearrange, relocate, or remove from the repository any original, printed, microform, or electronic document or artifact
- Use only procedures prescribed by the repository for noting corrections to any errors or omissions found in published works, never marking the work itself
- Keep note-taking paper or other objects from covering records or books, and avoid placing any pressure upon them, particularly with a pencil or pen
- Use only the method specifically designated for identifying records for duplication, avoiding use of paper clips, adhesive notes, or other means not approved by the facility
- Return volumes and files only to locations designated for that purpose
- Before departure, thank the records custodians for their courtesy in making the materials available
- Follow the rules of the records repository without protest, even if they have changed since a previous visit or differ from those of another facility

The listing provides the name of the publication, author, publication information, and Library of Congress and Dewey catalog numbers. It also lists the major libraries that have that book in their collections. WorldCat even highlights the name of your library since you "checked in" under your library's name.

The findings you discover in your literature search should be added to your to-do research list. You can visit one of those libraries to see the book, or you can ask your local library to procure it for you via interlibrary loan. The book may be available on microfilm at the Family History Library. You should keep a list of your WorldCat searches; otherwise, you'll find yourself searching for the same names. But new publications become available every day, so you may want to regularly review the list every six months or so.

FamilySearch

The Church of Jesus Christ of Latter-day Saints provides FamilySearch online *(www.familysearch.org),* which contains several options for genealogists (see Figure 11.3). This site allows you to search databases, learn more about family history research, and review the extensive holdings of the Family History Library.

Figure 11.3 FamilySearch Web site (Reprinted by permission. Copyright © 1999–2002 by Intellectual Reserve, Inc.)

The Share tab at the FamilySearch Web site allows you to review the following databases compiled by the library:

- Ancestral File
- Census, 1880
- International Genealogical Index
- Pedigree Resource File
- U.S. Social Security Death Index
- Vital Records Index

You can enter a name and search all databases, or you can look in each one separately. The Web site guides you to the features.

An efficient way to take advantage of this resource is with a FamilySearch worksheet (see Figure 11.4), which helps you to search the database in a methodical way and to avoid revisiting previously searched material. On the worksheet, list the ancestors you're researching; then, as time permits, search each FamilySearch database. Obviously, if you are looking for an ancestor from the 1700s, he won't be in the 1880 census or the Social Security database. Just write *N/A* in those columns. Keep the worksheet in your research notebook. Divide the worksheet by surname; eventually you will file it in the appropriate folder.

It may be necessary to alter the spelling or use just the last name to locate some ancestors. When I first searched these files several years ago, I found only three people out of about three hundred names searched. Today the databases are more extensive. Do not give up if your ancestors are not in these databases. This is just one stop on a long road of research.

The Search tab also provides access to research brochures on every state and many countries. Some brochures are specific to a state, but most provide general information for all researchers. Other guides have a combination—a state guide about the census offers general census information with a sprinkling of state-specific information.

If you are beginning research in a new location, an excellent, inexpensive resource is the Research Outline for that location, which provides the names of resources available for that state or country. You'll find an outline for each state and for various countries through the Family History Library Web site or your local Family History Center. Go to *www.familysearch.org*, click Search, and then click Research Helps. An

FAMILYSEARCH WORKSHEET

Name	Ancestral File	1880 Census	International Genealogical Index	Pedigree Resource File	Social Security Death Index	Vital Records Index

Figure 11.4 FamilySearch worksheet

alphabetical list states which Research Outlines are available. Some are printable in a PDF file. If a fee is listed, place the outline in your shopping cart.

You can also order the *Family History Source Guide* CD, which contains most of the Research Outlines. This CD is available for about six dollars.

PDF (Portable Document Format) was developed by Adobe software and preserves the original format of each page. The PDF document may be transmitted electronically, and its recipient will see that document exactly as you see the original.

FamilySearch is a fantastic Web site. Anyone doing family research should take full advantage of this site. Take the time to learn how to use the site, and record your findings. If the library catalog lists a book, your local or state research facilities may have it, as well. Family History Library books do not circulate off-site, but many are available on microfilm at your local FHL lending library. Make an extensive list of possible resources for your family, bearing in mind it may take a year or more to review all the items.

Family History Library Catalog

The largest genealogical library in the world, the Family History Library in Salt Lake City, provides a catalog of its holdings online at *www.familysearch.org* (see Figure 11.5) and on CD-ROM. Its collection of books, microfiche, and microfilm is outstanding. By referencing the library catalog, you can identify numerous publications about a particular county. The catalog also identifies family histories pertaining to many surnames. When you locate an interesting item, add it to your list. If the book exists at one facility, it is probably at another, perhaps in a library close to you—maybe even one listed on the WorldCat Web site.

The FHL catalog allows you to search by author, keyword, place, subject, surname, or title to locate the records needed for your research. If you know the film or fiche number or the call number of a book, there are search options for those, as well. To view the catalog, click the Library tab, then Family History Library Catalog.

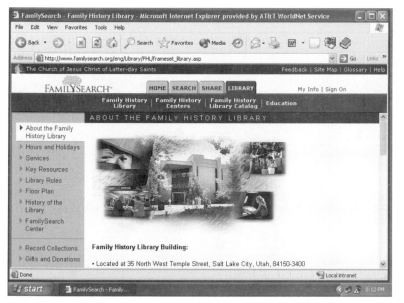

Figure 11.5 Family History Library Catalog Web site. (Reprinted by permission. Copyright © 1999–2002 by Intellectual Reserve, Inc.)

You can search by surname; just click the Surname option. On the next screen, enter the surname you're researching and click Search. You may find zero matches or hundreds. Read the summary of each book to determine which books or films best fit the family you are researching. The catalog provides a detailed description of each book. If you are interested in one of the matches, copy the name and call number. I keep my word-processing program open while searching this Web site so I can cut and paste the information I find.

To search by place or location, enter the name of the county. If you know the state, you can enter that on the second line. If you do not know the state, just enter the county name. A list of those counties and their states will appear. Since several states have a Washington County, for example, select the state that is your area of research. A list of subject headings for that county will appear. Check each category to review county records and determine whether they could apply to your ancestor. If your ancestor and several previous generations were born in the United States, there's no need to review naturalization records. But you should certainly review the basic sources—census, land, probate, wills, and similar records. With your word-processing program open, you can cut and paste new resources to your to-do research list.

The original records are available at the county courthouse, but the Family History Library houses books and microfilm of many of those records, including microfilm of original documents such as deeds, marriages, and probate records. Be sure to check the catalog. The microfilm is available from FHL for a nominal charge via the lending program at your local Family History Center or local lending library.

PERSI

The staff at Allen County Public Library in Fort Wayne, Indiana, compiles the Periodical Source Index (PERSI). Started in 1985, the project has been updated every year since. The index is a compilation of the titles of published articles in genealogical and historical society publications. Genealogists can search the index by surname, given name, or article title keywords. To search by location, you simply enter the name of the state or county, or article title keyword. You can also search for foreign locations. The index includes record types and methodology. Perhaps you want to first learn more about cemetery research in general, and then look specifically at cemeteries in Texas.

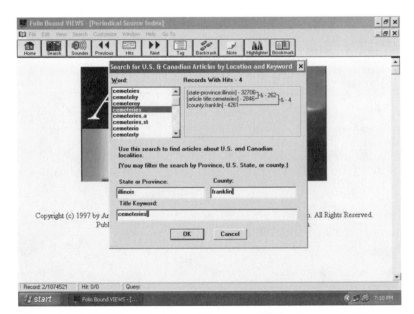

Figure 11.6 PERSI search screen (Courtesy of Allen County Public Library)

PERSI provides the names of articles written on those topics, but does not include the names and data that appear within the articles.

Allen County Public Library indexes current publications, as well as many older journals. A list of the publications included in the index is available on a CD or on a subscription database Web site *(www.ancestry.com)*. All the publications are available at Allen County Public Library. The name and address of the society that published the article is also available.

PERSI is available on a CD or at *www.heritagequestionline.com,* a subscription database site*;* most genealogical libraries can provide access to one of these. To obtain a copy of the original article, you can locate the journal in a genealogical or other library, contact the publishing society, or request a copy from Allen County Public Library.

Let's look at a few examples. If we want to find burials in Franklin County, Illinois cemeteries, we enter the location name and the word *cemetery* (see Figure 11.6). The chart in the top right corner shows the number of listings for Illinois, the number for Franklin, and the number for cemeteries. For the combination we've selected, there are four matches (see Figure 11.7). We copy those listings onto our PERSI worksheet (see Figure 11.8) for future research.

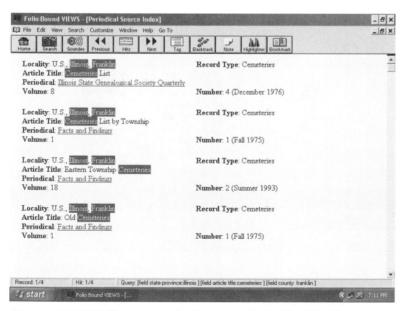

Figure 11.7 PERSI search results for cemeteries in Franklin County, Illinois (Courtesy of Allen County Public Library)

PERIODICAL SOURCE INDEX (PERSI) WORKSHEET

Name	Title of Article	Journal Name	Journal Code	Volume Number	Month	Year

Figure 11.8 PERSI reference worksheet

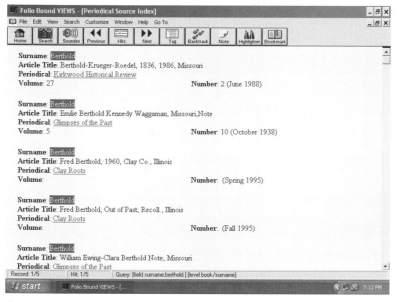

Figure 11.9 PERSI search results for the surname Berthold (Courtesy of Allen County Public Library)

A surname search for Berthold reveals five matches (see Figure 11.9). Three matches indicate the family was in Missouri where this family located after migrating from Germany. Be mindful that the vast amount of information published in these articles will probably never be published in full book format or on CD. This may be the only place we will find this data.

Before embarking on your research trip, take time to review this valuable asset. Search PERSI for entries pertaining to your area of interest. If you're searching for a Civil War veteran, there are certainly articles on that subject. If you are doing cemetery research, you're likely to find articles about cemeteries in the area you are researching. Review the index, and list on your PERSI worksheet those articles that look promising. The worksheet may contain numerous articles of interest. Your next step will be to try to obtain a copy of the article by writing to the society that published it or the local library. If you are visiting a library that has the correct journal and issue, you can make your own copies. When you plan a visit to the Allen County Public Library, a PERSI search should be at the top of your research list. As you locate each article, cross it off your worksheet.

Visit a Library

Libraries across the country are awaiting your visit. Each repository has a different collection, even though you'll find some duplication. Some libraries seek and collect genealogical resources, while others provide local history resources. Family historians need both types of collections. You must determine which facilities will be most helpful to you.

As a genealogist, you should follow the rules of each repository. Be aware of the opening and closing hours, and always be considerate of the staff. Staff members are happy to answer questions, but they want to go home promptly when their day is over. If the rules say use pencils only, do so. For these occasions, keep a mechanical pencil and extra lead in your supply bag. Some libraries restrict purses, bags, and three-ring binders. Use the lockers provided—without grumbling. For most lockers, you must use a quarter to lock the door, but it comes back to you when you open the locker. Even if they don't make sense to you, all the rules are in place at these research facilities because damage or theft has occurred there in the past. Learn the rules before visiting the facility, and prepare your lists and supplies accordingly. Clothes with big pockets often help.

While in any library, you should be courteous to the staff and other genealogists. Return the resources to the proper location so that the staff can reshelve the books. Follow the photocopy rules and limit the number of copies if others are waiting. When you are talking to other researchers or the staff, speak softly so you do not disturb other patrons. Cell phones should be used outside, never inside the library.

Photocopy cards are available in some libraries. They are wonderful. A copy card machine accepts coins or bills and places the same amount on your copy card. The card works like a debit card each time you make a copy. A one-time nominal fee is usually charged for the actual card, maybe fifty cents. After that, you reuse the card by adding funds as needed. Put your name on the card, but even then you may lose it, so don't put too much money on the card at one time, just in case. When you return home, store the card in a project folder or envelope designated for that facility. Then take the card with you the next time you return to that facility. If the library uses coins, take a supply of coins by filling empty pill bottles or film canisters; one with quarters, one with dimes, and another with nickels.

The first time you visit a library, request a tour of the facility or take a few minutes to walk around the library yourself. Look at the microfilm holdings, review the book

Library Checklist

Here are lists of specific items you should take to each research facility. The photocopy cards are available at some libraries and can be reused during each visit. A laptop with a lock and a digital camera are options at all facilities.

- **Allen County Public Library, Fort Wayne, Indiana**
  - PERSI to-do list
  - PERSI CD (if taking a laptop)
  - Photocopy card
  - To-do list from online catalog
  - Worksheets
- **Family History Library, Salt Lake City, Utah**
  - Change for lockers
  - Photocopy card
  - FHL CD (if taking a laptop)
  - To-do list from FHL CD or online catalog
  - Worksheets
- **National Archives, Washington, D.C.**
  - Change for lockers
  - NARA ID card or photo ID to register for NARA card
  - Pencils
  - Photocopy card
  - To-do list
  - Worksheets
- **State Library or Archives**
  - Change for lockers and parking
  - Pencils
  - To-do list
  - Worksheets

collection, locate the manuscript collection, and assess the availability of the computers, copiers, microfilm readers, and printers. Inquire about any check-in procedures or time limits for the use of the equipment. Also, locate the restrooms, drinking fountains, and emergency exits.

As you research in the library, you will probably have questions for the staff. In a regular library, the staff may not be genealogists. In a genealogical library, the staff is probably familiar with the collection; however, each staff member may specialize in a different area. One librarian may work with immigration records, another with military, and another reads French. You need to ask who can help with your type of question.

When asking the staff questions, be courteous—and get to the point. You may be fascinated by the details you know about your great-grandfather George Ferguson, who served in the Civil War in the Thirty-first Illinois Infantry, enlisted on 3 April 1863, and was discharged on 8 June 1865, and then returned to Southern Illinois before marrying Kate Lynch. But by the time you've shared these facts, the librarian's eyes have glazed over and you still haven't asked your question: "Do you have a unit history for the Thirty-first Illinois Infantry?" The staff doesn't care about all that other information. Be specific. Limit the focus of the question to a specific period, usually the year, and a particular place, perhaps the state. If you are asking about the 1850 census, the staff does not need to know your ancestor's name. They need to know 1850 and the state, period. The staff will appreciate your well-organized questions. With your to-do research list in hand, you are organized. You know what you are looking for and can work independently.

Many library catalogs are available on the Internet. If you haven't been able to access it from home, the catalog should be your first stop. Use your to-do list to locate the catalog numbers for the books of interest.

Once you locate the book, determine whether it has more than one part, perhaps even more than one index. How is the book indexed? If it's a probate abstract book, does the index cover only the deceased? Are you looking for a surviving spouse, child, or even a witness? You may or may not be able to find your ancestor. Look at the preface or introduction to determine what is included in the book and how it was produced.

When you locate a reference, photocopy the information. You should copy the title page, the information desired, perhaps the index, and any other pages required to understand and document the book.

Research trips are always fun. If possible, take a friend or relative who will assist you with the research and share your excitement when you find that long-lost ancestor. Before departing, compile your research to-do lists. Review the resources at your local library so you don't waste time out of town looking at information you could have studied at home. With all this preparation, you're sure to have a successful trip!

Now that you have completed some of your research goals and organized the contents of your heritage trunk, it is time to organize your genealogy by writing your family history. Plan your publication and proceed with the method that works best for you.

Part 3
Organize Your Family History for Publication

CHAPTER 12

Share Your Story

FAMILY HISTORIANS SPEND A LOT OF TIME LOCATING HIDDEN TREASURES. Some genealogists unintentionally hide the new findings in stacks of papers or file drawers, or they simply do not share the information with others. Don't be selfish; tell the world all about your family. Share those facts with family members and other genealogists. By preparing and organizing your family history for publication, you will identify your research strengths and weaknesses.

You started this journey by gathering your documents, photos, and heirlooms, and storing them in an organized manner. Then you organized your research by preparing worksheets. Now you should organize your data into a family history for publication. As you progress, you will repeat each step. After all, those files won't stay organized by themselves; whenever you learn new information, you will update the worksheets and prepare new ones. (see Figure 12.1).

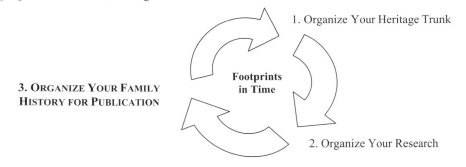

1. Organize Your Heritage Trunk

Footprints in Time

3. ORGANIZE YOUR FAMILY HISTORY FOR PUBLICATION

2. Organize Your Research

Figure 12.1 Phase three, organize your family history for publication

As you plan your publication, you should take some time to consider what your readers want to know. Try to avoid printing family group sheets or similar preprinted charts and long lists. They are boring to produce and read; narrative is much more inviting. The text should include interesting facts about your ancestors, making them come alive to the reader. A simple statement including the ancestor's name, birth, marriage, and death dates is fine, but that's just basic information. What did this person do for a living? Did he serve in the military? How many children did the couple have? What church did the family attend? Why did this family move from one location to another?

One person you don't want to forget in this family history is you. Family historians often become so consumed with our ancestors that we overlook the current generation. Although you shouldn't necessarily publish information on the current generation due to privacy issues, you certainly want to record the data. Who better to write about your life than you? Prepare a file folder with your name and start filling it with your thoughts, your biography, and your goals for the future.

This information can come one paragraph at a time. What are your hobbies? Do you like sports? Did you want to be a fashion designer, but ended up doing something else? Do you like to read, watch television, sew, garden, build furniture, or work on the car? Did you serve in the military? If you travel, where have you been? Have you visited all fifty states? Have you been to all of the continents? Maybe you like to stay home and try new recipes. Whatever it is, write it down. Since none of us know what is in store for us tomorrow, it is never too early to start this part of the project.

If you are a parent, grandparent, aunt, or uncle, write something about the younger generation. What happened on the day they were born? Was there a mad dash to the hospital? What did the baby weigh? Why did your parents select your name? Then when the children marry, write down funny stories about the wedding day and the events leading up to that day. If something currently costs one hundred dollars, imagine what that same item will cost when that couple is planning their children's weddings.

There are already generations alive now who do not remember a time without cell phones and remote controls. Write about life before some of our modern conveniences such as DVDs, computers, and even television. Describe your life as a child. Did you play hopscotch or Nintendo? How did your family cope with the heat before homes and cars were air-conditioned? Did you go on vacation with your family, perhaps driving to Florida or California? Do you remember the Mercury and Apollo space programs? Tell them about your high school years. Describe the changes in your hometown, the buildings, highways, parks, sports stadiums, the suburbs. All these

Standards for Sound Genealogical Research
Recommended by the National Genealogical Society

Remembering always that they are engaged in a quest for truth, family history researchers consistently

- Record the source for each item of information they collect

- Test every hypothesis or theory against credible evidence, and reject those that are not supported by the evidence

- Seek original records, or reproduced images of them when there is reasonable assurance they have not been altered, as the basis for their research conclusions

- Use compilations, communications, and published works, whether paper or electronic, primarily for their value as guides to locating the original records or as contributions to the critical analysis of the evidence discussed in them

- State something as a fact only when it is supported by convincing evidence, and identify the evidence when communicating the fact to others

- Limit with words like "probable" or "possible" any statement that is based on less than convincing evidence, and state the reasons for concluding that it is probable or possible

- Avoid misleading other researchers by either intentionally or carelessly distributing or publishing inaccurate information

- State carefully and honestly the results of their own research, and acknowledge all use of other researchers' work

- Recognize the collegial nature of genealogical research by making their work available to others through publication, or by placing copies in appropriate libraries or repositories, and by welcoming critical comment

- Consider with open minds new evidence or the comments of others on their work and the conclusions they have reached

things seem like trivia today, but they are just the type of details your family—and especially your family historian—years from now will read with delight. What special events have you attended? I attended the last baseball game played by Stan Musial, attended the 1964 World Series between the St. Louis Cardinals and New York Yankees, then saw Roger Maris play baseball as a Cardinal in the same stadium where Mark McGwire broke Maris's home run record, and watched the construction of the Gateway Arch, all in St. Louis.

If you ask a group of your friends, one by one, if they know how their parents met, "I don't know" will be the response of many. If only someone had recorded the fine details of their lives. One friend carries a tape recorder in the car with him. He records any random thoughts about his life and his family history. His daughter-in-law then transcribes the stories. It is important that we record our place in history.

Think about those special moments. How did you feel as a bride or groom as you were walking down the aisle at your own wedding? Describe holding your child for the first time. What was it like to lose a loved one? You are unique; your descriptions and stories reflect your personality and lifestyle, as well as the times in which you live. Your descendants will know something about you, more than your name, birth, marriage, and death dates.

Publishing Your Story, One Way or the Other

Set Goals

We all need something to inspire us to finish a project. Maybe a relative is old or ill and you want this publication completed for her benefit. Perhaps your parents started this project and you want to finish it in their memory. Whatever the reason, the important part is to finish!

Family historians often state that they will write their family history when they are finished. When will that be? Will you ever run out of ancestors? Will you live that long? Genealogy is a lifelong job; you never really finish. If you start writing today, you will have a work in progress. It will become clear where further work is needed, which part looks good, and what documentation is weak. Don't leave your family history hiding in a box in the closet for someone else to publish after you are gone.

Organizing and preparing your research for publishing is a major goal. You should begin by deciding what part of your family history you want to publish. As you do

References for Publishing

Publishing is an important part of genealogy. The following books will assist family historians:

- *The BCG Genealogical Standards Manual,* Millennium edition, by Board for Certification of Genealogists (Orem, Utah: Ancestry Publishing, 2000)

- *The Chicago Manual of Style: The Essential Guide for Writers, Editors, and Publishers*, 15th edition, by University of Chicago Press (Chicago: University of Chicago Press, 2003)

- *Evidence! Citation and Analysis for the Family Historian*, by Elizabeth Shown Mills (Baltimore: Genealogical Publishing Company, 1997)

- *Indexing Family Histories*, by Patricia Law Hatcher and John Vincent Wylie (Arlington, Virginia: National Genealogical Society, 1993)

- *Numbering Your Genealogy: Basic Systems, Complex Families, and International Kin*, by Joan Ferris Curran, Madilyn Coen Crane, and John H. Wray (Arlington, Virginia: National Genealogical Society, 1999)

- *Producing a Quality Family History*, by Patricia Law Hatcher (Salt Lake City: Ancestry Inc., 1996)

that, keep in mind that no matter how prepared you think you are, more work is ahead. So set a manageable and realistic goal. Determine the scope and format of the publication. Will it be a single-surname book or an all-my-ancestors publication? As you review other publications, record their formatting pros and cons. Organize, prepare, persevere: Your finished project will be great!

Copyright

Copyright concerns every writer. Information on this topic is available at *lcweb.loc.gov/copyright* and at *www.copyright.gov/circs/circ1.html*. You should respect the intellectual property of others, just as you would expect others to do the same for your work. Always obtain written permission from the author if there is any concern about using a quote or material. Be cautious in questionable copyright situations.

Standards for Sharing Information with Others
Recommended by the National Genealogical Society

Conscious of the fact that sharing information or data with others, whether through speech, documents or electronic media, is essential to family history research and that it needs continuing support and encouragement, responsible family historians consistently

- Respect the restrictions on sharing information that arise from the rights of another as an author, originator or compiler; as a living private person; or as a party to a mutual agreement

- Observe meticulously the legal rights of copyright owners, copying or distributing any part of their works only with their permission, or to the limited extent specifically allowed under the law's "fair use" exceptions

- Identify the sources for all ideas, information, and data from others, and the form in which they were received, recognizing that the unattributed use of another's intellectual work is plagiarism

- Respect the authorship rights of senders of letters, electronic mail, and data files, forwarding or disseminating them further only with the sender's permission

- Inform people who provide information about their families as to the ways it may be used, observing any conditions they impose and respecting any reservations they may express regarding the use of particular items

- Require some evidence of consent before assuming that living people are agreeable to further sharing of information about themselves

- Convey personal identifying information about living people—like age, home address, occupation, or activities—only in ways that those concerned have expressly agreed to

- Recognize that legal rights of privacy may limit the extent to which information from publicly available sources may be further used, disseminated, or published

- Communicate no information to others that is known to be false, or without making reasonable efforts to determine its truth, particularly information that may be derogatory

- Are sensitive to the hurt that revelations of criminal, immoral, bizarre, or irresponsible behavior may bring to family members

Guidelines for Publishing Web Pages on the Internet
Recommended by the National Genealogical Society

Appreciating that publishing information through Internet Web sites and Web pages shares many similarities with print publishing, considerate family historians

- Apply a title identifying both the entire Web site and the particular group of related pages, similar to a book-and-chapter designation, placing it both at the top of each Web browser window using the <TITLE> HTML tag, and in the body of the document, on the opening home or title page, and on any index pages

- Explain the purposes and objectives of their Web sites, placing the explanation near the top of the title page or including a link from that page to a special page about the reason for the site

- Display a footer at the bottom of each Web page that contains the Web site title, page title, author's name, author's contact information, date of last revision, and a copyright statement

- Provide complete contact information, including at a minimum a name and e-mail address, and preferably some means for long-term contact, like a postal address

- Assist visitors by providing on each page navigational links that lead visitors to other important pages on the Web site, or return them to the home page

- Adhere to the NGS "Standards for Sharing Information with Others" (see page 258) regarding copyright, attribution, privacy, and the sharing of sensitive information

- Include unambiguous source citations for the research data provided on the site, and if not complete descriptions, offering full citations upon request

- Label photographic and scanned images within the graphic itself, with fuller explanation if required in text adjacent to the graphic

- Identify transcribed, extracted, or abstracted data as such, and provide appropriate source citations

- Include identifying dates and locations when providing information about specific surnames or individuals

- Respect the rights of others who do not wish information about themselves to be published, referenced, or linked on a Web site

- Provide Web site access to all potential visitors by avoiding enhanced technical capabilities that may not be available to all users, remembering that not all computers are created equal

- Avoid using features that distract from the productive use of the Web site, like ones that reduce legibility, strain the eyes, dazzle the vision, or otherwise detract from the visitor's ability to easily read, study, comprehend, or print the online publication

- Maintain their online publications at frequent intervals, changing the content to keep the information current, the links valid, and the Web site in good working order

- Preserve and archive for future researchers their online publications and communications that have lasting value, using both electronic and paper duplication

Web Publishing

Several means of publishing are available to you, including Web sites. Web publishing allows genealogists to update as the research progresses. The material is available to millions of people at no cost, and unknown cousins may contact you. But privacy is a concern for everyone. If you publish on the Internet, be considerate of living family members. Do not print vital information about living family members on your Web site. Vital information here includes names, birth date and place, as well as marriage information. It certainly includes such information as Social Security numbers. If you would like to learn more about establishing and publishing a Web site, a complete instruction guide is available in the NGS series, *Planting Your Family Tree Online: How to Create Your Own Family History Web Site,* by Cyndi Howells, creator of Cyndi's List.

Miscellaneous Publications

Newsletters, holiday letters, journal articles, and monographs are a few ways you can share your family history with others. If you want to publish a hardback book, further information is available in the next section. Consider all your options, and determine which one will work for you.

Publications should include pertinent information about the current generation back to the founding ancestors. Inform readers about your grandparent's hometown area or the location of the family's first homestead. Share information about military experiences, occupations, religious beliefs, and migration patterns.

Different members of your family will want to read about specific lines and ancestors. Divide the family into groups. Who is interested in your maternal grandmother's side of the family, and who is interested in your paternal grandfather's line? Make a mailing list of family members for each branch of your family to determine the quantity of distribution. Create a newsletter on your home computer after learning a few desktop publishing skills. The production cost is low; photocopying and postage are the major expenses. Perhaps a sibling, cousin, or other family member will make a donation toward the expenses. Distribute newsletters to family members when information is available. Be sure to keep each publication pertinent to the family members. Your maternal family is probably not interested in your paternal line.

Family History Book

A hardbound published family history may provide the most complete version of your family history. Many genealogists are afraid to tackle this project, but why not?

Develop a chapter for each surname. Start with one surname and write the history of that family. When that chapter is complete, start writing about one of the other families. Before you know it, a book is taking shape.

Before you decide what you want your book to look like, review other family histories to see what you like and, more importantly, what you do not like. Family histories are available at local genealogical libraries, on microfilm from the FHL, and through interlibrary loan. Does the book have enough white space to make it easy on the eye, or is the text jammed together and hard to read? Is the typeface and formatting consistent, or does it change with every page?

You can format the book any way you like. If you are writing a small book about one surname, the decisions are easy. However, if you are writing about all of your ancestors, the decisions become more complex. Should you list all the surnames in alphabetical order with perhaps your focus surname first? That works well. You can group the maternal lines together and then the paternal lines together. Group the chapters however you like.

If your publication does not look good, readers will wonder if it is accurate. Have you ever read a book that states a woman was born in 1845 and married in 1850? If there are errors in the book, are there errors in the research? Polish the finished product so

Table of Contents Example

Many family historians ponder how to assemble their book. The first chapter should be the focus family (yours) with the other families listed alphabetically. If your book includes the family of a husband and wife, divide the book into two sections. The following example shows a portion of my husband's family and then a portion of my family. Each section starts with our respective surname.

Fleming	Carter
Aspley	James
Britton	Neal
Ferguson	Piatt
Hathaway	Rowland
Ice	Upton

Family History Numbering System

The *New England Historical Genealogical Register* (Register) and the *National Genealogical Society Quarterly* (NGSQ) each has a family history numbering system. The only difference between the two systems is who receives numbers. In the Register system, only the people who are carried forward receive a number. In the NGSQ system, everyone receives a number.

Both systems use a generation number for everyone in that generation. This number is placed immediately after the given name. The individual number is given to those carried forward in the Register system and to every person in the NGSQ system. The third set of numbers is the birth-order number; a roman numeral is given to everyone. Here are examples of the Register and NGSQ systems, each using the same family.

Register System

In this example, Samuel is number 2 and his siblings do not have a number.

1. John[1] James, born in Maryland and died in St. Louis County, Missouri, on 14 February 1834. He married Julia Creely in St. Louis on 4 February 1812.
    Known children of John and Julia (Creely) James:

    i. John[2] James, born 26 February 1814, St. Ferdinand, St. Louis County, Missouri.

    ii. Robert James, born 2 July 1815.

    iii. Julie Mae James, born 10 August 1819, died 25 August 1819.

    2 iv. Samuel James, born 25 July 1817.

2. Samuel[2] James (John[1]), born 25 July 1817 and died 28 July 1897, both in St. Ferdinand, St. Louis County, Missouri.

NGSQ or Modified Register System

Notice in this example that Samuel is number 5 and each of his siblings has a number.

1. John[1] James, born in Maryland and died in St. Louis County, Missouri, on 14 February 1834. He married Julia Creely in St. Louis on 4 February 1812.
    Known children of John and Julia (Creely) James:

    2 i. John[2] James, born 26 February 1814, St. Ferdinand, St. Louis County, Missouri.

    3 ii. Robert James, born 2 July 1817.

    4 iii. Julie Mae James, born 10 August 1819, died 25 August 1819.

    + 5 iv. Samuel James, born 25 July 1817.

5. Samuel[2] James (John[1]), born 25 July 1817 and died 28 July 1897, both in St. Ferdinand, St. Louis County, Missouri.

there is no doubt about the quality of the book and research. Consult a style guide to ensure that your style is consistent and your text is grammatically correct.

What should you include in the book? The text should include all of the data available. Select a style and numbering system that you like; however, do not invent your own numbering system! In addition to the text, include charts, maps, letter-heads, photographs, and signatures. What features do you like and not like in other family histories? Using your own design and creativity, combine the features and produce your own publication.

As a genealogist, you want every book to include an index. How many times have you picked up a book, ready to look at the index, only to find nothing? Your family history should certainly have an index of every name listed in the publication, every place name, and the major events. List your female ancestors by their maiden and married names with a cross-reference, since researchers often know one name and not the other. You can produce your index using your word-processing or genealogical software programs. If you don't want to use either of those methods, there is the old-fashioned way of making an alphabetical list, which actually gives you more flexibility.

If you do not use a computer and have several shoeboxes of note cards, it's time to start writing. Start by combining all your notes for each person on a separate piece of paper, expanding as needed. The goal is to compile all information available about that person in one spot. While compiling this data, make documentation notations. You may want to place the properly numbered documentation on a separate page. The documentation will serve as your footnotes or endnotes.

Endnotes are documentation placed at the end of a manuscript, consecutively numbered within the entire work or single chapter.

Footnotes are documentation placed at the bottom of a page, consecutively numbered within the manuscript.

While your family history is a work in progress, print a copy to review and take to research facilities. Print your history on both sides of the paper. Start each new chapter on the side with an odd page number. Use the *coil*—not spiral—binding available at copy stores. The coil binding allows the booklet to lie flat on the desk or fold to any page. It's also easier to turn the pages.

Documenting Your Research

The ultimate goal of a family history research project should be to write a family history. While that may seem like a daunting task at this moment, it will not be as you progress with the research. Documenting your sources is an important part of that process.

Many family historians do not believe it is necessary to document the sources because "it is just for my family." Then, as family interest expands, they have to reconsider that decision. You need documentation to join a lineage society or perhaps to prove to a skeptical cousin that you *really* are a distant cousin to Meriwether Lewis.

Every fact you write down came from someplace or someone. If your mother told you her birth date, she is your source. If a couple provides the names and birth dates of their children, your citation is an oral interview with Joe and Susan Smith. Be sure to include the date of the conversation in the citation. You may or may not pursue additional documentation. Document each fact by recording the author, publication information, and page number. Record the data in a word-processing or a genealogical software program. If you do not use a computer, record your documentation by hand.

All too often, family historians do not document their sources because it is too much trouble. By learning the basic documentation formats, you can streamline the process. Not only is it important to document for others, it is also important to document for yourself, as the family historian. When you share information with relatives, a cousin or aunt may challenge a statement. Perhaps you state Grandma died in 1904 at the age of eighty-four, but your aunt says it was 1906 at the age of eighty-two. To discuss this difference, you, as the family historian, must cite your sources. Your aunt may be relying on her memory, which may or may not be accurate. Who is correct? If you can cite the source, your aunt may suddenly change her mind. A death register, death certificate, or obituary is a great source. A statement from another family member is not as credible. Either way, knowing the source is critical.

Several sources may be needed to document something as simple as a person's name. Most records may list the ancestor as Arthur Swahlstedt. One city directory or the funeral home record may list his middle name or initial. Add the documentation listing the middle name. Multiple sources are wonderful.

If you make templates for various citations, you can then use the cut-and-paste process in your word processor. Use the same documentation in various citations. For example, you can use a census citation for the place of birth for the entire family. If the 1880 census states the father and mother were born in North Carolina, the two oldest children were born in Tennessee, and the last four children were born in Indiana, use the same citation for all of those facts. Type the citation once, then cut and paste for the following entries. Each citation has a long and short version. Use the long version in the first citation and the short version thereafter. Here are examples of the long and short versions of two citations:

Book Example

1. John Smith, *The Great Family History* (Baltimore: Whoisit Press, 2003), 2–5.
2. Smith, *Great Family History*, 2–5.

Census Example

1. John Smith household, 1860 U.S. census, Franklin County, Illinois, population schedule, Benton township, Benton post office, page 35, dwelling 101, family 104; National Archives micropublication M653, roll 177.
2. 1860 U.S. census, Franklin County, Illinois, population schedule, Benton township, page 35, dwelling 101, family 104.

With your word-processing or genealogical software program, you can make a file of your citations, both the long and the short versions. Then open the citation file and the family history file. Cut and paste the citation into the family history. That method certainly saves time and effort. However, be sure there are no typos in the citations. If there is an error, it will repeat when you cut and paste.

It may be necessary to make a few adjustments to the documentation when using a genealogical software program. Enter two or three citations, and then print out the examples. Do they look like what you expected? Do you need to make adjustments? Before you enter too much data, look at the printed versions and make adjustments as needed. Verify that the citations print the way you like them.

You will enter information in your genealogical software over several years, and it's important that you use a consistent formatting and documentation style. A style sheet helps you do that. The style sheet is where you record your decisions about the small details, as well as the major ones. Start one today, and continue adding new information. Print your style sheet on colored paper, or place it in a plastic sheet protector, anything so that it stands out on your desk.

Developing a Style Sheet

Entering data in a word-processing or genealogical software program offers many opportunities for variety. Some days you may choose to spell out the name of the month. Other times you abbreviate the month, using a three- or four-letter code. The same applies to numbers; do you spell out the numbers or use numerals?

Consistency is important in every project. Make a few basic decisions about the way your book should look, and record those decisions on a style sheet; your project will look better and be easier to read. When you read family histories in your library, you'll think of other style choices for your own publication. Of course, as you start this project it is impossible to know all the decisions you need to make. Thus, your style sheet is a work in progress. Keep it next to your computer and record all your decisions.

Genealogists use *The Chicago Manual of Style*, by the University of Chicago Press, as the standard style guide. This publication explains why authors should use a particular standard and provides some options. Genealogical software programs are databases where general information such as names, dates, and places are stored. They offer numerous event fields and the opportunity to use a note field for information about those events. Print the data in various formats such as a family group sheet or a book. In either case, the data should look good and read well. After all, you will share this information with others and its appearance reflects on you, the family historian.

The data in the note fields should be consistent. If you are referring to the American Revolution, do you type the words in full or do you use an abbreviation? Most likely, the answer is a little of both. Use your style sheet to make your publication look good and be consistent.

Names

It is necessary to make some decisions about the data. Should you include first and middle names as they become available? Should the surnames be printed in bold, ital-

What to Include in a Style Sheet

A style sheet or list should include anything that is important to the publication. In this book a leaf is found near the end of each chapter. That was a style decision by the publisher. You are the author and publisher of your family history. The following list contains a few suggestions to start your style sheet:

Spacing

- Margins
- Paragraph spacing
- Spacing before and after headings and subheadings
- One space at the end of a sentence

Punctuation

- Serial commas

Font

- Font and size of text
- Font and size of headers
- Font and size of subheadings
- Font and size of footnotes or endnotes

Footers and Headers

- Placement of page number
- Contents of the alternating header or footer

ics, all capitals, small capitals, or regular type? If you're using a genealogical program, you probably only have two options: regular type or all capitals. Since several generations will read the family history, use the ancestors' names, rather than your relationship to them. If a person is your grandmother, she is an aunt, great-aunt, sister, and possibly mother and wife to others. You should include nicknames with the given name, since some ancestors used the nickname extensively, but you must decide how you want to designate a nickname—perhaps in quotes, Harry "Red" Smith. Be consistent in your use of names; always refer to your ancestor by the same name, even if he had several names.

Places

Locations must be identified clearly and completely. If you mention Portland, is that Oregon or Maine? Should you abbreviate or spell out the state names? If you abbreviate, use the non-postal abbreviation. Use postal zip codes only when attached to an address, not in a place listing. We often abbreviate "United States." The preferred abbreviation is "U.S."—with periods and no spaces.

State Name Abbreviations

The left column shows the standard state name abbreviation, and the right column shows the zip code abbreviation. If you choose to abbreviate state names in your family history, use the standard abbreviation. Use the zip code abbreviation only for addresses.

Ala.	AL	Ky.	KY	N.Dak.	ND
Alaska	AK	La.	LA	Ohio	OH
Ariz.	AZ	Maine	ME	Okla.	OK
Ark.	AR	Md.	MD	Oreg.	OR
Calif.	CA	Mass.	MA	Pa.	PA
Colo.	CO	Mich.	MI	R.I.	RI
Conn.	CT	Minn.	MN	S.C.	SC
Del.	DE	Miss.	MS	S.Dak.	SD
D.C.	DC	Mo.	MO	Tenn.	TN
Fla.	FL	Mont.	MT	Tex.	TX
Ga.	GA	Nebr.	NE	Utah	UT
Hawaii	HI	Nev.	NV	Vt.	VT
Idaho	ID	N.H.	NH	Va.	VA
Ill.	IL	N.J.	NJ	Wash.	WA
Ind.	IN	N.Mex.	NM	W.Va.	WV
Iowa	IA	N.Y.	NY	Wis.	WI
Kans.	KS	N.C.	NC	Wyo.	WY

Include the county name, as well as the city and state. If you don't know the county name, go to the Geographic Names Information System Web site (*geonames.usgs.gov/ gnisform.html*) for assistance. The city, county, and state should be included for every event in your database and identified in your family history in your word-processing program. Separate the parts of the place names with commas—Chicago, Cook County, Illinois. Abbreviating "county" with "Co." is optional. If you do, it should read Chicago, Cook Co., Illinois. Whichever method you use, *be consistent.*

Dates

Abbreviations are often used for dates. Determine the date format to use. Will you enter the day, month, year, or month, day, year? The preferred date format in genealogy is the day, month, and year. Do you prefer to abbreviate the names of the months or spell them out? Run a test to see which one you like the best. Enter the abbreviated information for one person and the spelled-out version for another. Then print the data and decide which format you prefer.

Abbreviate or Spell It Out?

Which paragraph is easier to read? Be mindful that the reader stops each time an abbreviation is used even if it is a well-known abbreviation.

Mary Jane Smith was b. on 2 Sep 1842 in Boston, Suffolk Co., MA, and d. in Jefferson City, Cole Co., MO, on 8 Dec 1910. On 6 Feb 1862, Mary m. Jack Brown in Jackson, Hinds Co., MS.

Mary Jane Smith was born on 2 September 1842 in Boston, Suffolk County, Massachusetts, and died in Jefferson City, Cole County, Missouri, on 8 December 1910. On 6 February 1862, Mary married Jack Brown in Jackson, Hinds County, Mississippi.

Numbers

Numbers are another area where style varies. Do you list numbers in numerals or spell them out? Some people spell out all numbers below 101. Others spell out only numbers below 10. You decide which method you like and then *be consistent*. If you include a phone number, do you use parentheses around the area code or follow it with a dash or period? Some writers abbreviate a range of numbers, such as 1850–62; others include the full number, 1850–1862. Should ordinals be spelled out (first or second), appear as numerals with regular text (1st or 2nd), or appear as numerals with superscripts (1st or 2nd)? Genealogical dates are usually listed day month year without commas. Since family histories cover several centuries, you should include all four digits in the year. There are many decisions to make; just be sure to record them on your style sheet.

Numerals or Spelled Out Numbers?

Family histories usually contain many numbers. You must determine how to display the numbers. The two examples listed below demonstrate differences in number style, using the same text.

This is the 2nd time we have reviewed the 31st IL regiment, which had 32 people in the unit, with 2 serving as captains. The unit served in the Civil War 1861–5.

This is the second time we have reviewed the Thirty-first Illinois regiment, which had thirty-two people in the unit, with two serving as captains. The unit served in the Civil War 1861–1865.

Abbreviations

Abbreviations should be used carefully, if at all. Authors may use "b. m. d." for "born," "married," and "died." Does the average reader know what those abbreviations mean? Eliminating abbreviations will only lengthen the text a few pages. Most of the time, it won't even change the length of the paragraph. Besides, by the time you write this family history, the last thing you should be concerned about is saving one or two pieces of paper. Test drive a page of abbreviations versus a page of spelled-out text and numbers on a few family members. Which one do they find easier to read?

Symbols

Symbols are great in the right place; however, family histories are usually not the right place. If you list a percent, spell out "percent" (not %). The same applies to "cents" (not ¢). If you need to use the abbreviation for "number," perhaps in a citation, use "no." (not #). The word just looks neater.

Punctuation

You'll need to make some decisions about punctuation, including periods and commas. Years ago, typing teachers insisted on two spaces at the end of every sentence. Now that we have computers and proportional spacing, one space is standard after all punctuation marks. Try to break that old habit of two spaces after a period. When listing a series of words in a sentence, use serial commas. In the sentence, "The family has a dog, cat, and bird," the comma after "cat" is optional, but suggested. *Chicago* suggests that writers use serial commas, and most genealogical journals agree.

Should you use a hyphen, en dash, or em dash? Each has a special use! A hyphen is used between hyphenated words, such as mother-in-law. An en dash, a combination of two hyphens, is used between dates, 1950–2000, and between page numbers, 365–400. Do not use two separate hyphens, - -. That is incorrect. The em dash, a combination of three hyphens, is used in sentences to separate a change in thought—usually there is no space before or after the dash. On most word processors, including recent versions of Microsoft Word and WordPerfect, you can set the AutoCorrect option to convert the keystrokes of two hyphens into an en dash, and three hyphens into an em dash. Check your word processor's Help feature for further information. Using the correct dash is another detail that will make your publication look professional.

Fonts

What is more visible to the reader than the font size and type? The font should not be too small nor should it be too big. Consider your audience. Which font and size will your family members find easy to read? Maybe you like Times New Roman or

Examples of Fonts

Font selection is important in developing the style of your publication. Look at the difference in the following two samples:

Serif Fonts
Times New Roman and other serif fonts have curls at the ends of the letters. Readers find this type of text easier to read; it should be used in the text of the book.

Sans Serif Fonts
Arial and other sans serif fonts have straight-line letters and should be used in the headings or titles. Readers usually find this font more difficult to read.

perhaps Goudy. Text is usually set in serif fonts; sans serif fonts are often used in the titles, headings, and subheadings. Will titles, headings, and subheadings be in boldface, italics, or underlined? (Underline is passé!) Before making your decisions, print the same text using various fonts. Share these printouts with others, and take a survey. Whatever font you select, use only two fonts in the publication. More than that will detract from the text.

Format

White space is important to all publications. Should the family history pages be full-page text or in columns? Either way, allow ample margins, including at the binding edge. On each page, include either a footer or a header, but probably not both. Alternating headers can include the book title and page number on the even-numbered pages and the chapter title and page number on the odd-numbered ones. Your word processor will automatically alternate the headers or footers for you.

Paragraph style is another decision. Do you like the paragraphs indented or flush left? Do you like full justification or left justification with a ragged right edge? Do you like single-spaced paragraphs or lines with a little more space between them? When moving to a new paragraph, should there be an additional line between the paragraphs?

Paragraphs often extend from one page to another. Single words or lines should not extend to the next page. Activate the widow-and-orphan option in your word-processing program to avoid this formatting problem. Regardless of which paragraph style you choose, be sure to allow adequate white space on every page.

Graphics

Use graphics when they add something or enhance the text. Ancestors' photos add to the publication, as do signatures. A migration map helps the reader visualize the long and difficult journey undertaken by the ancestors. Graphics also provide relief for the reader and make the text easier to read. Clip art that illustrates part of your ancestor's life makes a page visually interesting. Decide whether you like the caption centered under a picture or left justified. Do you like the caption in italics or the same typeface as the text?

Talk to your printer before reproducing photos. Some printers prefer original (or copies) of photos, while others want everything electronically. Before publishing, obtain written permission to use any copyrighted photographics. Acknowledge the original owner of the photo in the caption: "This photo is used with permission of John Smith."

Sharing your family history with others is a very rewarding experience. Your story may bring tears to the eyes of a loved one, or it may bring back memories of the good old days. Try reading the family history to a blind cousin, reminding her of those days in Oklahoma when grass was belly high to a horse and she lived in a sod house. Can you think of a more worthwhile endeavor?

Researching your family history is a huge undertaking and not an overnight task that will be finished by the holidays. This is a lifelong project to savor and enjoy. Be patient; every day new records become available.

By organizing your heritage trunk, including papers and data, you have become a happier and more successful researcher. You know what information you have, where it is, and what it says. Heirlooms are stored safely. Photos are identified, stored, and shared with others. Remember that organizing your material is an ongoing process, as you continue to search for those elusive ancestors who left footprints in time.

National Genealogical Society Standards and Guidelines

THE NATIONAL GENEALOGICAL SOCIETY HAS WRITTEN A SERIES OF genealogical standards and guidelines, designed to help you in your family history research. NGS developed these as a concise way to evaluate resources and skills, and serve as a reminder of the importance of reliable methods of gathering information and sharing it with others.

The NGS Standards and Guidelines appear in this book. They also appear online at *www.ngsgenealogy.org/comstandards.htm.*

- Standards for Use of Technology in Genealogical Research (page 79)
- Guidelines for Genealogical Self-Improvement and Growth (page 103)
- Guidelines for Using Records, Repositories, and Libraries (page 236)
- Standards for Sound Genealogical Research (page 255)
- Standards for Sharing Information with Others (page 258)
- Guidelines for Publishing Web Pages on the Internet (page 259)

Glossary

Abstract: A statement that summarizes the essential facts in a record.

Agricultural schedule: A special census enumeration listing the head of household, the farm goods sold or produced, and livestock in the preceding twelve months.

Ahnentafel chart: An ancestor chart, beginning with the most recent individual and working back in time.

Allen County Public Library: An outstanding genealogical library located in Fort Wayne, Indiana.

Ancestor: A person from whom you descend.

Ancestor chart: A list or chart of ancestors from whom you descend.

CD-ROM: Compact Disk Read-Only Memory.

Census: An official enumeration of the population of a country, region, or state.

Certified Genealogical Instructor: An associate of the Board for Certification of Genealogists who presents an integrated series of classes that teach students to begin and continue their own genealogical studies. [Definition from Board for Certification of Genealogists, *The BCG Application Guide* (Washington, D.C.: Board for Certification of Genealogists, 2001), p. 15.]

Certified Genealogical Lecturer (CGL): An associate of the Board for Certification of Genealogists who delivers oral presentations that address genealogical sources, methods, and standards. [Definition from Board for Certification of Genealogists, *The BCG Application Guide* (Washington, D.C.: Board for Certification of Genealogists, 2001), p. 15.]

Certified Genealogical Records Specialist (CGRS): An associate of the Board for Certification of Genealogists who shares common research and analytical expertise, demonstrating through findings and written reports sound knowledge of the records within specific geographic, ethnic, subject, or time-period areas of interest and experience. [Definition from Board for Certification of Genealogists, *The BCG Application Guide* (Washington, D.C.: Board for Certification of Genealogists, 2001), p. 2.]

Certified Genealogist (CG): An associate of the Board for Certification of Genealogists whose work extends to broadly based genealogical projects whose goal is finding the evidence, assembling the proof, and compiling a coherent historical account of the identities and relationships of *all the descendants* of a particular ancestor or ancestral couple. [Definition from Board for Certification of Genealogists, *The BCG Application Guide* (Washington, D.C.: Board for Certification of Genealogists, 2001), p. 2.]

CG: See **Certified Genealogist.**

CGI: See **Certified Genealogical Instructor.**

CGL: See **Certified Genealogical Lecturer.**

CGRS: See **Certified Genealogical Records Specialist.**

Civil War Soldiers and Sailors System (CWSS): An index of some 5.4 million entries of Union and Confederate Civil War soldiers and sailors created by a cooperative effort among the National Parks Service, the Federation of Genealogical Societies, the Genealogical Society of Utah, and numerous other volunteer organizations across the United States *(www.itd.nps.gov/cwss/)*.

Citation: An authoritative source of information for a specific record.

City directory: A book containing a listing of names, addresses, and other information for residents of a city or county. City or county directories also contain listings for businesses, cemeteries, hospitals, newspapers, organizations, and schools, in a classified business section. Some include a crisscross or reverse directory of streets, allowing users to look up an address and determine the resident or business at that address.

Closed stacks: Library books shelved in a nonpublic area.

Collateral line: Persons with an ancestor in common, but who descend from different lines within that ancestor's family.

Correspondence log: A list of correspondence pertaining to genealogy, containing the name, address, phone, fax, e-mail, family surname, date of correspondence, and response.

County directory: See **City directory.**

Crisscross directory: See **City directory.**

CWSS: See **Civil War Soldiers and Sailors System.**

Cyndi's List of Genealogy Sites on the Internet: A springboard to more than two hundred thousand genealogy-related Web sites *(www.cyndislist.com).*

DAR: See **National Society Daughters of the American Revolution.**

Database: Any collection of specific information ranging from index cards to computerized programs.

Daughters of the American Revolution: See **National Society Daughters of the American Revolution.**

Death certificate: An official record that documents an individual's date and place of death and other details.

Descendant: A person whose descent can be traced from a particular ancestor.

Descendant chart: A list or chart of descendants. It begins with an individual or couple and moves down to children, grandchildren, great-grandchildren, and so on.

Direct line ancestor: A person from whom you directly descend, such as a parent, grandparent, or great-grandparent.

Endnote: Documentation placed at the end of a manuscript, consecutively numbered.

Evidence: The information that proves or disproves a statement.

Extant records: Available and surviving documents.

Family group sheet: A form that contains information for a single family; husband, wife, and their children, such as names, dates, and places of birth, marriages, and deaths.

Family History Centers: LDS genealogy research centers located around the world. Microfilmed records from the Family History Library can be ordered and viewed at any Family History Center.

Family History Library: The largest genealogical library in the world, run by the Church of Jesus Christ of Latter-day Saints (LDS or Mormons) in Salt Lake City, Utah.

FAQs: Frequently Asked Questions; a document or Web page that provides answers to questions that new visitors often ask.

Federation of Genealogical Societies (FGS): An umbrella organization society, made up of societies that serve the needs of member organizations.

FGS: See **Federation of Genealogical Societies.**

FHL: See **Family History Library.**

Finding aid: An explanation of documents that helps a user locate specific material within a collection of records.

Footnote: Documentation placed at the bottom of a page, consecutively numbered within the manuscript.

GAR: See **Grand Army of the Republic.**

GEDCOM: GEnealogical Data COMmunication; a file format that allows users to share genealogical data between genealogy database programs.

Genealogical society: A group of people who meet regularly to share an interest in genealogical research, education, and preservation.

Genealogist: A family historian.

Genealogy: The study of family history.

Given name: The first name provided by parents.

Grand Army of the Republic (GAR): A membership organization for Civil War Union veterans.

Grantee: The purchaser of property.

Grantor: The seller of property.

Heirloom: A valuable item in the family.

Hollinger box: An archival safe (acid-free) box used to store photos and heirlooms.

Interlibrary loan: A loan of a book from one library to another. Library patrons can borrow a book from a distant library through their own library.

Internet: A network of computers across the globe that facilitates data exchange, e-mail, newsgroups, etc. The World Wide Web is part of the Internet.

Library of Congress: The largest library in the world, with the mission of making its resources available to the American people and Congress.

Lineage society: A membership organization based on proof of lineage from a designated group of people.

Literature search: A search of published information on one subject.

Maiden name: The surname a woman has at birth and is known by before she marries. In some cultures, this is her first name; in other cultures, her last name.

Maternal ancestor: A person, male or female, from whom you descend through your mother.

Microfiche: A flat piece of approximately 4 x 5-inch film containing images of printed material.

Microfilm: A continuous roll of film on which images of printed materials are photographed at a reduced size.

Miracode: An index for the census similar to the Soundex, but providing county, volume, enumeration district, and the family number assigned by the census taker.

Mortality schedule: A special enumeration of the census listing individuals who had died within a certain period.

NARA: See **National Archives and Records Administration.**

National Archives and Records Administration (NARA): The U.S. governmental agency tasked with preserving the historical records of government.

National Genealogical Society (NGS): A service organization that leads and educates the national genealogical community.

National Society Daughters of the American Revolution (NSDAR): An organization composed of descendants of Revolutionary Patriots.

Naturalization: The process of becoming a legal citizen of a land other than where you were born.

NEGHS: See **New England Historic Genealogical Society.**

New England Historic Genealogical Society (NEHGS): A genealogical society focused on New England residents.

NGS: See **National Genealogical Society.**

NSDAR: See **National Society Daughters of the American Revolution.**

Obituary: A published death notice, usually in a newspaper, that sometimes includes a biography or personal details of the deceased.

Online catalog: A library catalog accessible on the Internet.

Open stacks: Bookshelves in a library that are accessible to the public.

Oral history: Historical information obtained from interviews of people with firsthand knowledge, often written down, audiotaped, or videotaped.

Paternal ancestor: A person, male or female, from whom you descend through your father.

PDA: See **Personal digital assistant.**

PDF: Portable Document Format; a file format used by Adobe software that preserves the original appearance of each page, even when the document is transmitted electronically.

Pedigree chart: See **Ancestor chart.**

Periodical Source Index (PERSI): A comprehensive index of journals and periodicals compiled by the Allen County Public Library.

PERSI: See **Periodical Source Index.**

Personal digital assistant (PDA): A handheld computer used to maintain contact information, calendars, to-do lists, and other organizational information.

Primary source: Firsthand information created at the time of the event.

Probate: Documents created during the disposition of an estate.

Query: An inquiry or search.

Repository: A place where documents, books, or other items are kept or preserved.

Research log: A document that records sources a researcher has checked and the results of any searches.

Research notebook: A notebook containing research outlines, notes, and worksheets.

Research report: A report that focuses on a particular research project, with a summary of the analysis, focus, results, and plans.

Reverse directory: See **City directory.**

SAR: See **Sons of the American Revolution.**

SASE: See **Self-addressed stamped envelope.**

Scanned image: A picture created by using a scanner to digitize the image.

Secondary source: Secondhand information; information created some time after an event or copied from another source.

Self-addressed stamped envelope (SASE): A stamped envelope addressed to you, usually provided by you in a letter with a genealogical request, to make it easier for the recipient to reply.

Sexton: A caretaker of a cemetery or church.

Shortcut keys: A user-defined series of keystrokes used to lessen the number of keystrokes required to type frequently used words and phrases.

Sibling: A brother or sister.

Slave census: A census schedule listing the slave owner and his slaves.

Social Security Death Index (SSDI): A searchable database containing information about deceased people who had Social Security numbers and may have received Social Security benefits.

Sons of the American Revolution (SAR): An organization composed of descendants of Revolutionary Patriots.

Soundex: A coded index based on the way a surname sounds, which groups similar names regardless of spelling.

Source: Any item or document relating to a person or event.

Source citation: A detailed list of information about a specific source (usually a source used to uniquely identify a particular event). This information is recorded on genealogical charts, forms, and reports.

Spreadsheet: A computer software program that organizes data for easy sorting and retrieval.

SSDI: See **Social Security Death Index.**

Style sheet: An outline of design and style decisions for a publication.

Surname: A person's family name.

Surname list: A list of surnames pertaining to the family history.

Timeline: A list of events in chronological order.

To-do list: Comments or reminders recorded in a genealogist's research logs or database notes about other resources to check, possible new names to search, etc.

Transcribe: To make an exact handwritten or typed duplication of an entire record, including headings, insertions, notes, capitalization, spelling, and cross-outs.

Vital records: Birth, marriage, divorce, and death documents that record those important life events.

Web site: A location found via a connection on the Internet.

Will: A legal document directing the disposition of a person's goods after that person dies.

Zip drive: A high-capacity storage device that can be internal or external to a computer.

THE BEST BOOK AVAILABLE WHEN YOU REALLY WANT TO KNOW

100 YEARS OF EXPERIENCE

The *Organized*

Includes CD of forms and worksheets

Family Historian

How to File, Manage, and Protect Your Genealogical Research and Heirlooms

ANN CARTER FLEMING, CG, CGL

Index

National Genealogical Society

. . . . the national society for generations past, present, and future

What Is the National Genealogical Society?

FOUNDED IN 1903, THE NATIONAL GENEALOGICAL SOCIETY IS A dynamic and growing association of individuals and other groups from all over the country—and the world—that share a love of genealogy. Whether you're a beginner, a professional, or somewhere in between, NGS can assist you in your research into the past.

The United States is a rich melting pot of ethnic diversity that includes countless personal histories just waiting to be discovered. NGS can be your portal to this pursuit with its premier annual conference and its ever-growing selection of how-to materials, books and publications, educational offerings, and member services.

NGS has something for everyone—we invite you to join us. Your membership in NGS will help you gain more enjoyment from your hobby or professional pursuits, and will place you within a long-established group of genealogists that came together a hundred years ago to promote excellence in genealogy.

To learn more about the society, visit us online at *www.ngsgenealogy.org.*

Other Books in the NGS Series

Genealogy 101
How to Trace Your Family's History and Heritage
Barbara Renick

A guide to basic principles of family research, this is a book the uninitiated can understand and the experienced will appreciate.

$19.99
ISBN 1-4016-0019-0

Online Roots
How to Discover Your Family's History and Heritage with the Power of the Internet
Pamela Boyer Porter, CGRS, CGL
Amy Johnson Crow, CG

A practical guide to making your online search more effective and creative. Includes how to know if what you find is accurate and the best way to make full use of the Internet.

$19.99
ISBN 1-4016-0021-2

A Family Affair
How to Plan and Direct the Best Family Reunion Ever
Sandra MacLean Clunies, CG

Family reunions can create memories and celebrate a common heritage. Here's how to do it with a minimum of fuss and maximum of good times.

$19.99
ISBN 1-4016-0020-4

Planting Your Family Tree Online
How to Create Your Own Family History Web Site
Cyndi Howells, creator of Cyndi's List

A guide to creating your own family history Web site, sharing information, and meeting others who are part of your family's history and heritage.

$19.99
ISBN 1-4016-0022-0

Unlocking Your Genetic History
A Step-by-Step Guide to Discovering Your Family's Medical and Genetic Heritage
Thomas H. Shawker, M.D.

An informative guide to completing a meaningful family health and genetic history. Includes the basics of genetics for the non-scientist.

$19.99
ISBN 1-4016-0144-8